NEGRO PERIODICALS
IN THE UNITED STATES

NEGRO PERIODICALS

IN THE UNITED STATES

SERIES I 1840-1960

Alexander's Magazine (1905-1909)

Colored American Magazine (1900-1909)

Competitor (1920-1921)

Crisis (1910-1940)

Douglass' Monthly (1858-1863)

Half-Century Magazine (1916-1925)

Messenger (1917-1928)

National Anti-Slavery
    Standard (1840-1870)

National Era (1847-1860)

National Principia (1858-1866)

Negro Quarterly (1942-1943)

Quarterly Review of Higher Education
    Among Negroes (1933-1960)

Race Relations (1943-1948)

Radical Abolitionist (1855-1858)

Southern Frontier (1940-1945)

Voice of the Negro (1904-1907)

SERIES II 1826-1950

African Observer (1827-1828)

American Anti-Slavery Reporter (1834)

American Jubilee (1854-1855)

Anti-Slavery Examiner (1836-1845)

Anti-Slavery Record (1835-1837)

Anti-Slavery Tracts (1855-1861)

Brown American (1936-1945)

Color Line (1946-1947)

Education (1935-1936)

Fire!! (1926)

Harlem Quarterly (1949-1950)

National Negro Health News (1933-1950)

National Negro Voice (1941)

Negro Music Journal (1902-1903)

Negro Story (1944-1946)

New Challenge (1934-1937)

The Non-Slaveholder (1846-1854)

Race (1935-1936)

Slavery in America (1836-1837)

AMERICAN
ANTI-SLAVERY
REPORTER

Nos. 1-8
1834

NEGRO UNIVERSITIES PRESS
WESTPORT, CONNECTICUT
1970

This reprint edition reproduces
the entire contents of the original publication,
as far as it has been possible to determine.

This work has been printed on long-life paper
and conforms to the standards developed
under the sponsorship of the
Council on Library Resources.

Printed in the United States of America

SBN 8371-3053-0

AMERICAN

ANTI - SLAVERY REPORTER.

VOL. I.]   JANUARY, 1834.   [NO. 1.

AMERICAN ANTI-SLAVERY REPORTER.

Six numbers of a periodical with the title, *Anti-Slavery Reporter*, have been issued during the last year gratuitously, and extensively circulated. This number commences a new series which will be published by the AMERICAN ANTI-SLAVERY SOCIETY. Though issued in February, it is dated, January, for the sake of conforming the volume to the year. The number for February will be issued during the month, and hereafter the work will make its appearance as near the first of each month as practicable. It will be filled with original essays, and authentic matters of FACT, adapted to probe American Slavery to the core. It will have nothing to do with Slavery "in the abstract." We are not at war with innocent imaginations but with wicked realities. May God grant us wisdom, energy, perseverance and courage enough to hold up, in its own meanness and cruelty, the system of American Slavery to the scorn and indignation of all honest men. For not till Slavery shall be made odious, as the consummation of *theft and robbery*, will it be exploded from this tyrant-ridden world. We have nothing to do with *dead* slaveholders,—we are not their judges,—but to the *living* we must speak plainly. We feel for them as fellow men ; we are their *best* friends. But we must not apologize nor flatter. If they do not choose to enter the door of eternal infamy which is opening before them, let them have the magnanimity to be JUST. Let them cease to make merchandize of God's image, and to "fare sumptuously every day" upon the avails of unrecompensed toil ! We take for our motto the language of the prophet, as expressive both of the duty and the consequences of IMMEDIATE EMANCIPATION : "If thou take away from the midst of thee the YOKE, *the putting forth of the finger*, and *speaking vanity*; and if thou draw out thy soul to the hungry, and satisfy the afflicted soul; THEN SHALL THY LIGHT RISE IN OBSCURITY, AND THY DARKNESS BE AS THE NOON DAY."

For the terms of subscription see the last page.

☞ *When gratuitous, please to read and hand it to your neighbor.* ☜

REVIEW

OF THE SPEECHES AND PROCEEDINGS OF THE RECENT ANNUAL MEETING OF THE AMERICAN COLONIZATION SOCIETY.

THROUGH the laudable zeal of the Editors of the N. Y. Evangelist and the N. Y. Observer, the public has been favored with very full reports of the late Colonization Anniversary at Washington. We are not aware that these reports disagree as to any important fact or expression. In the following pages, except when the reader is otherwise notified, we quote from the Evangelist, for brevity's sake. We earnestly commend this *expose* to all who prefer light to darkness, and are conscientiously desirous to do their whole duty.

In our opposition to the Colonization Society we have not been fighting against *men*, but against *false principles* and an *injurious plan*. There have been men connected with the Colonization enterprize whose memories are dear to all abolitionists. But we must say, they labored under a sad mistake. There are men connected with it still, whom we love and admire, and upon whose co-operation with us, at no distant day, we repose all confidence. The disclosures which we are about to review will open their eyes. We know that our feelings are not those of triumph over a fallen enemy. We once ourselves sympathized in some of the hopes which are now suffering disappointment. But we should be inhuman to conceal our joy, that one great obstacle to the freedom of the slave is likely soon to be removed—that a master delusion which has blinded the community to the wrongs of their fellow men is just bidding adieu to things sublunary.

As a scheme of benevolence the Colonization Society is *dead*.* It may, however, replenish its overdrawn treasury—it may conduct a greater business of transportation than ever—but still it is *dead*. It will never regain the confidence of those who really seek the freedom of the slave. Why? Not simply because the society

is "bankrupt" in *funds*, but because this bankruptcy was produced by a bankruptcy of moral principle. We speak of the society as it appears between the covers of its authorized publications. Its present calamity is the fruit of a system of concealment, a time-serving "expediency," an assumption, more dishonest than uncommon, that the end sanctifies the means. To conciliate slaveholders, the *right of property in slaves* was admitted, and thus the society *gave up forever the power of plain honest truth.* In the execution of its plan it was necessary to make the public believe the colony prosperous and happy; it was necessary to make the public believe, that after the emigrants were landed and *seasoned*, they could support themselves, &c. and under the strong temptation to produce this belief *at any rate*, the managers it seems have permitted their agents at the colony, year after year, to neglect making any definite returns, in the shape of bills of mortality, accounts of expenditures, statistics of agriculture, &c. Vague statements have been received by the managers in regard to all these important interests, bearing always in favor of the colony, and have been by them widely circulated. We charge this as a culpable negligence, upon the managers, and we call common sense to witness, whether men who were determined to be honest, and let consequences take care of themselves, could continue to support agents who should thus neglect to make accurate returns. Is there not a strong ground to presume, first, that the agents at the colony had nothing to report which would bear detail; and secondly, that the managers suspected this and connived at it? It seems to us cruel for the managers to blame the agents as being slack about returns—they trained them up to this very habit by publishing with great zest and exultation those " letters from the colony" which contained any thing but information. The public were deluded. They thought Liberia a paradise, or at any rate quite enough so, for black people. They poured their money into the colonization treasury ; and urged the managers to prosecute their grand enterprize of removing the whole colored population. The consequence was, that, from the latter part of the year 1831 to the first of 1833, 1198 emigrants had been despatched to the colony. And although the agents at the colony had found some difficulty in accommodating this large accession, we find the following language in the Annual Report of 1833.

"The managers are convinced that Liberia is now prepared to receive a much larger number of emigrants annually, than the means of the society have heretofore enabled it to colonize. They be-

* We are aware that some of the ablest friends of the society at the North cling to it in the hope, that by a *reform*, it will get out of the way of the Anti-Slavery Society and give up the business of removing the entire colored population or any considerable part of it. In fact, their plan is, to disclaim any action whatsoever in regard to slavery, to cease to send emigrants, and confine their labors to the moral and physical improvement of the colony. This is all as it should be. We lay down our arms [pens] the moment it is accomplished ;— but can it be accomplished? Does Mr. Gerrit Smith's giving up his resolution to amend the Constitution in an important respect, "*for the sake of harmony*," look like it? We do not believe the society will bear *reforming*. It has not the requisite moral stamina. It will die under the operation. Let the truly benevolent colonizationists form a *new society* for the physical relief and moral improvement of Liberia. At any rate, let them drop the odious *name* of colonization, when they drop the *deed*.

lieve there is no reason to apprehend that the resources of the society will ever exceed the demands for aid from those anxious to emigrate, *or the capabilities of the colony to afford accommodation and subsistence to those who may choose to make it their residence.*"

Now observe how much "*good men*" may be mistaken. Since that time the society has colonized but about 257, it has received upwards of $37,000, and is found to be in debt $40,000 ! ! Even if we add, as Elliott Cresson suggests, to the expeditions of the past year the ship Hercules of the preceding, we shall have but 437 emigrants, for whom, after deducting $10,000 for other expenses, we shall have $60 apiece, more by $20 or $30 than the estimated expense of transporting and *seasoning* an emigrant. Here then is a debt for the support of the colony, accruing within less than two years, over and above the estimates, of more than $40,000. Mr. Gerritt Smith says the debt would have been less by $10,000 if the managers had sent out sufficient supplies. But did not the managers know, more than a year ago, that "the rice crop had failed"? Did they not know that there was nothing like agriculture in the colony? Did they not know what sort of "materials" they had sent out to build up the colony? If they did not, it was not the fault of the abolitionists, nor indeed, of Gov. Mechlin.* But did the extraor-

* *Extracts from Gov. Mechlin's letters in the African Repository for Nov.* 1831.

"We have not yet adopted, to any extent, the agricultural improvements of civilized countries, &c.

* * * * * * *

"The crops of last year did not succeed well, in consequence of unusual drought : the rice suffered more from this cause than from any other ; as we do not here, as in the southern states, plant it in low situations, which can be readily irrigated from adjacent water-courses ; but, on the contrary, it may be seen growing in the greatest luxuriance on the highest grounds, depending solely for its prosperity on copious showers, which *usually* [not always] fall during four or five months in the year. We are, however, *getting into the way* of raising Indian corn, though not to an extent sufficient to rely upon it as an article of subsistence. The corn of this country is of an inferior kind, and not near so productive as that of the United States. * * * *

" Formerly, the public store was the only resource *thr* most of the people employed by the agency, *and ey were glad to receive their pay in goods at a* GREAT ADVANCE! * * * *

" I regret to learn you had pledged yourselves to send out six expeditions during the ensuing twelve months ; and I fear, if persisted in, this will in the end prove very injurious. I may be wrong, and you may have greater funds at your disposal than I am aware of ; but if you have not, great pecuniary embarrassments will certainly ensue. * *

But I have great hopes your treasury will receive an unusual influx of money, or you will spare us two or three of the *threatened expeditions.*"

N. B.—The letters from which we quote the above are dated in July, 1831.

In the Af. Repos. for Sept. 1832, we find the following in a letter from Gov. Mechlin, dated July 13, 1832:

"I have before urged the necessity of keeping a re-

dinary pressure of spontaneous emigrants carry the humanity of the managers beyond their prudence? We think not; for after they were fully aware of their insolvency, they "got up" an expedition confessedly as a lure to draw funds from New-York.

Now we beseech our readers to understand, that while we do blame the 'managers for their disingenuous policy, we would not hold them up as *peculiarly* dishonest. *We quote their faults only as illustrating the tendency of their scheme.* That scheme, we pretend not to deny, numbers among its friends many of the wisest and best men of our land ; and yet we should despair of selecting from them a board of managers any more worthy of confidence than that which has hitherto existed. There is a sort of insanity in the scheme itself, which is totally destructive of that straight-forwardness which

gular supply of trade goods in the public store. Our stock of cloths and many other important articles [Rum? spear-pointed knives?] is at present exhausted ; nor can they be purchased here, except on a very great advance on the first cost in the United States. Now is the time for purchasing rice and palm oil; the *natives* are getting in their new crops ; and if we do not avail ourselves of the opportunity, we will find great difficulty hereafter in procuring the quantity requisite for the subsistence of our people."

Under date of Sept. 8, 1832, Gov. Mechlin writes as follows. See Af. Repos. for Nov. 1832.

"You have doubtless, ere this, received drafts on the society to a considerable amount. This extra demand on your resources was, from the nature of circumstances, unavoidable. *The great number of emigrants that have been thrown upon our hands,* and the very scanty supplies that were sent out by the last expedition, as well as the expense necessarily incident to the erection of buildings for their accommodation, and other causes which will be more fully detailed in my communications per brig Liberia, have caused our disbursements for the few months past to be much greater than could possibly have been anticipated."

The following is from the said "communications per brig Liberia." It may be found in the Af. Repos. for Dec. 1832.

"I am at this moment issuing rations to at least one hundred persons, whose *six months have expired.* Some of these have been prevented by sickness from attending to their farms ; the crops of others are not sufficiently advanced to afford them subsistence ; but by far the greater number are women and children, who have been sent out without any male person to provide for them, and being unable to obtain a livelihood by tilling the soil, or any other occupation, have become a burden to the agency. Many in the *present expedition* [128 by the brig America,] are similarly circumstanced ; and what to do with them, I know not."

With the same letter, Dr. Mechlin transmitted "drafts to a considerable amount," for expense of "receptacles," "hospital expenses," the purchase of "rice and palm oil," &c. for which their "disbursements" he says, had been "far beyond what was anticipated." Dr. Mechlin may have grossly mismanaged the affairs of the Board ; but it cannot be denied that he gave them *timely* warning to desist from their mad scheme of transplanting our whole colored population. The plain, sober fact is, the managers had made foolish boasts, they had committed themselves —and their pride drove them over the cataract of bankruptcy with their eyes open.

we commonly call honesty. While the enterprise flourished, its friends assigned *too many reasons* for its prosecution; and now that it is brought to a stand, they assign *too many reasons* for its failure.

But we will not detain the reader from the report of the committee on the finances of the society. We quote it as follows, from the N. Y. Observer.

"The Committee appointed to inquire into the state of the financial concerns of the society, report as follows, that the debts owing by the society, now due, and that will fall due, by the first of May next, amount to a sum varying from $40,000, to $41,000

This unprecedented and alarming amount of debt against the society is accounted for, by the following reasons:

1st. The rice crop in the colony and on the coast generally, the last year, failed almost entirely; and by this Providence, a considerable share of the colonists, who would otherwise have been able to subsist upon their own means, were thrown upon the bounty and humanity of the government of the colony.

2d. The Ajax, which sailed from New-Orleans with 150 emigrants, lost 29 of them by the cholera; was double the usual length of time making the voyage, and arrived at the colony with but two weeks supply of provisions, instead of the usual supply for six months.

3d. An unusually large proportion of the late emigrants are improvident, and reluctant to betake themselves to agriculture.

4th. In some instances among the late emigrants, families without male heads have been sent to the colony—and, in many instances, the great mortality in the colony, during the last year has deprived families of their male heads and left them to the humane and expensive provisions of the government of the colony.

5th. The supplies of the colonial store have not been ample, as they ever should be. This deficiency, however, is not to be charged to improvidence in the Board of Managers; but to their pecuniary inability to do on this subject what they were very solicitous to do. This deficiency has made it necessary for the government of the colony to purchase at 100 to 200 per cent, profit, large amounts of supplies from merchants in the colony, and from vessels touching at the colony.

In view of existing pecuniary embarrassments of the society, the committee would advise that the society send out no emigrants the present year, unless under very special circumstances, and when the society would be put to comparatively small expense, in sending out and provisioning the emigrants. To guard against such heavy embarrassments in future, the committee advise, that the society do never, except in the extraordinary cases above referred to, send out emigrants whilst they are under a debt exceeding $10,000.

The committee hope that the Board of Managers will, as soon as the means at their disposal will allow, so far furnish the colonial store with goods and provisions as to preclude the necessity of purchasing them on terms so disadvantageous as those above referred to. This necessity having

existed for the last two years particularly, and which has been unavoidable on account of the large disbursements of the society for the expenses of emigration, has swelled the debt of the society to an amount of many thousand dollars greater than it would have been, if this necessity had not existed.

The committee are highly pleased to learn that the Board of Managers have adopted and are contemplating measures for bringing within ascertained and the narrowest limits, the compensation made to the officers of the society residing in the colony—and, also for avoiding the surprise of large drafts upon its treasury."

This report is really a very slim affair. "The rice crop failed in the colony." And for the very good reason that it is not cultivated. This ought to have been stated. Does the society pretend that there is any person in Liberia who in ordinary years gets his living by agriculture? Is it a very uncommon occurrence for the rice crop to fail on that coast? Why did not the committee tell the society plainly, that the colonists have always depended to a large extent on foreign importation for their provisions, and that while the colony was small they managed to purchase them by the proceeds of their petty trades, but now that, by a spasmodic effort, the colony has been overpeopled, there are multitudes, many of them women and children, who are "reluctant to betake themselves to agriculture" because they have no agricultural implements but such as *nature* has provided, and who must be supported at the expense of the society, or *starve*. We are told that the government of the colony had to purchase provisions at an advance of 100 or 200 per cent. on the cost in this country, but we are not told whether this is an unusual advance, nor whether any merchant can take the risks of transporting provisions to that tropical climate for less. We do not see what the loss of the 29 passengers of the ship Ajax, had to do with cutting short the supplies, nor indeed how the reduced number of passengers could contrive, by merely doubling the "usual time" of their voyage, so nearly to eat up the "six months" provision for the whole.* It really seems to us that the causes of expense assigned by the committee are mostly not temporary, but such as must cleave to the enterprize—and with the more force, the more rapidly it is pushed forward.

The committee advise, as a matter of economy, that "*no emigrants be sent out the present year.*" We would go further, and advise, that those sent out in former years be brought back. It will cost less to bring them home, than to support them there; and we presume their consent may be obtained as easily as it was in the first instance.

We cannot better, expose the society's scheme to the reprobation of the benevolent and ingenu-

* The Ajax was *eighty-two* days on her passage, and $2,300 of her outfit was paid by the Kentucky Colonization Society.

ous, than by quoting largely from the debate upon this report.

"Mr. Breckinridge said this report was not at all what he expected. He wished to know all about this business, how and when this debt had arisen, and by whose negligence, or mismanagement, or extravagance. He felt himself all in darkness about it. This debt was absolutely frightful, to him. It is over a whole year's income. And yet the committee propose to discontinue sending out emigrants for a whole year. He thought this would be like killing the goose that laid the golden eggs. For it is only to carry out emigrants that you can get money, to any extent. A few persons of a thorough missionary spirit, will give you money professedly to build up religion and education in the colony. But the most even of these will think there are so many other ways to give their money, that you will get but little. But the great mass of the people will not give you a dollar unless you connect with it the carrying out of emigrants. He hoped the report would be referred to the committee, for the purpose of having it made more explicit, and of having a more thorough examination. He wanted to know who these merchants are in the colony, that charge the society an advance of 100 or 200 per cent, in time of famine."

And why should they not so charge the society? Had not the society taught them the lesson by charging a similar advance to the colonists!

"Mr. Gurley said he believed he could explain the affair so as to show that it was no improvidence on the part of the managers that had brought this debt upon them. The society will recollect that two or three years ago the desire became very strong to see a considerable increase of emigration. It was thought the interest of the society required it, and the applications were also numerous and pressing. And the managers were willing to go even somewhat beyond their means with the confident hope that the community would sustain them. In consequence, at the close of the year 1832, they had increased their responsibilities beyond their receipts to the amount of from $12,000 to $15,000 and were calculating to enter upon a course of means to increase their resources commensurate to their want. But the early part of the year the demands from the colony began to come in most unexpectedly both for number and amount. He had not the means before him of an exact statement, but he believed that in four months they paid and accepted drafts from the agent exceeding $20,000, and that the whole of their acceptances on this amount were more than $30,000. The managers did not suppose they had been so very negligent in sending out supplies to the colonial store. The Hercules took out $6,000 in trade goods, [how much rum, gunpowder and tobacco, and how many "spear-pointed knives" and "brass blunderbusses?"] as they are called, which it was supposed would be worth from twelve to $20,000 in sustaining the colony. But the rice crop came short and the agent was obliged to purchase. It is plain there has been an accumulating debt at the colony, of which the managers were

for some of the bills received this year were for accounts that had been running on for several years. He had not examined particularly, but he was inclined to think there was some irregularity in the colony in regard to salaries. This amount then is not a demand for this year only, though it has come upon us all at once. The remote causes of the debt were doubtless these: the improvidence of many of the emigrants, and their neglect of agriculture; the unfortunate character of some of the materials sent out to build a colony; the agent was much of the time in feeble health; sickness prevailed to a great extent; both the physicians were absent, and the whole care thrown upon Dr. Mechlin: and under these circumstances it is impossible to suppose that the general administration of the colony could be so economical or so correct as would be desirable. There was one other cause, (for the society ought to be made perfectly acquainted with the whole truth;) during the early part of the year, there had been great debility, to use the mildest expression, in the operations of the Board. It arose, in part at least, from the excitement which grew out of the elections last year, and the introduction of several new members into the board, who were not accustomed to its proceedings. There was a cessation, of course, of holding meetings once in two weeks, and a substitution of an executive Committee, of very limited powers, not equal to the necessities of the case, and very many things were neglected; and among them, efforts to raise the means to meet our increasing expenses. In the course of the summer, I proposed to the Board a united effort to sustain the credit of the society, by a loan on the individual responsibility of the members. But it did not succeed. If done, to the amount of 15 or $20,000, he believed the revenue of the society could have been greatly increased. In his efforts at the north, his greatest difficulty was not in the fact that the society was in debt, but that we had failed, and our drafts were under a protest, and that whatever people gave would go for paying an old debt. Still he did not think affairs looked so very dark. There were many things, it is true, in the colony as well as here, to be regretted. But they were not such as to authorize despondency, much less despair."

Ah! Mr. Gurley, this mild, soft way of plastering over every body's faults may be very amiable in a popish forgiver of sins, but it will not do in a man who undertakes to manage the charities of plain matter-of-fact people. As we have shown in a former note, you knew long ago that the "remote causes of the debt," were in active operation, and yet you say, that in the early part of the year the demands from the colony began to come in most unexpectedly!!"

"Mr. Frelinghuysen was glad to hear this explanation. When the fact respecting our debt was first developed last night, it made his heart feel sick; especially because it will be employed so effectively against us. It will be seized with avidity by our adversaries, and pressed with great power. If I had not strong confidence in the goodness of our cause, and in Him who patronizes and protects every good cause, I would sit down in despair. While we were holding ourselves out to the public, as able to transport any number of emigrants for $30 each, and that the colony was prosperous, and the emigrants thriving and happy, these dis-closures came upon us. In the midst, too, of our conflict with the abolitionists, as well as in the midst of this triumph respecting the colony, we have gone in debt, in two years to the amount of more than $40,000. With a large portion of the community, this blow will be irretrievable at present. They will point to the foot of our leger, and pass upon us a sentence of reprobation. Still I will give way to no despondency. We have come now to a crisis in the history of the society, and if we improve it properly, we may date from this anniversary a new era of prosperity and success. I hope we shall not only re-organize our constitution, but adopt a new set of principles in the management of our affairs. Our Board, and all who are employed, must be made to have a deep sense of responsibility, that not a dollar shall be expended which shall not be satisfactorily accounted for. It must not be allowed to any agent to run the society in debt, or to draw bills without sending an account. They must go to their work with a sense of as deep responsibility as if they were next door to the Board, and feel that this money is drawn from the public charity, and every dollar must be stritly accounted for. And then we can go on. If I did not feel sure, said Mr. F. that this cause is deeply seated in the affections of the American people, I would move instantly to adjourn *sine die*. But I do believe all these things are sent upon us by the hand of Him who would draw our dependence away from all human contrivances. Let us now repose our cause on his arm, and he will bless us. Let the abolitionists clamor. Let fanaticism rage as it may. I cannot yet bring myself to believe, that Finley has died—that Mills has perished on the ocean in behalf of Africa, to no purpose. I trust that, when the secretary comes to publish his report, he will prepare a statement on this subject, so that the public may have what I apprehend will be a perfectly satisfactory explanation of this business."

What a precious compound of absurdity. This noble Senator "was glad to hear an EX-PLANATION," which covered up things. He had felt sick at the thought of being detected by the abolitionists. He confesses that the society is caught in the very act of deceiving the public and getting money under false pretences, and yet he professes to have confidence "in Him who patronizes every good cause ! ! !" What pious swindling !—Good courage—no despond-ency—indeed it makes us think of a couple of scared urchins in the dark ; "Jack," says one of them, "are you afraid ?" "No, I'm not afraid." "Nor I neither." How wonderfully courageous !

"Let fanaticism rage as it may," says he, "I cannot believe that cause will fail which two good men died in promoting." What is this but superstition—the very parent of fanaticism ? Last of all, he hopes the secretary will plaster this up nicely in the *annual report*, so that it will be "satisfactory." We are not master of English suitable to express our views of such a sentiment, and we shall not make the attempt.

No doubt the secretary will try his art. But it is too late,—the thing has been mended too many times already.

"Bishop MEADE said, When sinful, frail beings get into difficulty, we should first examine *our-selves*, and see why it is so. This examination should be very strict and faithful, and we should be careful not to ascribe our trouble to any wrong causes. I do not doubt that the secretary has given us a faithful exposition of the business, as he supposed. And so far as it goes, it is well enough. But all must be satisfied that the radical defect is in the colony. For during the last year, our expenditure on emigration has been less than usual. And the funds which have been contributed are greater than ever before in a year. We may dwell too long upon lamentation. When we fall, we should not lie lamenting, but rise and proceed on our way, as fast as possible. The Bishop thought a successful appeal might be made to the legislatures of the adjoining states, for aid in this emergency. With Virginia, our plea must be acknowledged just. Last year the legislature appropriated about $20,000 for colonizing her free people of color in Africa. And if it had not been for the imprudent and excessive zeal of rash friends, the appropriation would have been $100,000. As it was, they so trammelled it as to make it ineffective for the purposes designed. And, said he, I cannot but hope that now, if the legislature now in session can be approached through some of its popular members, they may make the appropriation this year in such a way as to relieve us. They will recollect this society has been carrying on its operations without legislative aid, and a kind of debt thereby contracted. Might not a similar application be made to Maryland ? And thus our society might be speedily extricated from this unexpected and sad catastrophe ; and we might say to our enemies, that though we have erred against the rules of prudence, yet He who originated this noble design has not permitted our errors to destroy the work.

Rev. REUBEN POST, of Washington, said that only a very small portion of this debt was incurred in the past year. All our expeditions have not cost over 10 or $12,000. The two which went from Virginia were sent at the urgent request of friends in Norfolk, Mr. Maxwell and others. The expense of those sent from New Orleans was defrayed, it is understood, by the Kentucky and other Western societies. The great amount were sent the year before last, chiefly from Virginia, and those very ill fitted to go. And the Board have resolved that they will not send any more unless the funds are provided in hand. Another circumstance was, that their whole affairs rested on one person, except that a part of the year he had had an assistant in the office. The Board had appointed several gentlemen from Virginia, and tried to engage them as general agents, but none of them would accept. And they have looked to this meeting in the hope that some persons might be found to take hold.

Mr. BRECKENRIDGE said, It is not the magnitude of the debt that disturbs me. But the causes assigned by the committee do not account for it, for most of them were, as it appears, posterior to its occurrence. The 769 emigrants sent out in 1832, if supported the whole year, could not have cost $40,000. Sir, if these drafts are wrongfully drawn, I say they should not be paid. Those who drew them ought to suffer. If drawn for expenditures not warranted by the Board, they should not have been accepted. If the managers do not know how it came, they ought to know, and they ought to suffer, and we ought to change our officers. FORTY THOUSAND DOLLARS is a small sum, in connection with such an object as the removal of our colored race to Africa. But it is the mismanagement by which the debt has been produced that I complain of. To me it seems perfectly nefarious that the merchants of our colony should charge *us* three or four hundred per cent. advance. And it has been stated, and published, that the agents whom we sent out and supported are these very merchants. I hope the report will go back to the committee, who are capable of searching to the bottom of the whole. There is an immense aggregate of blame somewhere; and I want to find out where it belongs, and put it there. I want to know who did it, and what for. Two years ago, I warned the managers against this Virginia business. And yet they sent out two ship loads of vagabonds, not fit to go to such a place, and that were coerced away, as truly as if it had been done with a cart whip. They were not driven by force. But after the Southampton affair, the legislature enacted severe laws, which required the free negroes to go through certain operations and forms of law in order to remain. They were ignorant and terrified, and you will not wonder at it if you look at the legislative reports of the slaughter. And so they fled to our agents, who took them and sent them away. And I think we have a just claim upon Virginia on their account, as well as just cause of complaint against those who let them go to our colony.

Sir, we are not only embarrassed but we are *broke.* And if we lose our character we lose all. But if we can come out now with a fair character, the public will sustain us and pay our debts.

Mr. GURLEY said, I cannot concur in the view that any part of this has come from the weight of business on myself. In regard to any business entrusted to myself by the Board of Managers, it has been done, and done faithfully. The difficulty is not with managers. Two years ago, they sent out full instructions to the agent, to enforce the strictest accountability, and demanding quarterly returns of all expenditures. But they had no returns with any regularity or to any extent. I believe one reason has been the sickness of the agent, and the weight of affairs that pressed on him. No strictness of instructions can secure a correct administration of affairs unless they are obeyed. I cannot concur in the entire unfitness of what are called the Southampton emigrants, or that we did wrong in receiving them, and sending them out, when they were coerced away. Our friends at Norfolk appealed to us, and said the people were persecuted, and that it was a matter of humanity to take them. Our agents said they were driven from the county, and had appealed to him and begged to go to Liberia, and certified that they were respectable and industrious. Our expeditions have been small this year. The Jupiter was fitted out at the earnest solicitation of the

New-York City Society. They stated to me that there was no hope of raising funds there unless some project could be started for a New-York expedition to send out emigrants. It was not the debt which embarrassed us, but the entire failure of our credit. Our friends at New-York said the best way was only to let it be known to a few warm friends, but to start an expedition, and then many will give for the project, and many others will give for the general purposes of the Society. I wrote to the managers on the subject, and they held a meeting, and gave their consent to the plan.

GERRIT SMITH hoped the motion to re-commit would not prevail. He could not see any good from it. As a member of that committee, he had spent several hours in examining the affairs and interrogating Mr. Gurley and Dr. Laurie, and he saw that to obtain the minute information called for would require the labor of many days, and he for one had not time to spend here to do it. We have arrived satisfactorily at the general causes, which the report unfolds, and we should not be greatly benefited by spreading out the details. It is certain there is a very bad system of operations, or rather there is no system at all. This debt is from five to ten thousand dollars greater than it would have been if there had been a constant supply of goods in the colonial store. In looking over the accounts of Colston M. Waring & Co. and others, with the Agent, I find prices charged two, three, and even four times higher than the cost in this country. The reason assigned by the treasurer for their not keeping the store supplied is not satisfactory. It might have been a little bold, perhaps, for this Board to incur a debt of a few thousands in order to send on supplies in season. But the result shows that it would have been economical. There is an excessive number of officers in Africa, and their salaries amount to a very considerable sum, not far from $5,000 a year. The colonial governor and the physician, whose salaries are very handsome, including what they receive from the government of the United States, one being $2,400, and the other $1,200, in addition to all this, they are allowed to furnish their whole domestic establishment at the public expense, and some of these bills are very large.

As Mr. S. was sitting down, several gentlemen begged him to go on, but he said he had rather not. He might misapprehend or mis-state something.

Dr. LAURIE said the salary the agent received from the society was only $80.

Mr. CRESSON said that having devoted five years of his life to the Society, without any compensation, direct or indirect, he supposed his explanations might have some weight. It will be observed, that one item of debt, amounting to one-fourth of the whole, is the charter party and expenses of the ship Hercules, in 1833. There had also been 1100 emigrants landed in the colony in a little more than 12 months, which had increased the expense of their accommodation. In short, to borrow a phrase from the negroes of Virginia, " It is as it is and it can't be no tis-er." The prices of provisions at Liberia, and on the coast were increased in consequence of the famine at the Cape de Verds. He was satisfied that none of the Society's agents had benefitted themselves by participating in any commercial transaction. Mr. Waring and Mr. McGill were not capitalists, trading on their own accounts, but commission merchants, and therefore bound to sell to the best advantage for the interest of their principals.— The debt could not have been avoided without starvation in the colony.

Mr. FRELINGHUYSEN said there was no need to send the report back for further particulars, in order to make a very sad statement indeed. We can't help it, and we must make the best of it. The managers should not accept drafts from the colony, unless preceded by advices, and accompanied by accounts stated. No merchant would have done it. They must make it a strictly ac-accountable concern.

BISHOP MEADE said if we called for these accounts, it might show those merchants that we disapprove of their conduct.

Mr. COXE thought it necessary to have some decided expression of opinion from the society.— There was a resolution of the Board already, not to accept of drafts unless preceded by advices and accompanied by accounts. He would ask the Board whether there has been no draft accepted without either? The managers are aware of the propriety of this course, but they do not act up to it. The attention of the Board has been called to this subject. I would ask also, if any member of the Board can tell how many officers we have at Liberia, and what are their expenses? For one, I believe it is impossible to get along, unless things can be placed on a proper basis. He hoped the society would take it up once for all, and if it should take a week, or a month, it would be a saving of time in the end, as well as a great saving of money.

Mr. GURLEY said there was one difficulty the Board had to encounter. They had not had correct information in regard to the expense of supporting emigrants in the colony. They had been told that $10 worth of goods in this country would bring enough there for each. And they had always made their estimate on this basis, for each expedition. But they have now found that their estimate was quite inadequate. As to the resolutions of the Board spoken of by Mr. Coxe, it was proper to say, that they were passed *after* this great amount of debt had come upon us, and in consequence of it. The letters of advice accompanying the drafts, have generally been very brief, and not explicit or full. The expense of the officers in the colony was doubtless an unfortunate arrangement. The full development of the course things were taking, never reached us till last spring or summer.

Mr. BACON said that in regard to the recommendation of the committee not to send out any more emigrants this year, one gentleman has urged that this was the way not to obtain funds. But Mr. B. believed it to be the only way in which affairs can be managed to revive the confidence of the public. And he hoped it would lead to a permanent change in the policy of the society in regard to sending out emigrants. Let us bend our efforts to make the colony what it ought to be, and what it might be, and we shall find the free people will begin to look at it in a different light,

and will spontaneously help themselves to Liberia. And whenever they became desirous to go, they did not need a society to help them. The free black who cannot earn $30 is not fit for the colony, and ought not to go.

The motion to recommit was withdrawn, and the report accepted."

We have dwelt thus long on the state of the Society's finances because it illustrates the capital defect of its morals. Mr. Frelinghuysen recommends the adoption of a "new set of principles." Honesty should be one of them. We can but glance at the interesting matters contained in other parts of the report.

The annual report, read by Mr. Gurley, of which we have some of the heads, is deceptive as usual. It represents the *Sabbath* as being well observed, many added to the church, &c. while it utters not one word about iniquities that have been practiced there in high places. If at some station of the American Board the leading missionaries had been guilty of numerous seductions ; if by their extravagance and profligacy they had brought religion into contempt, and unhinged the morals of the community about them, would the Board smooth over the matter to the public by saying "there are nine meeting houses ; the *Sabbath* is well observed, &c." Yet such is the sad fact in regard to the late leading authorities of Liberia, as we knew long ago from private letters from the Colony, and as we know now by the confessions of one of the standard bearers of Colonization just returned from the Anniversary. Indeed the report goes still farther in covering up matters, and says of Dr. Mechlin, "His self-denying services, and successful efforts for enlarging and improving the colony, entitle him to the grateful regards of the Society." *Self-denying !!* This appears from the facts we have just mentioned, from the salary of $2400, and from a bill of some $5,000 against the Society for his "domestic establishment !" Truly even the most "self-denying" governors are somewhat expensive.

The annual report, as usual, eulogizes Mr. Cresson, that veracious person who told the venerable Clarkson that *one hundred thousand* slaves were ready to be liberated, if seven pounds and ten shillings could be raised for the transportation of each, and then backed up the monstrous story, by another, that this state of things had been produced by the *faithfulness of the ministers of the gospel at the South !!* We put the question to Mr. Cresson, recently at Philadelphia, whether he made these statements to Mr. Clarkson. He replied that he merely stated these things as his *opinion !* What a happy retreat behind his own insignificance ! We know not which most to admire, the inexhaustible impudence of Mr. Cresson, or the unparalleled effrontery of the Society in sustaining him against the "organized opposition" of British philanthropists. No doubt the Society will receive the thanks of Lord Bexby, the Duke of

Sussex, and the whole body of West India slave-holders.

Robert S. Finley, Esq. at the anniversary in the Capitol, introduced a very pertinent and seasonable resolution relative to ardent spirits in the Colony. He was very happy as usual in refuting his own argument. "The Colony," he said, "had already done much to arrest the tide of intemperance, which for 200 years has been rolling over Africa like a flood." And yet the Colony has carried on an extensive traffic in ardent spirits,—a traffic which Mr. Finley says "is a greater crime than the slave trade, because it supports the slave trade." This is implied by Mr. Finley's proposing that "all future settlements" should be founded on "temperance principles." If Mr. Finley were only a doctor, he would probably prescribe brandy for *delirium tremens*. According to his statement the Colonists, selling 3,000 barrels of *rum* in a year, have outstripped the best of us in the temperance reformation, and have done wonders in breaking up the slave trade, and yet the sagacious Mr. Finley says, ardent spirits, are injurious to the colony! It is a little singular that the Col. Board should hesitate to pass a law excluding ardent spirits from the Colony for fear those moral people should refuse to sustain it.

Bishop Meade, of Va., made a speech in which there is nothing more remarkable than the following sentiment :

"The object of this Society is benevolent. Its object is to improve the condition of those who are formed *in some respects* after the image of God, but who are nevertheless *so* formed as to be liable to many calamities. And is not this benevolent ?"

Rev. Robert J. Breckinridge uttered sentiments which were probably as little relished by his audience as they were expected. Were it not that he now and then threw a sop to Cerberus, we might take him for a genuine abolitionist. He evidently lacks not courage. Some of his rebukes are enough to raise a blush on the palest face of "dough." He most fully confirms several of the positions of the abolitionists, as a few extracts will show.

"The view which I wish to present is this; the future prospects of the Society in regard to procuring proper emigrants. In the Providence of God, the free blacks have become hostile to us—intensely hostile. I know the fact, and it is useless to disguise it. I believe they are unalterably hostile. They have been made so, on system, by a great and growing party in our country, to which I am decidedly hostile. We owe thanks to God, that when the Society first started, and could not procure slaves to colonize, the free people of color were willing to go. The first four or five hundred who were sent out were chiefly free. And by their success we were enabled to demonstrate the feasibility of our plan of colonization. And now these free people of color, without just cause, and under the influence of wrong instructions, are going farther and farther from us. For the

last five years, we find among our emigrants, that the proportion of slaves emancipated for the purpose of colonizing has greatly increased. I was surprised to learn, by the report read to night, that of the emigrants from Kentucky, my native state, 90 per cent. were manumitted slaves, and from the whole valley 75 per cent. notwithstanding there are a hundred thousand people of color there. And this spirit among the free blacks will grow every day, because the party who have poisoned their minds will grow, because some states will take up the subject, and because *we* have grown wise by experience, and do not intend to let you send out your ship loads of free vagabonds to Christianize Africa. We had rather have those who are sent out by humane men, that will manumit their slaves from conscientious principles. If we cannot have men of good character, we want none. You do more hurt than good by every ship load of these free vagabonds."

The following sentiment is in accordance with the views of the abolitionists as expressed in the Declaration of the Anti-Slavery Convention. We believe it has not been sufficiently pondered by those upon whom the responsibility rests.

"As to any other means of abolishing slavery, I will say nothing of the power of the United States government, only that the constitutional authority which forbids the importation of slaves from foreign countries, is plainly competent to forbid their importation from other states. Congress have already exercised this authority towards several now flourishing states of this confederacy, and over all our territories lying north of a certain parallel of latitude. And the day when this authority shall be exercised over all the states, is the day that slavery terminates its power. Slavery cannot survive such a blow. This sir, is, I admit, an engine of vast potency against slavery. And it is not to be exercised until the good sense and piety and humanity of the nation shall call it forth."

We trust that the "good sense and piety" of the nation are now beginning to awake. Such language as the following from a Southern man is some proof of it.

"No man can read either the Old Testament or the New, but he must see it is hostile to slavery. And though you may say that, as Christians it is out of our province to urge such considerations upon the government, yet as Christians we may speak to one another, and admonish each other of wrong. And, sir, as the man who kills another is *prima facie* a murderer, and is held to clear himself by showing justifiable grounds for his deed, so the man who claims title in his fellow man, in his bones and sinews and blood, shall be considered *prima facie* a sinner, and shall be held to prove that his title has originated in such circumstances, and is held for such purposes, as are consistent with the spirit and principles of the gospel. And, sir, the Presbyterian church, of which I am a member, can bring forward three hundred thousand persons who will maintain this, and will act upon it.

I have spoken freely of the abolitionists, but it is not in unkindness. I agree with the slave-holder, that the free people of color must go away or perish. [Then they must *perish*, for he has elsewhere conceded that they *will* not go, and that the society *cannot* carry them.] And if any one doubts the truth of this, let him come to Baltimore, and I will show it to him. There he will find that our lawyers will not admit a colored man to the bar, nor our druggists to their profession. Our hack stands show few men of color. Even our draymen are nearly all white. We exclude the colored men from every employment in which men can rise. And they are there perishing for the want of daily food.

But the day is coming, too, when the other side of this subject will come up. If the slave-holder forces us to a stand in our present course, and compels us to decide whether slavery shall be abolished instantly, or endure forever, we come to a new position. And I, for one, am prepared to meet it. Let the slave holder beware how he drives us away. *We stand in the breach for him, to keep off the abolitionists.* We are his friends, but only to give him time. If we are driven away, *where can he find an ally?* Where in the literature of the whole world, in the public opinion of the whole world, in the religion of the whole world, will he find an advocate? The abolitionist is upon him. And if he attempts to maintain slavery as perpetual, every one of us will be upon him too. You, Mr. President, and I, and all of us will join the abolitionist in such a cause, against perpetuating slavery. Rather than slavery, with its horrors, shall exist forever in this country, let us suffer the evils incidental to its *instant* abolition. If abolition must be immediate or not at all, let it be immediate, come what will. For it is one of the plainest of all propositions, that slavery ought not to be perpetuated. If I am asked whether God made one man to own a title to another, I must reply, Nay. To me, it is self-evident, that the beings whom God made in his own image, he must have made free. We are the only friends of the slave holder, for we give him time, and that is all he can ask—TIME to act and abolish slavery. And in regard to the other branch of our labors, the colonizing of the free, we appeal to the humanity of the slave holder, and ask him, Will you drive this free man away, and not let us unite to provide him a home? Our brethren at the South will surely become our friends and the friends of our enterprise, I do not say if they will understand us, but if they will only so far command their feelings as to give us time to cry to them, "Strike, but hear us."

Give the slaveholders TIME! That is all they ask. The Colonization Society is always giving them *time*, and therefore the time to repent never comes. As for us, we think the time has come. It came long ago, and every hour's delay adds immensely to the obligation to repent *immediately*.

Mr. Breckinridge, it seems, received some significant growls from the lion, for making so free with his beard in his own den. But he is not easily frightened, and we trust the discipline he will receive from his slave-holding brethren will drive him off from some of his strange inconsistencies. He delivered a speech of a similar character before the Kentucky Colonization Society in 1831. It appears in the African Repository for August of the same year. It furnishes almost the only Anti-Slavery sentiments to be found in that periodical for nine years; but, on the 185th page of the same number, the editor of the Repository takes occasion to enter a Jesuitical disclaimer. He says:

"In the sentiments of this speech generally, we concur, but we wish it to be distinctly understood, that we consider slavery to be an evil, which can not, without producing evils greater than itself, be abolished, except by deliberate, cautious and gradual measures. The present generation did not produce, and are not therefore responsible for the *existence* of the present form of society in our Southern communities. If (!!) the state of things is wrong, it should be set right, but only with due regard to the rights and interests of all parties, &c."

When Mr. Elliott Cresson wished to persuade a certain distinguished Anti-Slavery man in London, that the Colonization Society was in fact, an Abolition Society, he presented him this number of the African Repository. The trick succeeded admirably, for, as was afterwards discovered *the leaf containing the* DISCLAIMER *had been nicely* CUT OUT! It is needless to tell the result of this unexpected discovery. If Mr. Cresson wishes to stick this additional feather in the cap of his disgrace, he may have the names of all the parties by applying at the Anti-Slavery office in New-York.

Mr. Gerrit Smith, whose philanthropy none will doubt, and whose offer to pay so large a portion of the Society's immense debt proves extraordinary honesty, made a very sensible speech. But we wonder how, with all his candor and means of information, he fell into certain mistakes. After commending the best intentions, he says:

I wish I could say as much in commendation of their publications, as I can of their intentions. And there are some of their documents which I much regard as admirable exhibitions of truth, which cannot be too widely circulated or too earnestly considered. But I am compelled to declare that many of them are also rash, ill-judged, uncharitable and slanderous, and not a few of them incendiary, to the last degree. I believe the sensible and good men among them (and I take a pleasure in acknowledging there are many such) feel it to be so too.

It should be understood that he was speaking not of individual abolitionists but of "the Anti-Slavery Society." We beg of Mr. Smith to put his finger on some of our slanderous and "incendiary" documents. We hold ourselves responsible only for what we publish. We suspect Mr. Smith may take to himself the reproof which he administers to us: "They have done the Society injustice by holding us too much responsible for the acts and speeches of indvidual members."

In regard to our charge against the Colony for trafficking in ardent spirits he is under a great misapprehension. ، He says,

They have also created a strong prejudice by harping on the fact that ardent spirit continues to be sold at the colony. On this subject I will say (and my neighbors, at least, know that I am not a friend to rum, and will therefore attach some value to the declaration) that I have, both at former times and now, inquired into the measures, which have been adopted by the Board of Managers from time to time, in relation to this subject, and I fully approve them. We are denounced for having omitted to make the attempt of suppressing the traffic in ardent spirit by law, with an ill grace indeed, until at least some one of our governments at home shall have set the example (so much needed) of shutting up the grog-shops in their jurisdiction.

Now we ourselves "fully approve" "the measures adopted by the Board of Managers" so far as they go. And we do not "denounce them for having omitted to make the attempt to suppress the traffic" by law, but for holding up the Colony as a missionary station, when they very well know that a law for the suppression of the traffic would be useless for the want of a proper public opinion in the colony to sustain it. While Mr. Smith cannot deny that the rum-traffic is carried on largely in Liberia, it is "with an ill grace indeed," that he ridicules us for making the colony "appear but a convenience for the slave-trader."

Mr. Smith also ridicules the assertion that "there are now in slavery 265,000 persons who would have been free but for the influence of the Society ;" in other words, that but for the Society, emancipation would have gone forward to this time at the same rate as it did before the existence of the Society. Now be this as it may, while Mr. Smith grants that the Society has stood somewhat in the way of emancipation, we do not see how he can say that the assertion "makes ridiculously large drafts upon public credulity."

The following concessions are honest and manly, and we feel no disposition to withhold a tribute of respect for the moral courage it took to utter them, on such an occasion as the Colonization Anniversary in the Representatives' Hall. We presume the Representatives of southern "property" will take care to give a casting vote against the repetition of such heresies in that sacred place.

But truth compels me to say, that this is not the character of all that the Anti-Slavery Society has charged against us. I would it were so. But to some of the charges we should make haste to plead guilty, and make haste to profit by the admonition. Fas est ab hoste doceri. They have told us many wholesome truths about ourselves and our influence, for which I thank them.

The opinion is gaining ground rapidly, at the

North, that our society obstructs the progress of emancipation. And I could wish that we had given no occasion. But we have given some occasion. We are not an Anti-Slavery Society. We have literally nothing to do with slaves. Our constitution confines us to another class of persons entirely. Whatever some of our members or agents may have said, our society sets up no pretensions to the abolition of slavery. And those who denounce us for not doing this, might with the same propriety denounce the Bible Society, or any similar institution, for not going out of their limits, to promote the abolition of slavery. But it is equally true that we are not a Pro-Slavery society. If there are. under any circumstances, any apologies to be offered for slavery, it is no part of our business to hunt them up. And if efforts are made by any of our fellow citizens, to abolish slavery, it does not become us to oppose those efforts. The objection has been well taken, I conceive, that we want to engross the field. I think we have tried to assume the position that slavery should be assailed only by indirect means, and that this society furnishes the only indirect means that can be allowed. Whether this position is true or not, I will not now attempt to discuss. But I will say, that we may as well abandon at once all hope of support from the North, as attempt to engross for our own society the whole of public sympathy and interest in regard to the abolition of slavery. The North will no more bear the attempt to make this engross the ground in regard to the abolition of slavery, than the South would bear to have it expressly oppose slavery. Both claim, and have a right to claim, that we should maintain a strict neutrality. And as, on the one hand, we are not to denounce slavery, so on the other, we are not to denounce any, even the wildest schemes for its abolition. So that our members may be either slave holders or abolitionists, without doing any violence to their principles or their connections.

But there is another objection against this society, which to my mind is still more weighty. It is, that it has been greatly, lamentably, wickedly deficient in pity for the free people of color. Their number in this land is more than four hundred thousand. They are scattered through all our states, but every where they have law, custom, and prejudice arrayed against them. They are persecuted at the North as well as the South. And whenever I hear the people of the North complain of the cruel treatment of the blacks at the South, I cannot but exclaim, O what hypocrisy ! It is the settled policy of my own native state of New-York. I am ashamed and grieved to confess it, but it is true, that the whole policy has been to keep this people vile, by withholding from them every inducement to well-doing. We make even the gift of freedom a mockery.

What will those presses, which have so abundantly reviled Mr. Garrison as the slanderer of his country, say to Mr. Smith, who has in a similar manner slandered his native state ?

We have room but for a single extract more of Mr. Smith's speech. He professes still to cherish the highest hopes of Liberia, "that fountain from which Africa, is already deriving her many streams of knowledge and improvement "

This is astonishing after Mr. Pinney has told us, "The natives are in fact menials, (I mean those in town) and sorry I am to be obliged to say, that from my limited observation, it is evident that as little effort is made by the colonists to elevate them, as is usually made by the higher classes in the United States to better the condition of the lower." Mr. Smith nevertheless wishes *all* the people of color to consent to go to Liberia. He acknowledges their right to a home here, and, we rejoice to say it, administers a deserved rebuke to those who have so often denied that right; but, after all, he thinks it best for them to go. He thinks the colony can be improved so as to make it all, tha', in our ignorance, we have fondly dreamed about it. We repeat, that we are beyond measure astonished at this, in a man so well acquainted as Mr. Smith with the materials of which the Board of Managers is composed, and who knows so well that the morals of the colony are in a wretched state. To hold on with such a board, for the purpose of reforming such a colony, is in our humble apprehension something like marrying a shrew to improve her temper. Such a thing may do well enough in romance, but we have no faith in it in real life.

"Let the measures of our society be prompted by a strong desire to relieve the distress of the free people of color, and I must beg leave to differ from my reverend friend who has spoken; I believe the people will become as unanimous in going to Liberia, as they are now unanimous in opposition. It is no wonder to me, that they have had feelings of jealousy towards us, and a want of confidence in the sincerity of our professions of kindness. We ourselves have given too much occasion for this, in our speeches and publications. We have looked too little to *their* benefit, and too much to the political and social advantages which we supposed would arise to *ourselves*, from the separation. And our project, which should have been held up as one of the purest and highest benevolence, has been degraded to a mere drain for the escape of this nuisance. Let us correct this, and place our society on its true ground; let us make Africa a desirable home for men of color, and they will find their own way to its shores."

In the speech of Mr. Terry who succeeded Mr. Smith, there is nothing remarkable. It is of the old sort—the common product of the colonization mill. In the language of the reporter,—

"He then moved a resolution, expressing that the meeting is cheered by the good effects of the colony on the surrounding native tribes, affording bright hopes that the light will spread farther and farther, until Africa shall take her equal rank among Christian nations."

What marvelous men! "cheered" by their very disappointments! "cheered" amidst the ruins of all their hopes! But this pitiful mockery is as much out of place as hypocrisy will be after the day of judgment. It reminds us of a passage in Pollok.

"Detected wretch! of all the reprobate, None seemed maturer for the flames of hell, Where still his face, from ancient custom, wears A holy air, which says to all that pass Him by, 'I was a hypocrite on earth.'"

What a comment on this resolution is furnished by the debate of the succeeding Thursday, in which Mr. Terry, the mover, admits that the colony is "in a suffering state,"—many persons "in a bad condition, and who might be relieved by the accommodation of '*cabins, similar to those used by the natives!*'" and Mr. Bacon said, "there was something to come out to which all this [the pecuniary embarrassment] was as the dust of the balance. There were things to come out, frightful in their import, but they could no more be concealed than the sun at noon day!" [See N. Y. Observer.] And "that the condition of the colony was such as must horrify every friend of the cause." *Why were not Drs. Mechlin and Todsen there to support this resolution by a narrative of some of the items of good done to Africa?* Excellent and self-denying missionaries! why are their labors for the benefit of the colony and the natives permitted to lie in obscurity?

We are now arrived, in the course of this splendid and "cheering" anniversary, at the set speech of "ELLIOTT CRESSON, ESQ." This wonderful man seems to be a sort of personification of the colonization scheme;—the tutelar divinity of the enterprize. Whenever he speaks of the society, he speaks of *himself.* He offered the appropriate resolution; "That the meeting rejoice in the formation of the British African Colonization Society, and would gladly co-operate with them in promoting the great objects in view." We hope Mr. Cresson will keep us duly advised of all the benevolent operations of this precious junta of antiquated aristocrats, under the patronage of his noble friends Lord Bexley and the Duke of Sussex. No doubt there are strong affinities between the two societies.

"Mr. C. said he could not but rejoice in the humble instrumentality which he had been permitted to have in producing this result. As for the slanders which had been heaped upon him for it, so far as he was personally concerned, he cast them off. But as an American he deeply regretted, that one bearing the name of citizen had dared to declare, before a British audience, that the American constitution was the vilest outrage upon humanity that was ever perpetrated."

And when Mr. Cresson heard this vile slander upon his country, why did he not rise and rebuke it! We have a faint recollection that Mr. Cresson was challenged by "one bearing the name of citizen" to defend his darling society,—"the bond of union among mankind," and that his *friends advised him to keep out of sight.* Doubtless they had their reasons.

But for ourselves we confess, we do not believe that any one bearing the name of an American ever made such a declaration before a

British audience. We must have some other proof than Mr. Cresson's assertion.

"He was happy, however, to be able to say, that such men as the excellent Clarkson, and the deceased and sainted Wilberforce, had fully approved the objects of the society. Pains are taken to make the American public believe that Wilberforce had denounced the society. The charge is untrue. In the vigor of his mind, three years ago, he *expressed* his ardent love for this society. His pretended signature to the noted "protest," was affixed when he was on his death bed, the very week of the termination of his valuable life. Subsequently, some of his nearest and dearest friends had reprobated the act which affixed his signature. Others had also stricken their names from the offensive document."

To Mr. Cresson himself we "have nothing to say" in regard to these statements. The man is incapable of shame. But to the hearers who listened to, and drank in such monstrous incredibilities we must be permitted to say, that our indignation at their prejudice has given place to a feeling half way between pity and contempt for the weakness of their intellects. The *lies*, to use a term more appropriate than polite, are exquisite ; but then, they are put together with very bad logic. A man frequently does a good thing on his "death bed" which he would by no means have done three years before. If we are not mistaken a poet has somewhere said, "Death is an *honest* hour." For the benefit of those who cannot see truth through so many thicknesses of falsehood, we subjoin a note on this passage by the editor of the Emancipator.

"We feel it our duty to affirm, positively, and solemnly, and on our own personal knowledge and responsibility, that this statement is untrue.— The original manuscript, drawn up by one of the protesting gentlemen, and to which is appended all the original signatures is now in this country. We have examined it, and so have scores of respectable gentlemen who will attest to the truth of what we say. No name is erased from it, nor has any request or order been received from either of the signers, (or from any one professedly on their behalf,) either to erase a name, or express a dissent. The signature of "William Wilberforce" stands in a bold and firm hand. No man, unless it be E. Cresson, denies that it is his real signature, written by himself. It was placed in the hands of Mr. Garrison, with all the signatures, before he was apprized that such a measure was in progress. The charge of forgery, if it were made, would be made on distinguished British Abolitionists. It is said, and cannot be disproved, that Mr. Wilberforce was in his usual health at the time of signing it, and was moving abroad for some time afterwards.—To this statement I affix *my* signature, which is not a "pretended" one, and I hereby challenge Elliot Cresson and all the Colonizationists on earth to disprove what I have here written. WILLIAM GOODELL. New-York, Feb. 1, 1834."

The plain fact is, that many excellent British abolitionists, "*three years ago,*" expressed their approbation of the Colonization Society, because they had been told by Mr. Cresson that one of its objects was "*to assist in emancipating all the slaves in the United States.*" This was the basis of their approbation. Mr. Clarkson himself used this very language in describing what he considered the objects of the Society in a letter to Elliott Cresson, Esq., which was partly published in the African Repository for Nov. 1832. But let it be pondered, *according to the settled policy of the Society, the language of Clarkson was suppressed*, and the words, "TO PROMOTE THE VOLUNTARY EMIGRATION TO AFRICA OF THE COLORED POPULATION OF THE UNITED STATES ;" was put in its stead.* All this to propitiate the South ! If an abolitionist had been found guilty of such a forgery, it would have been the *hic jacet* of his reputation, perhaps of his cause. It is the fate of deceivers to overdo. Consequently the dupes of Mr. Cresson soon began to find him out, and long before Mr. Garrison's arrival in England he was complaining of the "slander" and "opposition" of such men as Suart, Thompson, and Cropper ! But as soon as Mr. Garrison made his appearance with a trunk full of African Repositories and Annual Reports, the spell was broken ; the Immediatists of Great Britain saw through the trick, and the result was a *spontaneous protest* signed by Wilberforce and his compeers, resistless as a thunderbolt, and burning with the indignation of men who felt themselves to have been deceived. Mr. Clarkson was prevented from signing it, only by having committed himself to a perfect neutrality at an earlier stage of the development. It is to this storm of opposition that we owe the presence of Mr. Cresson in this country. He first took shelter under the gracious smiles of the Duke of Sussex and Lord Bexly, by whose munificence he was presented with a grand castle of moonshine, by the name of the British African Colonization Society. But even in this, he was not safe from the impertinence of such matter-of-fact people as Charles Stuart, Fowell Buxton, Daniel O'Connell and the like; he therefore prudently took ship for his native land.

It should not be omitted to the credit of Mr. Cresson's gratitude, that he has not forgotten his benefactors, but has sought for their names the distinguished honor of being enrolled on the Society's list of Vice Presidents. Can any one tell us why he has been unsuccessful in this laudable effort.

We shall have something to say of Mr. Bacon by and by. His public speech dissuades further expense in sending out emigrants, and with a sort of Hibernian logic admits that the Society has given *good grounds* for the "*misrepresentations*" of its enemies. Mr. Bacon has had the sagacity to discover that there is no

* Any person may be satisfied of this if he will compare the letter as published in the Boston Recorder, for Sept. 5, 1832, with the Repository.

use in keeping a "secret" that every body knows; and he accordingly concedes a great variety of facts which would otherwise be kept close.

Rev. Dr. Spring labored to show his Southern brethren that they might have confidence in the co-operation of the ministers of the North. They were not becoming abolitionists so rapidly as was supposed. In proof of this he referred to the vote of the General Assembly at its meeting last spring, in favor of the Colonization Society. He might have said further, that the committee of the General Assembly whose business it became to distribute to the members a quantity of abolition pamphlets sent on from New-York took upon themselves the responsibility of using them for "waste paper." This certainly showed a willingness, at that time, to "co-operate" with slave holders. The inferences derivable from Dr. Spring's facts, remind us of one which he drew on another occasion, when he said, "My confidence in the Colonization Society will never be shaken so long as I retain the memory of Samuel J. Mills!!"*

In regard to the vote in favor of Colonization, the Dr. says, "The same is true of the representative bodies of other denominations." We do not know that the Pastoral Association of Massachusetts would be regarded as such a body, but we well remember that at its meeting last spring in Boston the Rev. Mr. Plummer, of Virginia, delivered before it a large mass of pro-slavery cant in behalf of the Colonization Society. But no commendatory resolution was proposed, and the Association adjourned without loss of time. We presume this was considered a matter of prudence, inasmuch as a number of ministers were taking notes, and, if there was any truth in the glistening of their eyes, they would have dissected the Rev. advocate of slavery to the minutest fibre, if they had been permitted to.get at him. We have understood that some other ecclesiastical bodies that have met more recently, have failed to pass the vote of commendation. We trust in God that there are hundreds of ministers now in the land who would sooner have their tongues cleave to the roof of their mouths, than they would say with Dr. Spring, " You cannot elevate the negro here, but you can in Africa."

The Hon. Theodore Frelinghuysen, made a speech at the public meeting, which, as a specimen of colonization logic, deserves a separate review. We can do no justice to its merit in a passing notice.

" We have reached a peculiarly interesting period in the history of the Colonization Society. It has struggled through its early difficulties, it has outlived the scorn of its first years, when we find it is assailed by new and unexpected prejudices, and many of its wounds are received in the house of its friends. After the most unexampled prosperity, and when the colony has come up in advance of our most sanguine expectations, with the bless-

* At the Masonic Hall, in New-York, last June.

ing of heaven descending, and the wise and good of all nations smiling upon it, all at once the objects of the society, its friends and its patrons are denounced, and its plans declared to be a scheme of heartless cupidity, injurious to the people of color, and obstructing the progress of freedom."

This last sentence sounds strangely in juxtaposition with one which we have already quoted from his subsequent speech. He then said,

" While we were holding ourselves out to the public, as able to transport any number of emigrants for $30 each, and that the colony was prosperous, and the emigrants THRIVING AND HAPPY, THESE DISCLOSURES CAME UPON US!!"

What disclosures? Why, that the colony is in a wretched state, both as to its physical resources and its morals, and the society bankrupt to the amount of $40,000! As Mr. Frelinghuysen has probably been too busily engaged to watch the progress of the colonization controversy, these disclosures, perhaps, had not come to his knowledge, when he delivered his first speech, for if they had, they certainly would have saved him some of his arguments as well as a great deal of his fine rhetoric. As it is, they will save us the necessity of much reply. For curiosity's sake we must hold up a few paragraph's of this florid eloquence in the light of facts.

" I beg now that we may go back to first principles, and see whether there is any ground for all this. I would treat our foes charitably. But let us re examine our institution and its original design, and see whether there is any thing in it, that ought to provoke the frowns either of heaven or of our fellow-men. We owe it to ourselves not to remain silent spectators while this wildfire is running its course. We owe it to these misguided men to interpose and save them and their country from the fatal effects of their mad speculations.

" The objection is clamorously urged against us, and we find it even imported from abroad, in the shape of a British Protest, that the society is an obstruction to liberty. But what will be thought of this objection, when it is understood that a majority of that happy company whom you have planted on the shores of Africa, are liberated slaves, emancipated by Southern masters for the purpose of breathing the pure air of liberty? Yet this wild spirit of fanaticism denounces the colony as an obstruction to liberty.

But there is another objection still more strange. It is said that persuading these men, who are here writhing under our scorn, to seek themselves a new home in Africa, is an invasion of their rights. All this is the mere effusion of a sickly sensibility. Why should it be such a terrible thing to advise or aid men in seeking a new home? The whole earth is moved by this principle of colonization. Ever since the father of the faithful left his native Ur of the Chaldeans, emigration has become one of the established habits of mankind. The broken fragments of the Roman empire were colonized from the Northern hive. What are we here to-night, but living proofs of the benefit of colonization? Whence are these 15 millions of free and enlightened people? whence these splendid erections of art, these schools and churches, cities and towns, this wide spread empire, and all these blessed fruits of liberty? I see in this audience around me many respected colonists, who in former years left the graves of their fathers and struck their course to the great Western Valley, and having there assisted in training up those lovely sisters of the confederacy, they have now come hither to mingle their counsels with ours for the welfare of the whole. The whole Atlantic slope, from the sea coast to the mountains, is at this moment alive with colonists, who are pressing to the land of promise, to gather the grapes of Eshcol. And yet, barely to invite these degraded, whom circumstances have kept down, and will still keep down, to go home to the land of their fathers, is denounced as cruel oppression.

Strange that there should be none of the "pure air of liberty" fit for a black man to breathe, nearer to us than the coast of Africa! If there is, and they really may breathe it here at home, then we say, that a *society* which holds a contrary doctrine, obstructs liberty.

"Emigration is one of the established habits of mankind,"—So is oppression. Does it thence follow that we have a right to procure the emigration of those whom we dislike, by treating them as we would not be treated ourselves? We ourselves feel the benefit of colonization. Does it thence follow that those are righteous who expelled our forefathers from the old world?—Or even those who did not expel them, but who never rebuked their persecutors, and were so glad to get rid of them that they paid their passage? May *we* do evil that good may come? If the colored people go spontaneously to Africa, we shall not object; but thus far they have been duped away, and that is what we complain of. It may be, that they do not die faster in Liberia than they have done in some other colonies; but then they die faster than they would here at home, and what right have we to sacrifice human life to verify our theory of colonization?

"And yet Liberia, in 12 years, cheered by no royal favor, and sustained by no governmental patronage, progressing amid obloquy and scorn and indifference, now numbers more than 3,000 happy and redeemed souls, who there enjoy the privileges and hopes of freedom. Not only religion, but history thus sets her seal to the colony. The cause of liberty was never so effectually plead, as it is now plead by the colony. That is the great beacon of liberty; the wondering eyes of nations are turned to it, and the hope is cherished in the bosom of every philanthropist, that the redemption of Africa draweth nigh."

Sad mistake! How chilling the reality compared with the picture!

From the long and animated debate upon the alteration of the constitution, we learn that there is "A TOTAL WANT OF RESPONSIBILITY," *on the part of the Colony and its agents,* "to the BOARD OF MANAGERS." And that the "MEMBERS OF THE BOARD" "*really have not time to spare, to look into the business, and make themselves as intimately conversant with it as the* *case requires!!*" Really this is a pretty situation for a society that sends its agents all over the country to gather up the contributions of the benevolent,—the mites of the widows and orphans! No responsibility, forsooth! And of course, nobody knows what becomes of the funds! We confess we have for some time thought the society a *swindling* concern, but we hardly dared to whisper it, for fear of impeaching "good men."

A variety of remedies were suggested, which it is of no consequence for us to examine. We have no doubt of the mismanagement, but the disease is *immedicable.* The colony is a wayward child which cannot be managed by such a parent—a voluntary association made up of politics and religion, piety and prejudice, humanity and oppression. The society has soared up a little way, but the sunshine of truth has melted off its waxen wings, and it is now plunging into another element. The idea of a *benevolent* society managing a line of colonies—a trans-ocean empire—was too absurd even for the most sanguine originators of the scheme. They therefore looked to the ultimate interference of Congress. They intended to try an experiment and turn it over into the hands of the General Government as soon as it should prove itself successful. But, we are now told, that all hope of the interference of Congress is at an end. Nothing is left, but for those who have brought this precious bantling into the world, to support it as well as they can.

We should suppose that one of the managers, at least, was convinced of the utter impracticability of the scheme.

Rev. R. R. Gurley said, "He fully agreed in the expediency of seeking a new organization, and he rejoiced in the union of feeling that was witnessed. He should be able to show that all the debt and all the unnecessary expenditure in Africa, had resulted from no individual neglect or mismanagement, (!!) BUT FROM THE ABSOLUTE IMPOSSIBILITY OF DOING WHAT THEY WISHED TO DO."

This impracticability of the scheme, now so fully demonstrated, is the best thing about it. If it were within the limit of *practicabilities,* there is prejudice enough in the land to drive it through, cost what it might of toil or woe. Mr. Bacon mistakes in one point when he says, "The opposition to our cause is increasing and *is built up more for want of efficiency here and in Africa,* than from all other causes. And if *this* is not remedied, it will be impossible to hold it up any longer." The more efficient they are, the more mischief they do; and the more opposition will they excite from those who love their country and their race.

[We are obliged to postpone the remainder of this review till the next number. We regret this, inasmuch as the disclosures it contains are more important than any yet made.—ED.]

A PORTRAIT OF SLAVERY.

BY A SOUTHERN MAN.

We extract the following from an article in the last number of the African Repository by the Rev. Robert J. Breckenridge. The whole article is written with the impetus of a powerful, but undisciplined intellect; and, amidst a wilderness of clashing statements and crazy metaphysics, it bears the impress of honesty. Occurring as it does in the African Repository, it is as wonderful and interesting as a mountain would be thrown upon the flat and monotonous scenery of Holland. We regret that our limits forbid us to review the article at length, or to make more copious extracts. The writer wonderfully misapprehends the views of the abolitionists in regard to the matter of "*amalgamation.*" Abolitionism leaves every man to the free exercise of his taste, but it denies that any man has a right to withhold from another any right or privilege, to which he may be fairly entitled, lest the consequence should be, that he himself or some one else should violate the *present* dictate of his taste. Abolitionists neither encourage nor deprecate "amalgamation." It has nothing to do with their scheme. Neither the wishes nor the necessities of our colored brethren require it. If it shall succeed an act of equal justice, it will succeed in accordance with the taste of every individual concerned; and why need any one's taste be horrified at the prospect? It is the present system of amalgamation which ought to be dreaded, not that which may possibly ensue the establishment of equal rights.

What, then, is slavery? for the question relates to the action of certain principles on it, and to its probable and proper results; what is slavery as it exists among us? We reply, it is that condition enforced by the laws of one-half the states of this confederacy, in which one portion of the community, called masters, is allowed such power over another portion called slaves; as,

1. To deprive them of the entire earnings of their own labor, except only so much as is necessary to continue labor itself, by continuing healthful existence, thus committing clear robbery;

2. To reduce them to the necessity of universal concubinage, by denying to them the civil rights of marriage; thus breaking up the dearest relations of life, and encouraging universal prostitution;

3. To deprive them of the means and opportunities of moral and intellectual culture, in many states making it a high penal offence to teach them to read; thus perpetuating whatever of evil there is that proceeds from ignorance;

4. To set up between parents and their children an authority higher than the impulse of nature and the laws of God; which breaks up the authority of the father over his own offspring, and at pleasure separates the mother at a returnless distance from her child; thus abrogating the clearest laws of nature; thus outraging all decency and justice, and degrading and oppressing thousands upon thousands of beings created like themselves in the image of the Most High God!

This is slavery as it is daily exhibited in every slave state. This is that "dreadful but unavoidable necessity," for which you may hear so many mouths ut-

tering excuses, in all parts of the land. And is it really so? If indeed it be; if that "necessity" which tolerates this condition be really "unavoidable," in any such sense, that we are constrained for one moment, to put off the course of conduct which shall most certainly and most effectually subvert a system which is utterly indefensible on every correct human principle, and utterly abhorrent from every law of God,—then, indeed, let ICHABOD be graven in letters of terrific light upon our country! For God can no more sanction such perpetual wrong, than he can cease to be faithful to the glory of his own throne.

He who is higher than the highest, will, in His own good time and way, break the rod of the oppressor, and let all the oppressed go free. He has indeed commanded servants to be obedient to their masters; and it is their bounden duty to be so. We ask not now, what the servants were, nor who the masters were.— It is enough that all masters are commanded to "give unto their servants that which is just and equal;" and to what feature of slavery may that description apply? Just and equal! what care I, whether my pockets are picked, or the proceeds of my labor are taken from me? What matters it whether my horse is stolen, or the value of him in my labor be taken from me? Do we talk of violating the rights of masters, and depriving them of their property in their slaves? And will some one tell us, if there be any thing in which a man has, or can have, so perfect a right of property, as in his own limbs, bones and sinews? Out upon such folly! The man who cannot see that involuntary domestic slavery, as it exists among us, is founded upon the principle of taking by force that which is another's, has simply no moral sense.

DONATIONS

To the American Anti-Slavery Society, received up to Feb. 15, 1834:

Benj C. Bacon, $5; W. L. Garrison, 2; Isaac Knapp, 2; David Thurston, 1; Jas. Loughhead, 1; Enoch Mack, 1; E. L. Capron, 5; J. M. McKim, 1; C. Gillingham, 1; Amos A. Phelps, 1; D. E. Jewitt, 0,50; Jas. F. Otis, 1; Samuel J. May, 3; C. W. Denison, 2; A. L. Cox, 1; Nathan Winslow, 5; Thomas Shipley, 3; Isaac Winslow, 5; Robt. Purvis, 10; Jas. McCrummel, 1; H. P. Wakefield, 1; J. C. Barbadoes, 1; Jos. Cassey, 10; Jos. Southwick, 3; Evan Lewis, 0,50; Jno. Parkhurst, 1; Jas. White, 1; J. R. Cambell, 2; D. T. Kimball, jr. 5; J. Sharp, jr. 5; A. Kingsiey, 10; J. G. Whittier, 3; John Prentiss, 1; Levi Sutliff, 1; Milton Sutliff, 1; B. Fussel, 1; S. S. Jocelyn, 1; Jas. Mott, 5; D. Cambell, 1; Beriah Green, 1; E. Wright, jr. 1; John Rankin, 100; A Friend in Philadelphia, 500; Students of the W. R. College, 28; E. P. Atlee, 5; D. L. Child, 2; Joshua Coffin, 1; No. 3. 0,50.   W. GREEN, Jr. Treas.

TERMS.

☞ This periodical will be furnished to subscribers at $1 00 per annum, done up in a neat cover; or 50 cents, without the cover. To those who take several copies a discount will be made as follows: 15 per cent. for 10 copies, 25 per cent. for 25 copies, and 33 per cent. for 100 copies. To Auxiliary Societies it will be sold at $2,00 per hundred. Payment to be made in all cases in *advance.* Letters, POSTAGE PAID, addressed to the "Editor of the American Anti-Slavery Reporter, No. 130 Nassau-st. New-York," will be attended to.

S. W. BENEDICT & CO. PRINTERS, 162 Nassau street.

AMERICAN

ANTI - SLAVERY REPORTER

VOL. I.]   FEBRUARY, 1834.   [NO. 2.

THE MORAL CHARACTER OF SLAVE-HOLDING.

If there is any one principle which is vital to the Anti-Slavery cause, it is that SLAVE-HOLDING IS A SIN,—that it is essentially MAN-STEALING,—that it is the highest act of piracy upon human rights. If we succeed in convincing this nation that there is truth and reason in this high denunciation,—if in accordance with this conviction we lodge in the hearts of our fellow-citizens an abhorrence of slavery deep and irrepressible, we shall have gained our object—we shall have removed from our country what is commonly confessed to be its foulest stain, its sorest evil, its deadliest curse.

The slavery which we have in view is perfectly distinct from family government and from legal guardianship. It has nothing in common with family government, for the slaves are not held as such because they owe their existence to their masters, nor are they held during a limited minority, but for life. It is not a system of guardianship, for the pretended wards have never been assigned to their masters by any judicial tribunal. The well known characteristics of slavery as it exists in our country are, that it subjects to involuntary servitude for life, human beings who have never been charged with being guilty of any crime; that it makes them the mere PROPERTY of individuals, from infancy to the grave; that it so utterly subjects a whole race to the condition of brutes, that multitudes of them live scarcely ever suspecting that they are men. From the extreme ignorance in which slavery has kept them, they, in many cases, apparently acquiesce in their subserviency. They become a sort of willing machines. But the mass of the slaves, notwithstanding their having been born to such a condition, long for liberty, and are held in subjection only by the terror of the lash and the gibbet.

Now, taking that which belongs to another, without his consent, is *stealing.* But what belongs to another, if not his own person? If it be not self evident that a man belongs to himself, it is impossible to prove that any thing belongs to him. The proposition that one man can hold another as his property, fundamentally subverts the right of property. Admit it, and you cannot prove that any product of human industry is the property of the producer, for it does not appear that the powers and instruments by which he produced, were his own. That every man belongs to himself, and that all men enter and pass through life under equal responsibilities, are *axioms,* essential to the well being of society. Blot them out, and distinction of property ceases. The will of the strongest takes the place of law,[*] and the human race sinks to the level of brutes. The difference then between retaining a man in slavery, and any common case of stealing is, that in the latter, the thief takes a *part*, in the former, the *whole.*

Perhaps it may be considered that the word *stealing,* implies a secrecy in the abstraction of property. The open violation of right is denominated *robbery.* It is not very important to decide which of the two involves the most guilt. In the common

[*] All that prevents the rapacity of slaveholders from fastening on *white* victims, is the principle of *honor* among *thieves.* "You are *white,*" say they, "then you are *one of us,* walk in and share the plunder;"—but wo to you if your hue be too dark.

apprehension, a distinctive meanness attaches to the former. The open highway man, who demands the traveler's purse, with cocked pistol, is considered a depredator of nobler style than the one who adroitly abstracts the same thing without notice. And why should not the same distinction be made between the African trader, who at the peril of his life tears the full grown prey from a savage shore, and the American slaveholder, who safely steals the helpless infant, and cunningly contrives to keep it through life ignorant of the theft?

If a man withdraws a few dollars from the pocket of his neighbor, he is put under the face of society as a villain. This is all right. God intends that every man shall support himself by his own labor. But what shall we say of him who puts his hand carefully and deliberately over the whole existence of his fellow man, and withdraws from it all but the bare animal? Is he less a thief than the other? If so, it is because he has stolen more!

But it may be said, that we view the matter in the "*abstract.*" No: we are looking at slavery as it takes place every day in practice. There is no subject in the world which is less a matter of "abstract" speculation. We will not say that slavery in the "*abstract*" might not admit of a plausible defence; but all the circumstances under which it exists, in this country, conspire to aggravate its guilt and seal its condemnation.

1. *It is perpetrated upon whole families, from generation to generation.*

Were the crime committed upon scattered individuals, it would end with their lives. But the practice of enslaving or stealing whole families, and handing them down from father to son, gives a sort of eternity to the crime. It thrusts a race out of the pale of humanity, and subjects them to a forever deepening degradation. Take a single family, enjoying the privileges of freedom, and follow it in all its branches down through five hundred years. Into what a population does it spread; how many noble lives does it embrace; what an amount of physical, intellectual, and moral excellence, does it bring into being. Such fruits never grow from slavery. The man who lays his felonious hands upon this family, and brings it into hereditary bondage, steals from themselves and the community the whole of this value. The same is done by the man who retains in such bondage a family of slaves. The question is not, merely, whether the slaves are physically as comfortable as they would be if free; but whether they are in a condition to develope the powers which God has given them. God has scattered the gifts of intellect without respect to rank, or color, or race. But upon an enslaved race they are bestowed in vain. The man-stealer wages war with the plan of God. He bids darkness when God has bidden light. Had the slaves in America been free since the Declaration of Independence, and been partakers with the white population in the privileges of education, it is past belief that there would not have risen among them many minds of whom this nation would have reason to be proud. Slavery has stolen from our country all these. What holder of a slave can say that he is not robbing his country of more value than his own existence has conferred upon it. What can repay the world for blotting out the light of more than two millions of minds?

2. *It enhances the guilt of slaveholding that it is practiced by many.*

A single slaveholder might do as much mischief to his victims, alone, as if surrounded by thousands. But his example could avail little to sanctify the crime. Public opinion would be against him. He would be abhorred and shunned. But when great multitudes come into the practice then it is honorable, and over and above committing the wicked deed, each must answer for an effectually contagious example. Look at the case of our country. Were there but one slaveholder in it, having but one plantation cultivated by slaves, there would not be another man in the nation who would not regard him as a man-stealer, and shun his company and his crime. But now there are tens of thousands of slaveholders—all honorable men, and millions of people even in the free states, for this very reason, think that slaveholding, under all the circumstances of the case, is right, and are ready to commit the foul outrage. They in heart sin the same sin. Who then dares to say that it is not worse in the sight of God to go with the *multitude* to *do* evil, than to go *alone?*

Again, we can easily imagine the case of a solitary slaveholder, who should, by kind treatment, make his slaves, in many respects, happy. In depriving them of their liberty, he is guilty of man-stealing, but not of murder, perhaps not of cruelty. But the practice leads to cruelty, and when indulged in by multitudes, an immense and fearful amount of violence and torture is the result. Now when a man joins a multitude of slaveholders, although he may treat his slaves with all the kindness of which their condition admits, he adds to his mansteal- ing, the crime of upholding by his example a system of enormous cruelty. For the very goodness of the man is thrown as a cloak of sancity over the whole carcase of abomination. His negative, righteousness; his not doing as wickedly as he might, is magnified into a plea for the benefit of the most outrageous trangressors. Every slave- holder, then, over and above his private vi- olation of the eternal rule of right, is charg- able, under present circumstances, with abetting all the sin that grows out of all the slaveholding around him.

Moreover, the light shed upon the sub- ject of slavery by the extensiveness of the experiment, is incomparably stronger than could come from a solitary instance. It is true, the slaveholder is not now surrounded with the moral influence of public opinion, deterring him from the sin,—the pulpit is dumb, and no frown of popular indignation lights upon him; but he *must* hear the aw- ful voice of God's providence speaking, far and near,in insurrection,massacre,and deeds of vengeance at which humanity shudders. Suppose a solitary slaveholder from behind some ridge of the Alleghanies should to-day for the first time, learn the horrors involved in the slavery of *two millions*, might he not say, if I had known all this I would never have held a slave?

3. *It greatly increases the guilt of the pre- sent slaveholders, that the system has been* **ENTAILED** *upon them.*

Their fathers tried the system and found it bad. They saw clearly that it tended to brutalize men. The very plea on which they made the entail was, " these miserable slaves are unfit to take care of themselves. But surely, had they been treated according to the precepts of Christianity, since they were brought from a heathen shore, they would have been elevated to be useful members of society. Slavery has added to the ignorance of barbarism the vices of ci- vilization. All this was seen by the sons, yet they adopted the sin of their fathers.

While the heavens are gathering blackness, and the bolts of divine vengeance are ever and anon falling upon the guilty; they per- severed in the sin. Well might the Savior rebuke this generation as he did that which slew the last of the prophets. Upon you shall be visited all the stripes, and anguish, and blood, of the poor Africans, from the time your ancestors dragged them from their native shores, to the time when you yourselves shut up the word of God from them, and sought to banish from your land every vestige of liberty beneath a black skin.

But look again at the presumption with which this robbery is justified. With all the sins of their ancestors voluntarily assumed, the present slaveholders dare to plead the very guilt of their fathers in extenua- tion of their own. "We were born slave- holders. What shall we do? We did not introduce the system." They would have us believe that because they were regularly trained to this business of man-stealing, they really know no better! Ah! they might easily learn better, but "they hate the light because their deeds are evil." "This," say they, "is a *delicate subject.* Be it known to all who are disposed to intermed- dle, that we will not be interfered with in our domestic affairs." Carry the case for- ward to the last tribunal. The eternal Judge charges the oppressor with having withholden wages from the laborer. "In- deed," replies the astonished culprit, "my father told me that the laborer himself was my *property;* and I knew no better!" "But when you were told better," the Judge would ask, if we may suppose that he could bear with such contempt of his authority, "Why did you not listen?"

Granting, for the sake of argument, the ignorance of the slaveholders, what does it prove but that their system is intolerable? Why, it is so bad, that in an age or two it totally obliterates conscience; it disables men to distinguish between their own rights and the most sacred rights of others. What a horrible thing for society would be a sys- tem of petty larceny, which should, in two or three generations, make the adepts in it really think every thing their own, on which they could lay their hands? Just such a thing, according to the favorite plea of its apologists, is slavery in the universe of God. But really, the plea reverses the decisions of common sense. It assumes that knowledge does not increase by experience; that each generation is more igno-rant than its predecessor.

4. *The guilt of slaveholding is increased by being committed according to law.*[*]

A law which consigns a race of men to the place of goods and chattels, mere merchantable commodities, is the highest insult to that Being whose law is, "Thou shalt love thy neighbor as thyself." It sanctions iniquity. He, therefore, who, under protection of such a law, possesses himself of human bones and sinews, adds *rebellion* to injustice. He not only revolts from God, but he joins a standard of revolt. It is a wicked thing to forsake the post of duty, but it is still worse to go over to the marshalled enemy. Moreover, there is a deliberation about legalized wickedness which strips it of all right to excuse itself by the infirmities of human nature.

Remembering that in our country the people make the laws, let us turn to some of the laws which pertain to slavery, and see if we can estimate the amount of cool, determined, calculated wickedness which it must require to carry them into practice. The tenure by which the slaves are held is thus described in the new code of Louisiana.

"A slave is one who is in the power of a master to whom he belongs. The master may sell him, dispose of his person, his industry and his labor: he can do nothing, possess nothing, nor acquire any thing but what must belong to his master." [Civil Code, Art. 35.]

The following is from the laws of S. Carolina:

"Slaves shall be deemed, sold, taken, reputed and adjudged in law to be *chattels personal* in the hands of their owners and possessors, and their executors, administrators, and assigns, to all intents, constructions, and purposes whatsoever." [See Stroud's Sketch, p. 23.]

Such is the tenure by which *two millions* of human beings are held and handed down from father to son, as though they were things without souls.

Again, see how cruelly the protection of

law is withdrawn, by refusing to hear a *colored witness against any white* man. The question in regard to the witness, which *decides whether he should be heard,* is not, Is he honest, intelligent, credible? but, Is he *white?* It is not whether he has an open heart, but whether he has a fair *skin!* In Virginia an act of assembly has these words, "Any negro, or mulatto, bond or free, shall be a good witness in pleas of the commonwealth, for or against negroes or mulattos, bond or free, or in civil pleas where free negroes, or mulattos shall alone be parties, AND IN NO OTHER CASES WHATEVER." Similar laws exist in several other slave states, and in one of the FREE ;[*] but in the slave states where there is no express law, the same thing is sanctioned by the universal practice of the courts.

The following are a specimen of the laws which check the upward tendencies of mind in the slave. The Revised Code of Virginia hath this enactment, viz. "That all meetings or assemblages of slaves or free negroes or mulattos mixing and associating with any such slaves at any meeting house, or houses, or any other place, &c. in the night, or *at any school or schools for teaching them reading or writing either in the day or night,* under whatsoever pretext, shall be deemed and considered an *unlawful assembly;* and any justice of a county, &c. wherein such assemblage shall be, either from his own knowledge or the information of others, of such unlawful assemblage, &c. may issue his warrant directed to any sworn officer or officers, authorizing him or them to enter the house or houses where such unlawful assemblages, &c. may be, for the purpose of apprehending or dispersing such slaves, and to inflict *corporal punishment* on the offender or offenders at the discretion of any justice of the peace, not exceeding *twenty lashes."*

By the act of South Carolina, "Assemblies of slaves, free negroes, mulattos and mestizos," "for the purpose of *mental instruction,"* are declared to be unlawful, "and the officer dispersing such unlawful assemblage, may inflict such *corporal punishment,* not exceeding twenty lashes, upon such slaves, *free negroes,* &c. as *they may judge necessary* for detaining them from the like unlawful assemblage in future."

The following is from a Savannah paper:

[*] Wo unto them that DECREE unrighteous DECREES, and that write grievousness which they have PRESCRIBED; to turn aside the needy from judgment, and to take away the RIGHT from the poor of my people, that widows may be their prey, and that they may rob the fatherless! Isa. 10 : 1, 2.
Shall the throne of iniquity have fellowship with Thee, which *frameth mischief by a* LAW? Ps. 9 : 20.

[*] Ohio!!!

"The city has passed an ordinance, by which any person that teaches any person of color, slave or free, *to read or write*, or causes such persons to be so taught, is subjected to a fine of *thirty dollars* for each offence; and every person of color who shall *keep a school* to teach reading or writing is subject to a fine of thirty dollars, or to be imprisoned ten days and WHIPPED *thirty-nine lashes ! !*"

Thus, is the written revelation not only withheld by law from *two millions* of human beings but if any of them by their own unaided endeavors should presume to open the book they are rudely thrust away, as if it were a profanation for *them* to meddle with letters. Thus have a company of men dared to place themselves between God's light and *two millions* of immortal minds. Forsooth the cultivation of the mind is dangerous to their claim of PROPERTY. But they tell us they do not shut out the souls of their slaves from heaven. No they give them *oral* instruction ! ! Now, we ask seriously what the message of God can do, when it comes through mouths which daily swallow the unrequited labor of the poor?—Such *oral instruction* is an abomination in the sight of God ! It is the very thing for which His curse has fallen upon the Pope of Rome.

Now all the apologies which are plead for the so called pious slaveholders, who merely hold their *slaves in trust*, &c. may be good enough for slavery *in the abstract*, but they will not justify any for participating in this system of *practical* SOUL ROBBERY. The man who holds slaves, under the present system, obeys a law which excludes from men the written revelation. If we could *imagine* a system of slavery in which the slaves should be instructed and made wise, under such a system there might be some excuse for the slaveholder. But under the present system he is found in the ranks of an army of *practical* rebels against the laws of the Eternal.

It may be said by those unacquainted with this subject that these laws are inoperative—the inanimate relics of a darker age. Such is not the fact. It is not to be expected that laws for the security of *property* should grow obsolete except when superseded by others for the same purpose. Up to this moment these laws have been increasing in rigor. They must do so till the spell is broken—till the iniquitous

pretence of *property in man* is given up.

5. *The guilt of slaveholding is enhanced by being committed against a race of peculiar color.*

Under any system of slavery some individuals must gain their liberty. If these can become incorporated into free society, their elevation will materially affect the rigors of the system. But the slaveholding spirit naturally tends to exclude them. If it can lay hold of any physical peculiarity in the slave it will effect its purpose. The complexion and features of the negro race furnish the requisite peculiarity, and are seized upon by the spirit of slavery as the basis of a prejudice against color which tends powerfully to support the system. Throughout our whole country, men of the same complexion and features as the slave are held to be a degraded race, and are destined by the customs of society to continue such.

That this prejudice takes its origin in *slavery* and not in *nature*, is proved by the fact that it does not exist in Europe. African color and features do not exclude a man, who is *in other respects qualified*, from the best society either in Great Britain or on the continent. An ancient historian describes the Ethiopians of Africa as having the wooliest hair of all men, and in another passage he speaks of them as the most beautiful of all men.*

We conclude then that the criminality of slaveholding is enhanced by selecting victims of a different color from ourselves, because from that very circumstance they are consigned to a more hopeless degradation.

6. *Our guilt as a slaveholding nation is mightily enhanced by the fact that we have the revelation of God in our hands.*

He who can read the whole Bible and suppose that it gives any countenance to holding men contrary to their will, and for no fault, under laws by which they may be sold as beasts, and which require this very Bible to be kept out of their hands, must be strangely blind. There never was a book which from one end of it to the other did so thoroughly cut up all slavery by the roots.

---

*Οἱ μὲν γὰρ ἀπ' ἡλίου∘Αἰθίοπες, 136 τριχές εἰσι · οἱ δὲ ἐκ τῆς Λιβύης, οὐλότατον τρίχωμα ἔχουσι πάντων ἀνθρώπων. *Herodotus. Book VII. Sec. 70.*

Οἱ δὲ Αἰθίοπες οὗτοι, ἐς τοὺς ἀπέπεμπε ὁ Καμβύσης, λέγονται ἔιναι μέγιστοι καὶ κάλλιστοι ἀνθρώπων πάντων. *Herod. B. III. Sec. 20.*

The Old Testament enjoined upon the Hebrews a system most carefully guarding against involuntarily domestic servitude, by the frequent recurrence of days of release.

The New Testament has established a commentary upon the divine law, which makes slavery as much out of place on earth as it would be in heaven. It denounces the heaviest woes upon those who "bind heavy burdens," and who keep back the wages of the laborer; and places all men on a broad equality of rights, under the same responsibility to God and having no master but Him.*

To be more particular, we find in the Old Testament code the following law. "He that stealeth a man and selleth him, or if he be found in his hand, he shall surely be put to death." Ex. 21: 16. Common sense teaches that this law condemns the *buyer* as well as the *seller* of a *stolen man.* All those passages which recognize the right of one man to the service of another must be interpreted in consistency with this law. The Hebrews were permitted to hold as servants their own countrymen for the space of six years, and the heathen who dwelt about them till the year of jubilee, when *liberty* was to be proclaimed to *all* the inhabitants of the land. Hebrew servants were to be treated in all cases as if *hired.* Heathens might be held as bond servants. Now, how could the Israelites come in possession of these servants? It is inconsistent with the law we have quoted, to suppose they could purchase them of those whose claim originated in fraud. The following passage throws the needed light on the subject. "If thy brother that dwelleth by thee be waxen *poor* and be sold unto thee, thou shalt not compel him to serve thee as a bond servant: * * * * Both thy bond men and thy bond maids, which thou shalt have, shall be of the heathen that are round about you, of them shall ye buy bond men and bond maids," &c. The poor brother spoken of in this law plainly *sold himself.* A subsequent verse, using this very expression, takes it for granted that a Hebrew might do so, even to a stranger. The scope of the passage then is this: "Thou shalt not make a bondman of a HEBREW *who sells himself* to thee on account of his poverty, but thou mayest make a bondman of a

HEATHEN *who sells himself* to thee. There is not a particle of proof on the record that the Israelites were ever permitted to hold any in *bondage* except such heathens as *sold themselves.*

And the law made provision against the oppression of such slaves, for not only * was the jubilee a limit to their servitude, but if at any time they embraced the Hebrew religion and were circumcised they were to be treated in all respects as Hebrews, or if they should flee from their masters, the law forbade any Israelite to give them up. If it be asked why a distinction was made between Hebrew and heathen servants, we reply, the God against whom the heathen had sinned had a right to punish them as he saw fit. He did not please to give them an equality with his people while they retained their idolatry. But the same Being has broken down the partition wall which separated between Jew and Gentile. He has made all mankind Hebrews in re-

* The expression, "and they shall be your bondmen *forever,*" may seem to clash with the law of jubilee. But the discrepancy is only *apparent.* The emphasis should rest on "*they*" rather than on "*forever.*" As much as to say, The law that *Heathen,* and not *Israelites,* shall be your bondmen is perpetual. The individual heathens who had sold themselves to any Israelite might be retained by him or his heirs subject of course to the law of jubilee. But the passage furnishes no evidence that the children of such persons could be held as bondmen for life either by the master or his heirs.

Calmet, in speaking of the word "forever" in Deut. 15 : 17, says, "according to the commentators, till the year of jubilee, for then all slaves, without exception, recovered their liberty. The Rabbins add, that slaves were set free also at the death of their masters, and did not descend to their heirs."

Says Grotius, on the word "forever," "Durationem significat quantam fert materia subjecti." That is, it signifies as long a duration as the thing spoken of will bear.

If it should be contended from the silence of Lev. 25 : 46 about the heathen bondman going out at the year of jubilee, and from the apparent antithesis of that verse with the 40th, that he did not come under the law of release, even all this may be admitted without materially weakening the force of the argument. There is still no evidence that a man could be made a bondman except by his own consent, or that he could be sold without his own consent, or that his children could be held as slaves for life. But we apprehend the reason why the jubilee is mentioned in one case and not in the other, is, that the Hebrew servant on the arrival of the year of jubilee was in duty bound to return to his patrimonial possession so that his family might not be lost in Israel, while the heathen bondman was at liberty to do as he pleased. The mere silence of one passage is not sufficient to restrict the unqualified command, "Ye shall proclaim *liberty* throughout the land, to *all* the inhabitants thereof." Indeed so far as *personal liberty* is concerned we do not see how this could apply to any other than heathen bondmen, for no others were in *fact* to be deprived of it. See Lev. 25 : 39.

---

* Lev. 25: 10. Mat. 23. James 5: 4. Mat. 7: 12.

gard to their treatment of each other in these respects.

But suppose we should grant to professed Christians the same superiority over pagans, which the Hebrews enjoyed in regard to the neighboring nations. Would the planters hold their slaves by the Hebrew laws? First, they must release all those who had not within fifty years sold themselves or consented to serve as bondmen on certain conditions. Next, they must not hold as a bondman any professor of the Christian religion. Again, a right to the parent could give no right to the child except by the consent of the parent during the child's minority. And again, the master could not sell his bond man without his consent. And after all, if the bondman should flee from his master to the protection of some of our northen states, it would not be lawful for us to yield him up to his master. We confidently ask the slaveholders of the south, Will you adopt the Hebrew slave laws, instead of those which you yourselves have framed for the security of what you call your domestic relations? If you will, we promise not to trouble you further with our sort of abolition.

But the jealousy with which human rights are guarded in the word of God is obvious from the whole tenor of the Old Testament history as well as the prophecies. Oppression was the sin which frequently brought down the Divine wrath upon the nations—Jews as well as Gentiles. The Jews themselves were devoted to destruction because they would not observe the humane limitation of their law in regard to the servitude of their brethren. Jer. 34: 17.

"Woe unto them that decree unrighteous decrees," says the prophet Isaiah, "and that write grievousness which they have prescribed; to turn aside the needy from judgment, and to take away the right from the poor of my people; that widows may be their prey, and that they may rob the fatherless!" If this does not describe the slave-holders of the present day, it is impossible to describe them.

Isaiah, in his 58th chapter, utters the most terrible denunciation against the house of Jacob. What was their sin? Had they forsaken the worship of God? No. They fasted abundantly, and afflicted their souls, and wondered that God did not see nor take

knowledge. But the prophet's eye discovered under all this sanctity "the fist of wickedness," and he commands them in the name of the Lord, instead of "bowing the head like a bulrush," to "loose the bands of wickedness"—to "undo the heavy burdens, —to let the oppressed go free"—yea, "to BREAK every YOKE." What! BREAK the old yokes?—the yokes "entailed" upon the present generation?—turn loose an ignorant and degraded population?—emancipate all the slaves at once, "without regard to consequences?" Yes, and the prophet tells us what will be the consequences. "THEN SHALL THY LIGHT BREAK FORTH AS THE MORNING, and thy health shall spring forth speedily." "Then shalt thou call and the Lord shall answer." "If thou take away from the midst of thee the yoke, and the putting forth of the finger [let the people of the North mind that] and speaking vanity, * * * * then shall thy light rise in obscurity, and thy darkness shall be as noon-day." Aye, "and they that shall be of thee shall build the old waste places." Let the slave holders look round upon their desolate fields and decayed habitations and ruinous towns, and remember this.

But we must hasten to the New Testament. The doctrine of human rights there inculcated is irreconcilably opposed to the whole system of laws by which American slavery is continued. "Thou shalt love thy neighbor as thyself," says the Divine expounder of the moral law. "Thou mayest scourge thy neighbor, for no fault, on the bare back as long as thou pleasest, provided life be not taken nor limb broken," says the American slave law—"Aye, and take life too, if no white man see thee!"

"Whatsoever ye would that men should do to you, do ye even so to them," says the Savior. Yes, the slave holder replies, I will do to my slave as I would wish my slave to do to me if he were the master and I the slave. The command was not intended to destroy the relation of master and slave, but merely to regulate the relative duties. And any robber, whatever, might as well say the same. Common sense exclaims, "If I were retained as a slave,—a piece of property, under any treatment, I should think myself injured, therefore I will not hold a slave." If the golden rule does not forbid the enslavement of men, unconvicted of crime, upon earth, then, for any law there to the contrary, there may be slavery in heaven—and all the infernal apparatus for extorting reluctant labor may be there too!! It is not in the power of language human or divine to express a stronger moral guarantee of freedom than the golden rule.

Does the New Testament any where command the involuntary servant to obey his master, because the latter has a right to his services, or a property in him? Never. It commands the endurance of injuries for the gospel's sake   But it enjoins upon all masters to give unto their servants that which is JUST and EQUAL. It counsels slaves to use their liberty, if they can get it.

The apostle Paul was so confident that Philemon, who had doubtless been converted during the absence of his slave Onesimus, would make the latter a free man on his return, that he sent back Onesimus to him for the very purpose of giving Philemon the pleasure of manumiting him voluntarily. He exhorts Philemon to receive Onesimus, not as a *servant*, but as a *brother* beloved, both in the *flesh*, and in the Lord. And this he does for love's sake, though if he had pleased he might have commanded it as a matter of *right*.* With all the courtesy which the apostle shows to this converted slave-holder, we have a distinct recognition of the right of the slave to his liberty, and a broad hint that slave-holding is as " *unprofitable*," as it is wrong.   What would an American slaveholder say upon receiving such a letter by the hand of a runaway slave? Would he not think it an officious meddling with the " delicate question?" Would he not be very likely to destroy the incendiary letter, call the writer a fool for his pains, and after flogging Onesimus, in terrorem, sell him to the speculators, lest he should spoil the other slaves with his new notions?

But the slaveholders refer us to 1 Tim. 6: 1. The apostle there says, and so say we, " Let as many servants as are under the yoke, [slaves like their own, they understand, of course,] count their own masters worthy of all honor." And why? Because the masters really deserve it? Because they have a right to it? No,—mark the reason— " that the name of God and his doctrine be

* τὸ ἀνῆκον, which is rendered *convenient*, Phil. 8. might properly be rendered *right*, as will appear from comparing Eph. 5 : 4, and Col. 3 : 18, where the same word occurs.

not blasphemed." The apostle settles no question of right here ; but urges obedience even to the sacrifice of personal rights, that the gospel may not be hindered.   " And they that have believing masters, let them not despise them because they are brethren, but rather do them service." And why? Because the masters could if they pleased compel their services? No ; but because they are faithful and beloved, partakers of the benefit." The apologists for sin are mistaken in their text. It is as much as if the apostle had said, " Bondmen, when your masters become Christians you will be freed from compulsion of course, but do not on that account withdraw from their business, but rather still continue to do them service from Christian love.* They are " faithful," and you will not be losers.

But it is said, " Christ and his apostles did not preach the immediate abolition of slavery ; they left the gospel to work its way against slavery silently and gradually." In reply to this we have but to ask one or two questions.

Was one sixth part of the Jewish nation held by the rest as mere merchantable stock when Christ appeared? Did the apostles travel in any country where half the people might not assemble to hear them preach, nor be taught to read one of their epistles? Did hundreds of the churches planted by them, in their day contain members, who owned large plantations cultivated by *slaves*, who willed their slaves to their children, having kept them ignorant of letters according to law? If this was not the case, then it is plain why they spent their main force upon the prominent sins of their time, leaving us to apply the great principles of the moral law, which they had inculcated in general terms, to the abolition of American slavery.

* Let it be understood that we have not a word of censure for those masters who disavow compulsion, and merely receive the service of those who obey the precept of the Apostle. Such masters may be pretty well known from their not having *overseers*, armed with *pistols, dirks, whips,*&c. and from their not using any thing of that kind themselves. They never advertise for runaways ; nor raise money by selling off human stock to the speculators.

A caviller may perhaps say, " Your reasoning here makes the Apostle contradict himself, for in another place he says, 'If thou mayest be made free ; use it rather.' Not at all : for the service of a *Christian* master for love's sake *is* using liberty. But the Apostle referred to another sort of masters ; and by comparing the two texts we learn that servants were faithfully to serve their masters till they could obtain their freedom of which they were gladly to avail themselves.

But what if Christ and his apostles were on earth now? Would they apologize for slaveholders? Would they preach smoothly? Would they shun the wrongs and woes of *two millions* of oppressed brethren, as a subject "too delicate" for public discussion? Would they talk about a slaveholding, cast-loving prejudice as being beyond the power of the gospel to correct? Those ministers of the gospel who do not cry aloud against the injustice that is done to their colored brethren, both at the North and at the South, and who refuse to pray for them from Sabbath to Sabbath, we must say, do not declare the *whole* counsel of God. We would not be censorious, but we must call their attention to the curse of the compassionate Savior upon those who tithed mint and cummin and all manner of herbs, and neglected the weightier matters of justice, mercy, and faith. The Bible has turned the darkness in which the Savior found the world into noon-day. There is no hiding place now for oppression. The rights of man are written upon the broad firmament in sun beams. He who can make merchandize of his brother, at this time of day, deals murderously with his conscience. He who can plead scripture for the deed, mocks Jehovah, and impudently flings back His commandments in His face!

7. *We are the more guilty in our slave-holding for being republicans.*

We declared most solemnly when our political liberty was at stake, "that all men are created equal; that they are endowed by their Creator with certain inalienable rights; that among these are life, LIBERTY, and the pursuit of happiness." We take glory to ourselves among the nations for this declaration. But the more than half a million of slaves that then existed received not the benefit of it. They have given birth to *two millions*, and we as a nation have grown rich, and in a degree by their unrecompensed toil. We still boast of our declaration of inalienable rights, and hold it up as self evident truth—in regard to *ourselves*, to the least iota. But still when the bondman pleads it, we begin to make exceptions,—we stammer,—we prevaricate,—we play the hypocrite! The wrongs which we daily perpetrate upon colored Americans, are incomparably greater than those, to redress which, our fathers banded together, with swords in their hands, pledged never to sheath them but with vic-

tory. We say, and we say it truly, that God designed men to govern themselves. But there is nothing which does so much thwart this purpose,—there is nothing which brings so much scorn upon our institutions, as our hypocrisy in holding slaves. We are a scandal to the cause of republicanism, and unless we repent and reform, we shall ruin the noble experiment which God has entrusted us to make,—we shall *prove* traitors to the high hopes of a tyrant ridden world.

The history of our diplomacy shows, that we have not only trodden down the rights of our colored brethren at home, but we have thrown obstacles in the way of their liberty abroad. We refused to recognize the independence of Hayti, for no reason but that its inhabitants are BLACK; and hence, a recognition of their nationality, might have a bearing upon "the delicate question!" We have frowned upon the rising republics of the South, *because they freed their slaves!* Ah! we could forgive them any fault but that! Their consistency with their principles has turned *our* brotherly kindness into vinegar and gall. Instead of welcoming them to the floor of nations, with open hand and outstretched arm, in the sight of all Europe, as we should otherwise have been proud to do, we shrunk back and aped the prudishness of "*majesty*," and were only drawn along to a recognition in the wake of *royal* England, by a consideration of *dollars and cents!!* Alas! for the chivalry of Bolivar! It was tarnished with the vulgar humanity of negro emancipation.

8. *All excuse is taken away from our sin, by the fact that emancipation, having been tried in various instances and on large bodies of men, has uniformly been found to be safe.*

Our limits forbid us to enlarge on this point. Honest men believe that honesty is the best policy. But the common run of politicians have inverted the maxim. With them, policy is the best honesty. When they are urged to do a humane or a right thing, they must stop, of course, to inquire how it will affect their own interests.* And if the prospect should not be flattering in that direction, they forthwith see a multitude of evil consequences, like hungry lions, in the way. The moment that the equitable disenthralment of *two millions* of slaves is spoken of, they see visions of pillage and murder, bloody bones and mangled carcases, from one end of the land to the other. Wild anarchy and grisly famine, stalk together over the ruins of our greatness. And all this from the simple fact of restoring to a portion of the people their "inalienable right" *to be governed by the same laws as the rest.*

It is enough to say that not a solitary fact in the history of the past goes to warrant any such frightful apprehensions. This may be seen by those who will take the trouble to examine the publications of the various anti-slavery societies of England and America, and especially a pamphlet by Thomas Clarkson, giving a history of all the cases that have occurred.

9. *The greatness of our guilt is proved by the very* REMEDY, *which has been proposed for the evil.*

The whole community has become so steeped to the core in this iniquity, that many who would reform it, dare not speak against it in audible tones. Some reformers of this stamp, a few years ago, cast about for the best plan of operations for the removal of slavery. They hit upon one which has been quite popular. And what does it amount to? A plan for *avoiding the*

slave, we say the people ought to relieve it, and for this purpose should be taxed in proportion to their share of the plunder. For ourselves we are willing to pay more than our share. But in all honesty, let the *slave's claim* be settled *first.* Let the booty be restored to its true owner and let the principle of "honor among thieves" do its work afterwards. We protest against putting a concession to the slaveholder's claim of compensation in the fore-front of our moral attack upon slavery. The impiety of hiring sinners to repent is only equalled by its absurdity. To those whose minds are troubled with the claim of *compensation,* we would recommend the following illustration, borrowed from a British abolitionist :— "Suppose now, that an Irish pauper, in the days when Irishmen worked their horses by the tails, had been interfered with by the parish officers with a view to put an end to his barbarous practice, and had answered, ' If your honors stop my allowance till I give over working my horse by the tail, I hope you mean to pay me what I gave for him, *and allow me to work him in harness besides.'* This is a fair statement of the compensation proposal. Every body knows, that what they demand to be paid for, is the mere pleasure of working by the tail; it is simply the gratification of those evil lusts and passions, which can be gratified under a system of slavery, and cannot be gratified so well under a system of free labor."

obstacles to emancipation—obstacles created and sustained by the slaveholders themselves. How does it operate? By transporting those who are already free, or such slaves as the masters may please to send across the Atlantic,—an operation which they themselves confess is *adapted* to give strength and permanence to the system of slavery by removing the principal disturbers of it.* At the same time they "*hope*" that the planters will become so much enamored of the scheme, as to carry it beyond the stage at which it will only strenthen slavery—that they will even manumit the entire mass of their slaves, gradually, and permit them to be sent out of the country !! In seventeen years, by this plan, as many slaves have been transported to Africa *as are born in two or three days;* and hence it is thought to be a very *practicable* plan ! Nothing but a blinding and wicked prejudice against the people of color, could hide the absurd and false assumptions of this scheme.

1. It is not true that the residence of the free blacks here is an obstacle to emancipation. There are, it is true, penalties attached to emancipation in many of the states, and colonization, it is said, enables those who are so disposed to evade these laws. But will a majority of the people who make the law, enter into any scheme to evade the law ?

2. The liberation of slaves on condition of going to Liberia, is not emancipation but *exile.*

3. The transportation of a part will irevitably make those who remain more valuable, of course the masters will be less disposed to spare them.

4. To reduce the mass of the slaves, more than the annual increase must be taken off, but this would be certain ruin to the colony. Indeed we may say on the best authority, that the removal of one out of one hundred of the annual increase for the last year or two, *has ruined* the colony already, if that may be said to be ruined which had never been established except in imagination.

5. The scheme contemplates no agitation of the " delicate question" of slavery, hence,

6. It uses no moral influence against the

* See African Repository, Vol. I. page 227 and 15th Am. Report Archer's Speech.

system, so that slaveholders may patronize it, if they please, altogether to promote slavery. Thus it becomes, at best, a plan for the abolition, not of *slavery*, but of *slaves*,— or rather of *black* slaves,—or more properly still, of *free blacks*.

7. It undertakes to unite the very elements of discord, without changing their character,—to compromise the most opposite principles. It yokes philanthropists and slaveholders to the same car. The latter wish to draw it moderately ; the former will have worked in vain, if they do not run away with it ; but practically the car is not likely to be drawn fast enough for the purpose even of the slaveholder.

8. The action of the plan upon the free is altogether uncalled for, and is regarded by them as cruel and abusive.

What can be stronger proof of the deep and deadly taint of slavery throughout this nation, than the popularity of such a plan ? and the universal justification of it on the ground that our prejudices against the colored race are too strong ever to be conquered ?

We have not brought into view the pretence that the removal of our colored population will evangelize and civilize Africa. If there be any force in this plea for colonization, it shows still more clearly our wickedness in trampling down here not only human beings, but the very salt of the human race—men who are qualified for the grandest moral achievements.

Finally, if our view of this subject be correct, whatever may be said of slavery in the *abstract*, or of slavery as it existed in ancient times, or as it may exist in any supposable case, slavery, as it actually does exist, in republican, Christian America, is a soul murdering sin ;—it is the consummation of all that is atrocious and cruel and mean in the violation of human rights ! It is not a thing to be treated " delicately," to be kept out of sight, to be nursed with apologies, and pruned with expedients. It is tyranny, fierce and relentless, not in the distant thunders of a throne, but brought home to the "business and bosoms," the bodies and souls, of *two millions* of our brethren, in blasting, scorching, scathing energy, by ever present despots. It is the tyranny of a proud and haughty nation, bearing down upon a feeble, speechless minority, in the spirit of reckless prejudice and mean hypocrisy.

Who is it that inquires what *plan* we propose ? Has he a conscience ? Has he warm blood in his veins ? Has he a fibre that is human in him ? Nature cries out with ten thousand tongues—the very stones of the street cry out—ABOLISH THE SYSTEM! CEASE TO STEAL THE IMAGE OF GOD ! Let us join the chorus, —that is all,—let us join the mighty chorus, till the nerves of the oppressor tremble, till his grasp relax from the throat of our BROTHER.

LETTERS FROM THE SOUTH WEST TO MR. TAPPAN.

LETTER I.

NATCHEZ, 1833.

" *So I returned, and considered all the oppressions that are done under the sun : and behold, the tears of such as were oppressed, and they had no comforter ; and on the side of their oppressors there was power ; but they had no comforter.*"

It has been almost four years since I came to the south west ; and although I have been told from month to month, that I should soon wear off my northern prejudices, and probably have slaves of my own; yet my judgment in regard to oppression, or my prejudices, if any are pleased so to call them, remain with me still. I judge still from those principles which were fixed in my mind at the north ; and a residence at the south, has not enabled me so to pervert truth, as to make injustice appear justice.

I have studied the state of things here, now for years, coolly and deliberately, with the eye of an uninterested looker on ; and hence I may not be altogether unprepared to state to you some facts, and to draw conclusions from them,

Permit me then to relate what I have seen, and do not imagine that these are all exceptions to the general treatment ; but rather believe that thousands of cruelties are practised in this Christian land, every year, which no eye that ever shed a tear of pity could look upon.

Soon after my arrival I made an excursion into the country to the distance of some twenty miles. And as I was passing by a cotton field where about fifty negroes were at work, I was inclined to stop by the road side to view a scene which was then new to me. While I was in my mind, comparing this mode of labor with that of my own native place, I heard the driver with a rough oath, order one that was near him, who seemed to be laboring to the extent of his power, to "lie down." In a moment he was obeyed; and he commenced whipping the offender upon his naked back, and continued to the amount of about twenty lashes, with a heavy raw-hide whip, the crack of which might have been heard more than half a mile. Nor did the females escape. For although I stopped scarcely fifteen minutes, no less then three were whipped in the same manner; and that so severely, I was strongly inclined to interfere.

You may be assured, sir, that I remained not unmoved. I could no longer look on such cruelty; but turned away and rode on while the echos of the lash were reverberating in the woods around me. Such scenes have long since become familiar to me. But then the full effect was not lost; and I shall never forget to my latest day, the mingled feelings of pity, horror and indignation that took possession of my mind. I involuntarily exclaimed, O God of my fathers! how dost thou permit such things to defile our land! be merciful to us! and visit us not in justice, for all our iniquities and the iniquities of our fathers!

As I passed on I soon found that I had escaped from one horrible scene only to witness another. A planter with whom I was well acquainted, had caught a negro without a pass. And at the moment I was passing by, he was in the act of fastening his feet and hands to the trees, having previously made him take off all his clothing except his trowsers. When he had sufficiently secured this poor creature, he beat him for several minutes with a green switch more than six feet long; while he was writhing with anguish, endeavoring in vain to break the cords with which he was bound, and incessantly crying out, Lord master! Do pardon me this time! Do master, have mercy! These expressions have recurred to me a thousand times since, and although they came from one, that is not considered among the sons of men, yet I think they are well worthy of remembrance, as they might lead a wise man to consider whether such shall receive mercy from the righteous judge, as never showed mercy to their fellow men.

At length I arrived at the dwelling of a planter of my acquaintance with whom I passed the night. At about 8 o'clock in the evening I heard the barking of several dogs, mingled with the most agonizing cries that I ever heard from any human being. Soon after the gentleman came in, and began to apologize, by saying that two of his runaway slaves had just been brought home, and as he had previously tried every species of punishment upon them without effect, he knew not what else to add except to set his blood hounds upon them " And," continued he, " one of them has been so badly bitten that he has been trying to die. I am only sorry that he did not; for then I should not have been further troubled with him. If he lives I intend to send him to Natchez or to New Orleans to work with the ball and chain."

From this last remark I understood that private individuals have the right of thus subjecting their unmanageable slaves. I have since seen numbers of these " ball and chain" men, both in Natchez and New Orleans, but I do not know whether there were any among them except the state convicts.

As the summer was drawing towards a close, and the yellow fever beginning to prevail in town, I went to reside some months in the country. This was the cotton picking season, during which the planters say, there is a greater necessity for flogging than at any other time. And I can assure you that as I have set in my window night after night while the cotton was being weighed, I have heard the crack of the whip, without much intermission, for a whole hour, from no less than three plantations, some of which were a full mile distant.

I found that the slaves were kept in the field from daylight until dark, and then if they had not gathered what the master or overseer thought sufficient, they were subjected to the lash.

Many by such treatment are induced to run away and take up their lodging in the woods. I do not say that all who run away are thus closely pressed. But I do know that many do; and I have known no less than a dozen desert at a time from the same plantation, in consequence of the overseer's forcing them to work to the extent of their power and then whipping them for not having done more.

But suppose that they run away—what

is to become of them in the forest? If they cannot steal they must perish of hunger—if the nights are cold, their feet will be frozen; for if they make a fire they may be discovered, and be shot at. If they attempt to leave the country, their chance of success is about nothing. They must return, be whipped—if old offenders wear the collar, perhaps be branded, and fare worse than before.

Do you believe it, sir, not six months since, I saw a number of my *Christian* neighbors packing up provisions, as I supposed, for a deer hunt; but as I was about offering myself to the party, I learned that their powder and balls were destined to a very different purpose; it was, in short, the design of the party to bring home a number of runaway slaves or to shoot them if they should not be able to get possession of them in any other way.

You will ask, Is not this murder? Call it, sir, by what name you please, such are the facts—many are shot every year; and that too while the masters say they treat their slaves well.

But let me turn your attention to another species of cruelty. About a year since, I knew a certain slave who had deserted his master, to be caught and for the first night fastened in the stocks. In those same stocks from which at midnight I have heard cries of distress, while the master slept, and was dreaming perhaps of drinking wine and of discussing the price of cotton. On the next morning he was chained in an immovable posture, and branded in both cheeks, with red hot stamps of iron. Such are the tender mercies of men who love wealth, and are determined to obtain it at any price.

Suffer me to add another to the list of enormities, and I will not offend you with more.

There was, some time since brought to trial in this town a planter residing about fifteen miles distant, for whipping his slave to death. You will suppose of course that he was punished. No, sir, he was acquitted, although there could be no doubt of the fact. I heard the tale of murder from a man who was acquainted with all the circumstances. "I was," said he, "passing along the road near the burying ground of the plantation, about 9 o'clock at night, when I saw several lights gleaming through the woods—and as I approached in order to see what was doing, I beheld the coroner of Natchez with a number of men, standing around the body of a young female, which by the torches seemed almost perfectly white. On inquiry I learned that the master had so unmercifully beaten this girl that she died under the operation. And that also he had so severely punished another of his slaves that he was but just alive.

But, sir, you must not suppose that there are no laws for the protection of the slave. There are such laws; but of what avail they are, I have not yet been able to understand. It has always appeared to me that the masters are as independent as though there were no other beings in the creation but their slaves and themselves. And you know, sir, how dangerous it would be to entrust unlimited power to any set of men—however upright they might be at the time—for they would be sure to abuse it, especially if it had reference entirely to their own interest.

Yet these men say they treat their slaves well! It is folly to use words without meaning; but I fear, that, in this polite age, we use too many words in a sense altogether different from their right meaning. I have seen hundreds of slaves treated as my cattle and horses shall never be treated with my consent. I do not pretend to say, that every one is branded with red hot irons, that every one is shot, or that half of them are whipped to death. But I know that some of them are, and I doubt not but thousands of such cases have occurred, and will occur again if this system of oppression is not broken up.

And what is the exact number of such deeds that it is necessary to present in order to persuade the people of New England that slavery in this country is opposed to humanity and the spirit of the gospel? I am told that they are in the habit of considering these enormities as exceptions to the general treatment. Let them be called exceptions, or by any other name in the English language, enough of them have already defiled the land to condemn slavery forever. How many murders is it necessary should occur on the high seas to make the term piracy apply with propriety to such deeds? If the crew of any vessel plunders another crew of all their effects, murders the captain and some of the men, and treat the remainder *well*, by putting them to sea, in an open boat, after having given them each a hundred lashes, shall not these plunderers be called pirates—because they will not kill the whole, but treated a part *well?*

By this example you may understand what is meant by good treatment to slaves. It is not treating them so badly as they might be treated, but only giving them a hundred lashes each to show them the value of discipline—plundering them of all the avails of their labor, because they might in their ignorance make a bad use of their money—depriving them of intellectual and moral instruction, out of a tender regard to their happiness—and depriving them of their liberty, because they are ignorant and totally unfit to have justice done them?

The truth is there is no possible way of treating slaves well. The root of the tree is most unholy, and all the branches will ever be unalloyed iniquity. Then pluck it up by the roots; better that a little soil should be somewhat moved for a time, than that pestilence and death should devour millions of human beings. And the longer it is delayed the firmer will it be fixed in the earth, and the farther the branches extend the more effectually will they shut out the light of heaven. Cannot justice be done in Christian America, as well as in barbarous Africa? For fifteen years Africa has been looked to by many great and good men as the only hope of the oppressed. But fifteen years has relieved but three thousand, while more than half a million have been born to servitude.

What man in his sober senses can once imagine that it is within the range of probability to deport to a foreign land only the yearly increase? Twenty such colonies as that at Liberia could not receive them. And that is pointed out as the most flourishing colony that has existed since the days of Queen Dido.

Why then trust to this broken reed of Egypt. Allow that the few who go thither will be benefited, allow that through their means Africa will become christianized and the slave trade ended—What then? Should not our own domestic slave trade be abolished too? Why should we not christianize two millions in America as well as the same number of the natives in Africa. In short, why should not this whole crying sin be stopped at once?

I have seen men, while reading of forc-ing children from their parents in Africa, and of the awful middle passage, filled with the utmost indignation. Do not these same men well know that in Maryland and Virginia thousands are raised every year for sale, and forced from the dearest ties of life, when they are sold for the deadly climate of Mississippi and Louisiana? I have seen mothers shudder, while hearing of infants being exposed to the monsters of the Ganges.

But ye who feel for those that sit in darkness, and under the shadow of death—ye whose hearts are by nature given to pity, Do you ever think that 60,000 infants are every year in this happy land born to slavery? Born to learn every vice, to be at the will of another all their days, and then a great part of them to die without the consolations of religion. Well may you weep for these unhappy ones, and well might you weep for yourselves, if you knew that you contributed to such misery, in paying a premium on the products of slave labor.

O how prone are we, while enjoying all the comforts of life, to forget that misery and sorrow are the portion of millions. In the quiet walks of life we behold joyful faces, and commune with hearts of gladness. But we need not go to Rama to find "lamentation, and weeping, and great mourning."   X. Y. Z.

REVIEW OF THE COLONIZATION SOCIETY.
Concluded.

But we must answer to a very serious charge, brought by Mr. Bacon. He proceeds to say,

"The party which is now arraying itself as the Anti-Slavery, or more properly the Anti-Colonization party, is a growing party at the North. Gentlemen who are now leading characters in it, have a design to make it a political party. I have reason to believe they mean to make adhesion to their sentiments a test of office. And there will not be wanting political desperadoes who are willing to be arrayed under that banner. And if we do not rally, and move forward, the people at large will ere long be carried away by that wind of doctrine."

How does Mr. Bacon know what are the "*designs*" of the leaders of the Anti-Slavery party? What reason have they given him to believe that they "*mean*" to do this or that? We ask, who are these men?—what have they done?—what are their *principles?*—what is their *practice?* Are the leaders of the Anti-Slavery Society office-seekers? are they a set of men to be found in political squabbles? are they noisy demagogues, who love to swim in the front wave of popular turbulence? We appeal confidently to all who know them if there is a single man, who sides with them, or is approved by them, who has ever sustained any such character. If Mr. Bacon would reflect, but for a moment, he must see that it is superlatively mean, thus to throw odium upon a class of men, who have banded themselves together, with no other arms than the truths of the Gospel, to fight their country's giant sin. Mr. Bacon very well knows that the abolitionists of our country are men who honor the law of God by giving it a supremacy over their whole conduct. They do not put on their religion for a Sunday suit,—they design to have it cover whatever they do, during the whole week; is it for Mr. Bacon, then, to charge them with deep intrigues, with being the accomplices of " political desperadoes?" Before the final adjournment of the meeting, Mr. Bacon was pointed to the passage in the Address of the New-York City Anti-Slavery Society, where they say,

" Let it be distinctly remembered that our object is purely moral. It is to deliver our colored brethren from slavery, and our white fellow citizens from the sin of oppression, the fair fame of our country from the stinging reproach of hypocrisy and tyranny, and ourselves and posterity from the judgments of an offended God. Should interested politicians seek to avail themselves of the slavery question to promote the views of party, we disclaim their interference. While engaged in a purely benevolent work we will not suffer the reproach of being actuated by political views."

But even this could not cure him of his fault-finding. He bursts out into a fresh tirade of abuse, in which he shows his teeth at what he calls " the great Coryphœus" of the " party," a terrible fellow, " whom a national convention was assembled to glorify,"* and who spends most of his " time and breath in calumniating the constitution and laws of the United States." He undertakes to vilify " the Anti-Slavery party in England" as " a political party altogether," and quotes our sending memorials to Congress for the abolition of slavery in the district of Columbia, especially inasmuch as the petitioners in New Haven omitted him, as proof positive of our " political" designs! Well, as Mr. Bacon says, in another place, " it is of no use to keep back the facts." We will, therefore, out with the whole of them, and make a clean breast. While we have no design to dabble in the ballot-boxes, or count noses with the mobs of the nobility, who turn out to suppress abolition meetings, we do " mean" to work under the politics of the whole country, night and day, without intermission or respite, till there shall be such a complete over-

* Mr. Bacon seems to be very sensitive on the subject of glory. We recollect to have seen in a Quarterly, in which Mr. Bacon sometimes writes, a very splenetic prediction, that a man who had been imprisoned in Baltimore, would reap a great harvest of "glory" from his bonds. Mr. Bacon should know, that those who have the good fortune to be commended and caressed by slaveholders, ought to be contented with their own " glory."

turn, that those, who have built their immortality by defending the " present relation" between human flesh traders and their merchandise, shall find themselves a thousand fathoms deep in the rubbish of oblivion. This we confess for ourselves; for the " Coryphæus" and " the leaders" we have nothing to say.

Mr. Bacon thinks to prove that Elias B. Caldwell did not mean what he said, on a certain occasion, about the benefit of keeping slaves in ignorance, because he had an *excellent character*, to *his* certain knowledge. This is probably about the best of colonization logic, and serves admirably to show " the *delirium*, into which minds educated and sane, can suffer themselves to run, when they inscribe on their banner the motto of " IMMEDIATE EMANCIPATION," and set up, instead of the Eagle, the head of Garrison."

We confess, we always agreed with Dr. Franklin in preferring the *turkey* to the eagle, and much more should we prefer a human face, if it were that of an honest man, who had always been true to the noble " motto of IMMEDIATE EMANCIPATION." We are not ashamed of our banner yet, Mr. Bacon. *You* may worship the *king of birds* if you please, but *we* venerate an " *honest man*" as " the noblest work of God."

We must bring this article to a close by quoting from the graphic pencil of Mr. Bacon, the present picture of the colony.—[See New-York Observer for Feb. 8, 1834.]

" Mr. Bacon rose and said that the general condition of the society had been adverted to this evening and in every debate since they had met. He wished now to call the attention of the meeting to that subject. The society was bankrupt to the amount of $40,000: and new drafts were coming due from month to month, and this 40 might soon be found to be 60,000. The further they went the deeper was the difficulty. They had sounded first and found twenty fathoms; they sounded again, and found, not fifteen, but thirty fathoms. The further they had gone on " sounding their dim and perilous way," the darker was the prospect, and the deeper the abyss. This was not only true in reference to the state of the society here, but the condition of the colony was such as must horrify every friend of the cause. He had read a report from the acting governor of Liberia, Mr. M'Gill, written with considerable talent; and he had also seen a letter on the other side, and the lightest side was dark enough. He believed that it would require an expenditure of $50,000 during the present year to put the colony on a footing of prosperity. The fort which had been erected there was going to ruin, and the flag-staff had rotted away and been down three or four months, and there was not moral force in the colony to replace it. In consequence of this neglect, no signals could be made. The government schooner, which had been obtained for the colony, principally by the aid of a gentleman near him (Mr. Cresson), was rotting at the wharf, for want of new coppering, and the African worms were eating it through and through. It would be of no use to keep back the facts. The society had its enemies in the colony as well as here, and they were in correspondence with persons in this country. This, then was our condition, and he would say, without intending to inculpate any individual, that the society had arrived at this state through sheer want of management. How else could it have been? A governor was there whose expenses were to be paid, year after year, amount to what they might. He had looked at some of the particulars of these accounts, and had found a charge of $60 for a set of dining-tables. He had showed this item to Bishop Meade, who remarked that he had never had a table in his house which cost more than $5. He had seen a letter from a woman in the colony, who wrote thus:— "It is hurtful (painful) to see people begging for work to support their lives." What a state of things was this! Here was a new colony, in which every kind of labor ought to be in demand, where there were two harvests in a year, roads to be made, and every kind of improvement to be carried on, yet the people could not get employment. There was evidently great want of management in the colony. He did not charge the late governor with unfaithfulness, but he, was exeedingly inefficient, and as far as he had looked into the accounts, exceedingly reckless in his expenditures. Why had this debt been permitted, year after year, to accumulate, until, like an avalanche, it had fallen on us, and over-whelmed us?— There was also a want of management here. He did not charge any individual with neglect, but there was no responsibility. When drafts came, they were paid, and no one knew for what. It had been said that this was necessary to sustain the credit of the Society at the colony. He saw that there was a swarm of officers on salary in the colony. Among these he was surprised to find a register of deeds at $500 a year.— He thought that any settler, when he received his fee simple, would be willing to pay his sixpence to register his title. There was also a housekeeper for the governor at $104 a year, and a steward at $144. He had never dreamed that things were so bad as this. They in the north were aware that things were not going on well in the colony. By the vessels which came in, they had received rumors to that effect, and they had put the best face on the matter as long as they could, until truth had come in too much strength to be resisted. They had come 300 or 400 miles from the north, to see if by their representations they could bring into the society that responsibility which was necessary, for in the north the Philistines were upon them, and the cause there would be ruined unless they could restore public confidence in the society.— They had not said a word since they had been here on what was called the delicate subject. The south would not catch them coming here and making proclamations about slaves.

And here the matter stands. The pungent rebukes of Mr. Breckenridge fell idle, as from a coat of impenetrable mail. There is a great fault, but nobody is to blame! The efforts of Mr. Gerrit Smith to reform the society into a "benevolent" institution were all frustrated. The nice art of Mr. Bacon in setting sails, though he displayed some marvellous evolutions in managing the wind, has left the ship among the breakers. The whole reform consists in making some more *salaried* officers, reducing the number of the board of managers, and raising the terms of membership.*

We have one question to put to all the friends of the slave, to all Christians, to all honest men : Will you any longer throw your money into that bottomless gulf instead of devoting it to the work of showing this nation its sin, and of dis-enthraling your brother, the victim of cursed prejudice, at your very door ?

* Some very pertinent questions were proposed, by Mr. Gerrit Smith, and were directed by the society to be answered by the secretary. A true answer will bring the society to the end of its pilgrimage so far as Christianity and benevolence are concerned.

KIDNAPPING ACCORDING TO LAW.

Many citizens of New-York will not have forgotten, that about the first of last October, four men were taken on a charge of stealing a boat, and conveyed from this city to Northampton county in Virginia, where one of them was sentenced to be *hanged* on the 10th of January. If this sentence was not executed, we think we should certainly have heard of it from one whose interest it was to inform us of such a fact. The others we are credibly informed, were sold to the " *speculators !*"

Since that, several grievous cases have occured. But the most atrocious and diabolical, was that which took place last week. A little past-midnight between Friday and Saturday, a man by the name of Haywood, furnished with two constables, proceeded to the house of a colored man by the name of Lockley. After rummaging and pillaging and destroying every thing which looked like a " free paper," he seized and dragged off Lockley, his wife and child, and lodged them in Bridewell. The next morning at 11 o'clock they were brought before his *honor* the Recorder, and the *honorable* counsel for the *right honorable* claimaint proceeded to read the affidavit of the said claimant, setting forth that these three persons were the " property" of his deceased father and were now claimed in behalf of his mother, and that they absconded from Raleigh N, C. in December 1832. The claimant being called by the respectable appellation of Dr. Haywood, stepped forward and swore to the identity of the persons and the correctness of the affidavit. All this was considered very satisfactory by the Recorder, but at the urgent request of the prisoner and two or three of his friends, he was allowed till 2 o'clock P. M. to bring up avidence in his defence. At that hour the parties appeared before the Recorder. Several witnesses were brought forward who testified that they had known Lockley, his wife and child—a fine boy about 12 years old—as residents in this city long previous to the time specified in the affidavit. In short, as it appeared that they were well known in this city previous to December 1832, they could not have absconded in that month from Raleigh. But what did the Judge in this case? Be it remarked that Mr. Recorder had said at the opening of the case that it was a very plain one, if Lockley could not prove, his residence here previous to December 1832, he (the Recorder) should make out a certificate, *but if he could*, he should discharge him. But mark, gentle reader, as soon as the proof was produced, the Recorder adjourned the trial to the 31st of MARCH; that the said Dr. Haywood might obtain further evidence !!! As might be supposed, that *respectable* gentleman has decamped *in person* to the south for further evidence, leaving his three victims, where he himself deserves to be, in that den of abomination situated on the western side of the Park.

Truth and humanity require of us to make this publication at the present stage of the business. There is no safety, as experience has proved, in letting such things alone.

S. W. BENEDICT & CO. PRINTERS, 162 Nassau stre.

AMERICAN

ANTI - SLAVERY REPORTER.

VOL. I.]   MARCH, 1834.   [NO. 3.

THE following interesting narrative was drawn up by the venerable Isaac T. Hopper, and has been published by him in a very beautiful tract. By his permission we present it to the readers of the Anti-Slavery
Reporter. We have only to remark that the same process of legalized kidnapping, which is here disclosed,
is still in active operation. How long before we shall open our mouths for the oppressed? How long
shall *man-stealing* nestle and flourish beneath the Constitution? How long shall the safeguard of the white
man's rights crush to the dust the rights of the black man?

NARRATIVE OF THE LIFE OF THOMAS COOPER.

Thomas Cooper, the subject of the following narrative, was of African descent,
and was born a slave in the state of Maryland, where he continued to reside until he
was about twenty-five years old. During
his servitude, he experienced many hardships, being scantily clothed and fed, and
compelled to labor very hard, and was
obliged to lodge in a little hut, which was
so open, that it did not shelter him from the
cold in winter; but although his body was
held in cruel bondage, his mind was free,
and he frequently put up his prayers in
secret, to his merciful Creator, for deliverance from his sufferings; believing that all
are the work of one Almighty hand, who
hath placed them in various situations, and
that he was disposed to extend equally his
care and protection to all.

About the year 1800, Notly, (for this was
his name while a slave,) left his master's
service, and went to Philadelphia, and hired
with M—— & E——, who kept a lumber
yard, in which he was employed; here he
conducted with fidelity and industry, and
soon gained the confidence and esteem of
his employers.

After some time he married a respectable

When gratuitous, please to read and hand it to your neighbor.

woman of his own color; they lived together several years in much harmony and
affection, and were esteemed, by their
neighbors and acquaintances,as orderly and
industrious people, until a person who had
gained the confidence of John Smith, (for
upon his arrival in Philadelphia, he had
assumed this name,) betrayed him, by in-
forming his master where he was to be
found. This man soon after came to Philadelphia, and had poor John arrested and
carried before one of the Aldermen of that
city, and upon proof that he was a slave,
an order was granted to convey him back
to Maryland.

His employers were humane men, and
greatly commiserating his condition, and
sympathizing with his wife and children,
offered to pay a large sum of money for his
freedom, that he might be restored to them;
but no entreaties would avail with his cruel
master; he was deaf to the voice of pity,
and poor John was handcuffed, and a rope
fastened to each arm across his back, to
which another was tied, one end of which
the master held in his hand; and mounting
his horse, rode off, driving John before him.
All this took place in the presence of his
wife and children, who witnessed the horrid transaction with the utmost distress.

While they were fastening the fetters
upon John, he was engaged in talking to
his wife. He counselled her to take care
of their children, whom, he said, he wished
to remember their father; expressing a
hope that by industry and frugality, she
would be able to keep them at school, until they were old enough to be put out,
when he wished them placed with persons
of good character and industrious habits;
and he cautioned her against indulging
them in idleness, saying, that he wished
her to remember his advice, as it was not
likely that they would ever meet again.

He then addressed his children, saying,
"You will now have no father to take care
of you; be good children, obey your mother, and be sure that you never do any
thing to grieve her; don't play in the
street, or with naughty children—be industrious and faithful in whatever you are set
about."

He continued his speech until his master
raised his whip, when he set out on his
journey—his wife and children wept bit-
terly; and although he manifested great
sensibility, he retained his composure.

John and his wife, by industry and frugality, had acquired a little property: they
lived in their own house, and had been, for
several years, enjoying as much comfort as
their hearts could desire; but in an instant,
as it were, all their hopes seemed blasted,
and they parted in the deepest anguish and
despair not expecting ever to see each other's faces again.

The writer of this was present at the
examination before the Alderman, he saw
John fettered and torn from the bosom of
his wife and children.

The circumstances of the case were well
calculated to awaken feelings of sympathy
and tenderness; and at this distant period,
his sensibility is excited at the recollection
of the distressing scene; it made impressions which time cannot remove, as long
as memory lasts.

John's wife was now left with four small
children to provide for, and he was conveyed, in the manner above described, to
the city of Washington, and there offered
for sale to persons who bought slaves on
speculation, to be transported to Georgia,
or some other southern market. But even
in Washington, where slavery is tolerated
by laws, there were those who could not
with indifference, behold inhumanity like
that which this poor slave was doomed to
endure, and they rebuked his master for
his cruelty. This was very unexpected
to John, and inspired him with a determination to make an effort to regain his liberty; for his feelings were acute, and his
affections warm,although his skin was black.

Manacled as he was, he made out to trip
up his master's heels, and he fell to the
ground. John then ran to the woods: but
in a few hours, he was pursued by his av-
aricious master, with a company he had
collected to assist him, and it was not long
before he was discovered concealed in the
bushes. As soon as he found that he was
seen by his pursuers, he ran into a swamp,
where he was hunted like a fox, until the
darkness of the night released him from the
chase.

He then made the best of his way to the
house of a man of his own color, whose
sympathy was excited on seeing an innocent fellow-being bound with irons and
cords, like the worst of criminals. This
man was an old acquaintance, and knowing
John's integrity, soon found means to rid
him of his fetters, and he once more felt

himself at liberty. His friend and benefactor hastened to set before him the best his table afforded, and after taking a hearty meal, for he had eaten but little since he left Philadelphia, he again set out for that city ; but the journey appeared very hazardous, as he had several rivers to cross, and expected persons would be stationed at the bridges to arrest him ; he, however, determined to make the attempt.

He knew it would not be safe to be seen, and therefore hid himself in the bushes during the day, and pursued his journey in the night. After suffering much with hunger and fatigue, he arrived safely in Philadelphia, and went immediately to see his distressed family ; it was a joyful meeting: but John well knew that he would be again pursued, and could not be safe to remain long under his own roof; accordingly he left his family, and went to the house of a respectable citizen, well known as the black man's friend, and whom we shall call Philo Christian ; here he was kindly entertained.

The yellow fever was then in the city, and the family had removed into the country, except a colored woman, who remained in the house to attend upon Philo, whose engagements required that he should be mostly in the city during the day, and not unfrequently during the night also.

John was placed in an upper room, the door of which was kept fastened. He had been in this place but a very little time, before his master with two constables, came in pursuit of him ; and Philo being absent, they proceeded to search the house; and, on coming to the door of the room where John was, and finding it fast, they demanded entrance.

In a little time Philo came home, and being informed by the colored woman what was taking place, he immediately went up stairs, and found the intruders consulting how they should gain admittance. Philo instantly ordered them out of his house, upon which one of the officers replied, "This gentleman's slave is in your house, and if you do not immediately deliver him up, we will get a warrant from the mayor to search it." He again requested them to leave his house, and added, "the mayor dare not grant a search-warrant for my house." They then withdrew, and in a few minutes the officer returned, with a message from the mayor, requesting to see

him. Philo promptly waited upon the mayor, who lived near by, when the following dialogue took place:

Philo.—Hast thou business with me ?

Mayor.—Yes, this gentleman, (alluding to John's master, who was present,) says, his slave is in your house ; is it so ?

Philo.—I think thou hast just informed me, that man says he *is;* dost thou not believe him ?

Mayor.—Well, but I wish to be informed by you, whether he is in your house or not.

Philo.—I think the mayor, upon a little reflection, will see, that he has no authority to ask me this question, and of course, I am not bound to answer it ; if he is in my house, and this man can make it appear, I am liable to a very heavy penalty, and no man is bound to inform against himself; and the conduct of these people has not been so civil, that I feel myself under any obligations of courtesy to satisfy them. Hast thou further business with me ?

Mayor.—Did you say that I dare not grant a warrant to search your house ?

Philo.—Indeed I did, and now repeat it, neither thou nor any other magistrate in this city ; without intending any disrespect to those in authority, I am a man of reputation, I am not a suspicious character.

Mayor.—(Smiling) I don't know that, I am inclined to think in the present case you are.

Philo.—Hast thou any thing further to say to me ?

Mayor.—I believe not.

Philo.—Farewell.

The avarice of his master, together with his desire for revenge, induced him to pursue every stratagem that he could devise to recapture poor John; and among others, the following was resorted to : one of the party procured a suit of clothes, such as are worn by Friends—a hat with a round crown and broad brim, and a plain coat. Thus attired, he made his way to John's house ; upon entering, he saw his wife, bathed in tears, sitting in their once peaceful and happy cottage, with her children round her, the youngest by her side, looking its mother in the face, and, by its gesture, seeming to inquire the cause of her grief.

But all this had no effect to soften the heart of this man, whose object was lucre, as a reward for apprehending the unhappy fugitive. With affected sympathy and kindness, he inquired where John was to be found, saying, that his master was in pursuit of him, and he wished to see him, in order to assist him in getting out of the way : but this artifice, although ingenious, and must have been attended with some expense and trouble, proved unsuccessful; for the woman was on her guard, and declined giving him any information, but referred him to her friend, Philo Christian, as the most suitable person to advise with in the case. He became greatly enraged at this disappointment, and gave vent to his anger in profane wicked language ; declaring, as he withdrew, that he would have John, if he was to be found upon the face of the earth.

John remained under the protection of his friend about a week ; during most of this time, persons were seen lurking about the premises watching for him, but at length they disappeared. Supposing they had concealed themselves, a person was procured, who, some little time after dark in the evening, suddenly ran out of the house, where John was ; but he had proceeded but a short distance, before the apprehensions, which were entertained, that the enemy was in ambush, were realized, for they suddenly rushed from their hiding places, and seized upon the man that was running.

Finding that they were mistaken in the person, they released him ; but John's friend made application to the mayor, had them arrested, and compelled them to enter into bonds for their good behavior. The next evening, the same person went out as before, and was not interrupted; the following evening, John left his hiding-place, and got safely into New-Jersey.

Here he hired with a farmer, and, altho' he was within about eight miles of his home, he was an exile from it ; he remained in this situation several months, during which time, by his good conduct, he gained the confidence and esteem of the family where he resided. It was their practice on first day afternoons, to collect together and read portions of the Scriptures, and other religious books, and John was permitted to sit with them, which he esteemed a great privilege, and often expressed his gratitude for the favor ; he was also permitted to take his meals at the same table with the family. Instead of being elated

by this familiarity, it made him more humble.

After it became known that John had returned to Philadelphia, the person who had betrayed him, became greatly alarmed; and his fears so wrought upon his imagination, that he frequently dreamed that he saw John in the house, with a knife in one hand, and a torch in the other, and that he was about to kill him and burn his house; and he would sometimes cry out in his sleep, and start up in his bed ; so true is the saying, that, "wickedness condemned by her own witness is very timorous, and being pressed with conscience always forecasteth grievous things." But he had no cause to fear ; John had no desire to revenge the wrong that had been done him ; for he had learned that it was not right to render evil for evil, but, contrariwise, blessing.

His affliction was great at being obliged to live separated from his wife and children, for whose welfare he felt a deep interest; at length he ventured to rent a small house, in a retired situation, not far distant from the village of Haddonfield. He now hoped to be permitted to enjoy the comforts of domestic life unmolested, and yet he was in constant fear of the man-stealers ; this often interrupted his slumbers in the night, and even when at his work, he would startle at the rustling of the leaves ; so that he passed his days in fear, and his nights were constantly seasons of terror.

After some months, the place of his retreat was again discovered, and his master came to Philadelphia, with the intention to proceed to New Jersey to arrest him.— John's friend Philo heard of this circumstance, and immediately apprised him of his danger. He had already suffered much, and now finding himself again pursued, was driven almost to despair, and determined to resist by violence. The morning after receiving the information that his master had discovered his place of residence, and was coming to arrest him, he rose early, loaded his gun, and, with a determined resolution, prepared to defend himself.

It was not long before he beheld his master, with two other persons, advancing along a lane towards his house ; he placed himself in his door, and, upon their near approach, he called out, "don't cross that fence, for the first man that does, I will shoot him." So unexpected a salutation, coming from a man with a gun in his hand, struck them with terror, and they soon turned back to procure assistance.

In the meantime John went to Philadelphia, which was within about five or six miles of his home, and informed his friend Philo of what had transpired; his friend reasoned with him on the great impropriety and inconsistency with the Christian character, of putting the life of a human being in jeopardy. John seemed to be convinced of the correctness of the views of his friend, and therefore resolved again to fly for safety; and, with the advice of Philo, concluded to remove his family to Boston, in hopes of finding an asylum there, where he might live in peace.

A vessel was then lying in the river Delaware, which was expected to sail for that place in a few days; and the merchant who had charge of her, pitying his distress, offered him a passage free of expense, which he gratefully accepted; and, although he had never been at sea before, he made himself useful, and fully compensated the captain for his passage, by his labor.

His friends freely gave him certificates of his good character, which he found very useful in procuring employment among strangers; and in a few days after he arrived in Boston, he hired with a lumber merchant of that place. Now finding himself in circumstances to provide for his family, his employer, at his request, wrote to Philadelphia, desiring them to come to him; his wife accordingly disposed of their property in that city, and took the money she received for it, with her children, to Boston, where she again met her husband.

About the time of his leaving New Jersey, he changed his name from John Smith to that of Thomas Cooper, and by this name he was always afterwards known.

He often noticed, and greatly lamented the bad conduct of the people of his own color, as well as that of those of a different complexion. And, with a view of making himself more useful, he joined in religious communion with the Methodists, and in a short time became a popular preacher among them, and visited some of the West India islands as a minister.

After his return from the West Indies, he made a similar visit to Nova Scotia. In these places, it is said, he was very useful,

not only by his exhortations, but by his pious example; his religion being that of the heart, and not of the head only, his preaching had much effect on his hearers.

Not long after his return from those visits, he concluded to go to Africa, the birthplace of his fathers; and, for this purpose, took shipping with his family, and safely arrived in London, the metropolis of Great Britain. He was received with much kindness by a number of philanthropists, who were made acquainted with him and the object of his visit; and his children were placed at school, at the expense of a Friend in London, well known as a benevolent man, and a friend of the afflicted. Thomas Cooper soon became a man of much note, and preached to large congregations in that city. While there, he made a selection of hymns, which were published in a large duodecimo volume, and his friends had his likeness placed in the book, as a frontispiece.

After remaining about a year and a half in London, a passage was procured for him and his family, to Africa, as appears by a note in the hands of the publisher, of which the following is a copy, viz.

"J——— A——— informs his friend Thomas Cooper, that he has this day paid for the passage of T. C. and family to Sierra Leone, per the Echo, Captain Row. The vessel is not expected to sail till the third week in this month.

34 Gracechurch street,

10mo. 3d, 1818.

THOMAS COOPER,

Borough."

Thomas Cooper remained in London rather more than a month after the date of the above note.

When about to take his departure from London, for Sierra Leone, he had a meeting, at which, it is said, there were several thousand persons.

Soon after this meeting, Thomas, with his wife and children, sailed for Africa, and arrived at Sierra Leone, after enduring many hardships on the passage, in consequence of tempestuous weather. They were cordially received by the inhabitants, his fame having reached there before him.

How different now were his feelings, from what they were, when in his own country. There in continual dread of being torn from his family and friends, and of being reduced to the most degrading and abject slavery ; now, enjoying, without fear of molestation, the sweets of liberty, in the bosom of his family, and among his friends, who rejoiced in having such an acquisition to their colony. He immediately entered upon the object of his mission, and ·had meetings among the people—all classes flocking to hear him.

But this happy state was of but short duration ; for Thomas had not been more than two or three years in Africa, before he was taken ill with the fever, which has so often proved fatal to strangers in that hot climate, and fell a victim to it. His wife and children, by this afflicting event, were again left destitute, and that too in a land of strangers; but with the consoling reflection, that it was a dispensation of Providence, which had bereaved them of a husband, a father, a protector, and a friend ; and although the separation was painful, yet the survivors had comfort in the reflection, that he was now gone to a state of happiness, where the voice of the oppressor is heard no more.

Perhaps few men have ever lived, who experienced greater changes in their condition in life, than the person whose history we have been writing ; we have seen him a poor menial, suffering for the want of food and raiment, exposed to cold, and writhing under the lash of the tyrannical slave-driver ; again, we see him a minister of religion, pleading with the people to forsake the evil of their ways. and showing in his life, and by his own example, how far superior a life of virtue and integrity is, to that of vice and crime. The consequences of the latter are always disgrace and misery ; while the sure reward of the former is the favor and applause of the wise and good, and in the end, quietness and assurance forever.

After the death of Thomas Cooper, his wife and children returned to London, and from there to Philadelphia.

NOTE.—The results of this experiment of colonization, for such in a qualified sense it may be called, are worthy of remark. Mr. Cooper as a missionary may have done good enough to balance the sacrifice of his valuable life. But his widow and six children very prudently returned to Philadelphia, where we are happy to say they are now living very comfortably. Who shall say that they ought to have remained on that pestilential shore ?—ED.

LETTERS FROM THE SOUTH WEST
TO MR. A. TAPPAN.

LETTER II.

Having noticed some of the physical evils incident to slavery, permit me now to call to your mind some of the moral. You are aware, sir, that the slaves are prohibited from learning to read and write. And indeed that every kind of knowledge is kept from them as much as possible. Reading and writing are prohibited by law,—and although religious instruction is not unlawful ; yet there are few planters here who will permit it. And surely, it ought not to be expected, that those planters who care nothing for religion themselves, should be anxious that their slaves should be instructed in the truths of the gospel. I know not whether there are laws in any of the states against teaching them religion, except in Georgia—and even there none are prohibited but men of color. But whatever may be the laws, those planters with whom I have conversed on the subject say that religion strikes at the root of slavery. They say it teaches the slave that God is no respecter of persons—and that all men, masters and slaves, will be judged and awarded, not according to their condition in life, but according to their works. And that hence, if they are taught the religion of the bible so as to understand it, they will be discontented with their present condition ; and should they not understand it, they would become mad fanatics.

I remember that during this present year there appeared to be some degree of seriousness manifested among the slaves of my neighborhood. And as they were not permitted to meet together for prayer meetings where it was known—they sometimes assembled at midnight in the recess of some woodland :—and even there they were found out by the patroles and compelled to remain at home. But were religious instruction encouraged by the masters, even then it would be next to impossible to have religion prevail to any extent among the slaves. The first things they learn are to lie and steal, and to do many other things not to be mentioned. And there is no moral influence to counteract these propensities. Most of them have very vague notions of a future retribution ; and public opinion, which exerts an influence so powerful in a land of equal rights, has no force at all upon the slave. He feels his degradation—he knows he has no reputation to lose, and hence he has seldom any sense of shame. Perhaps he thinks he has a right to plunder the man who makes it the business of his life to plunder him. And there are many things which he feels the want of, and has no means of obtaining, but by deceiving and stealing.

There are indeed some pious men in the 'cities of the plain,' who instruct their slaves in religion ; but they do it with but little better success, than did pious Lot warn his neighbors. Such is their moral darkness that they cannot see the way of life, and so far as they can understand the truths of the gospel, they know, that the deeds of their teachers are in opposition to its precepts. But the number that is taught, is comparatively small. I have never known one plantation in ten where there was any religious instruction given at all. Do you wonder then, that those beings who are treated in every respect according to the caprices of covetous men—whipped like brute beasts—without intellectual or moral instruction—do you wonder that such beings should be degraded. Do you wonder that they should be unfit for freedom ? When does any man imagine that they ever will become fitted under such treatment ? Hear what our *wise* men say. " The slaves must not be free because they are unfit for freedom. They must not be instructed and pitied, because then they would be free." Therefore slavery must continue forever.

Now, sir, suppose they are, and always have been unprepared for emancipation ? Are we hence to infer, that no mode should be introduced to prepare them for freedom ? Are we hence to infer that they cannot be made better ? that because they are weak, we can be justified in oppressing them to the very extent of mortal endurance ? From many conversations that I have had with men both at the north and the south—and from many publications that I have lately read, I should imagine that I ought to infer all these monstrous results. Nay, more, that the righteous judge will not condemn us for doing any thing that we have the power to do, if it only be profitable to ourselves.

Again, allow them to be unfit for freedom. Who has rendered them so ? Who has brought them into their present state of ignorance and degradation, and kept them

there ? Every white man knows the true answer. We ourselves were not born into the world with all our present knowledge,— every man knows that he has had to strive by long and unremitting exertion, in order to arrive to any degree of knowledge. And he might know if he would reflect but a moment, that the powers of the mind increase with every new acquisition. He might know also that he has arrived at his present state of moral excellence under long and assiduous teaching, and by the continual influence of the principles of the gospel upon him. No one should wonder then, that the slave is not morally upright, as his whole treatment has been opposed to every thing holy.

Does not the sin then lie at our door? And will not the day of judgment reveal the truth which so many men are now slow in believing, that the blood of these men will be required at our hands ?

You must have observed, sir, that almost every argument brought by the slave party in favor of continuing the system, is only an evasion of the main question. They endeavor sometimes to convince themselves, (and indeed what is more easy than for a man to convince himself that he is correct in what he ardently desires ?) they endeavor to convince themselves, that the sin, if sin there be, lies further back than the present generation. They tell us that England, who now makes such strong declarations against slavery—employed in a single year no less than one hundred and thirty vessels in the trade. And that the English, French, Dutch, Danes, and Portuguese, are to answer for all the iniquity of the present generation. They tell us also, that Boston, Bristol, Newport, and many other towns, were enriched in fastening slavery upon the south. They tell us too of Polish Boors, Livonian Serfs—and English manufacturers. But what does all this amount to ? Go back, ye equivocators, if you please, to 1480, when the first fort was established at D'Elmina ; or if you prefer, go back to the time of the Moors, who first introduced African slaves into Spain, or to the time of Joseph, and bring up the long catalogue of crimes and oppressions. Measure the rivers of blood unrighteously shed in the horrible traffic ; count the number of groans, and the millions of the eternally lost of our own country ; and then tell me, whether you seriously intend to do these same things;

and to build the sepulchres of the prophets? Do you seriously intend to say, that you will oppress men in America because they are oppressed in Europe?

Christianity should lead to the freedom of the world, as well as to the preaching of the gospel to every creature. It did lead to the abolition of slavery in Europe at the close of the twelfth century, when mankind were much less entangled than they are at present. And the charters of freedom were given ' pro amore dei, pro mercede animæ.' In the spirit of Christianity, that excellent people the Quakers, so early as 1696, condemned the slave trade, and passed for many successive years resolutions against slavery itself.

In our own country Benezet and Woolman deserve to be held in everlasting remembrance, and to be imitated by all the great and good until there shall be no more oppression on the soil of America.

How long shall we delay to do justice, because we are unwilling to forego the profits of slave labor! Shall we continue in our oppressions until compelled by the judgments of heaven to let the oppressed go free? Until some signal calamity shall overtake us in our iniquity, and we find it too late to devise any means for justice or safety?

May God, in his mercy, stay these evils, and lead our northern and southern fellow citizens to unite in the bonds of love in wiping away this defiling stain from the land.

X. Y. Z.

———

LETTER III.

It may be supposed by some, that the people of the south have some constitutional peculiarities, which distinguish them from the inhabitants of the nothern states. South of the Petomac and the Ohio, few public works are found. Men seem to live more for themselves. They have a high sense of personal honor; but little industry or enterprize. North of these rivers, the people are rather distinguished for their industrious habits, and their enterprising spirit. Great public works are seen throughout the country, though there is less individual wealth; and religion exerts a powerful influence over the minds of the mass of the population. Now, although men differ ve-

ry widely in their feelings and habits, yet I must think, under the same circumstances, they would be very much alike. There are hundreds of people in Mississippi and Louisiana, having all the characteristics of southerners, who were originally from New England. And these men are said to be more cruel to their slaves than the emigrants from the old slave states. However this may be, I doubt not that, had the labor always been performed by slaves in N. England, the people would have been very similar to the inhabitants of the southern states. I make this assertion, because I believe, by those laws which the Almighty has established, it follows of necessity, that slavery must be a deadening blast to the moral character of any community.

Yesterday I was walking on the bluff at Natchez with a gentleman of my acquaintance, while a young man was carried to his grave who had come to his death by his own hands. " This young man," said my friend to me, " is but a melancholy example of too many youth of this country. He began with attending all the sports which are practiced by those of his age : fox-chasing, deer-hunting, and horse-racing, none of which are done without more or less drinking, until at last he lost all he had in gambling, and then shot himself, that he might not endure the reproaches of his relations, and the taunts of his associates."

We extended our walk along the bluff, until at length we descended to the level of the river, where the hills retire some little distance and form a most delightful retreat. And while we were speaking of the great number of duels which had lately occurred in Alabama, my friend said to me, " Do you know that even this lovely spot was a few years since defiled with one of the most horrible duels that was ever heard of? The principals," continued he, " and all the seconds, joined in the fight, and were most shockingly cut and stabbed with knives and swords." " But," said I, " can public opinion sanction such deeds?" " Public opinion," replied he, " is but light here against what you call enormities at the north. All men do not even here value a man any the more because of his delicate perceptions of honor. But to show you what the people in some places, at least, think of shooting a friend, I will relate a case that occurred in the neighborhood last year. In the village of Washington a deadly quarrel ensued between two young men, on account of a young lady. They crossed over into Louisiana, fought, and one was killed—brought back by his friends to the village, and buried in the sight of the people. The murderer married the object of his unrighteous strife; and how much she, her friends, or the people of the village reproached him, that deed may tell."

But let us consider for a moment how that peculiar state of things is brought about.

So soon as the child learns any thing he learns to command, and in too many cases to do as he pleases. Hence he becomes haughty and overbearing, not only to slaves, but also to those no less excellent than himself. He also is soon made acquainted with the wealth of his father, and that he shall in a few years come into possession of a fortune. He sees that labor is disreputable. Hence he not only becomes proud, but idle; and you know, sir, that the idle will always find something worse to do than dry study or vexatious business. And you know, too, that in all places, those young men who meet together to kill time, are likely to become the worst of citizens. I would suppose that a pirate might as soon become a religious man, as that an idle boy, brought up on a plantation, might become virtuous and merciful. I have heard boys no more than eight or ten years of age talk of shooting run-aways, with all the coolness of old soldiers. In addition to what they learn on the plantation, the common sports of the country are admirably adapted to make the young men intemperate and prodigal. Idleness, haughtiness, licentiousness, luxury, effeminacy, and irreligion follow in one ruinous train, and draw, with strong cords, all that might have been lovely and excellent, on to sure destruction. They foster every evil propensity to vice, and urge on many souls to perdition. Do you say that the young men should be brought up with habits of industry, and then they might escape from the contaminating influence of vicious companions. The sons of gentlemen will never be made to labor where none do so but slaves, intemperate mechanics, and profligate overseers. Where such men alone labor, it must be disreputable, and a southerner would sooner lose his life than his reputation.

It is common for the young men to meet often for hunting and fishing; and were I to judge from those parties which I have had an opportunity of attending, they have a most pernicious influence. During my first summer at the south, some fifteen of us met on the banks of St. Catharine's creek to catch buffalo and cat fish. I found in the course of the day, that the object was not so much to take fish, as to drink whisky. I need not detail all the particulars; it may be sufficient to say, it was no place for a sober man. I also soon after attended a deer hunt. It was among the long wave like hills on the borders of the river, where in passing over the summits you look down upon the river, the lakes, and interminable forests at the west. It was indeed a scene of unequaled nature in her wildest dress. And I could not help contemplating how beautiful are the works of God, where man has not been able to defile them! But in ihe midst of all this enchanting scenery intemperance was not wanting; and such intemperance as would have disgraced the very wild beasts that seek those thickets for shelter.

Such is the training of the youth. From their earliest years up to manhood, there is little in it all that leads them to consider the true end for which God created them.

But I will not trouble you with the recital of the thousand ways to death, which are here opened to the thoughtless and the young. Permit me only to relate some conversation which I lately had with one, who, from his profession, should follow mercy and truth. This man told me that he had come to the country with all the prejudices which I seemed to have; but that, after some years he began to think slavery a necessary evil; and that his having slaves so far from augmenting the evil, might actually lessen it; inasmuch as he might treat them better than those from whom he obtained them. "But," said I, "how could you thus expose yourself to covetousness? Was you not aware that no man can tell what he might be, under different circumstances? Was you not aware also, that many of your brethren had come into the possession of this species of property with precisely your feelings, and that these same men afterwards rather followed gain than the good of the slave? Not that they did not mean to do well; but they soon found that for some reason or other, it was easier to make cotton, than, under existing laws, to improve the slave." "It is true," said he, "we find them so degraded, that without the lash and close keeping, they will become most perverse and unprofitable. Religion is the only thing we are allowed to teach them; and I find among my slaves such ignorance and obstinacy that I almost despair, under the present state of things, of being able to improve them. I frequently preach to them in the plainest manner and then ask them to repeat to me something of what I have been saying; but I never found one in ten that could tell me a word of it." "Well," said I, "if what you say is true, ought not such, at least, as are now free of slaves, to consider it a sin, to purchase them, how much good soever they may imagine they can do them? I will argue the question with you not in relation to dollars and cents; but with reference to a future judgment; and without any offence, I should hope, as you are a preacher of the gospel. I am now clear of such property, as you was two years ago. Do you believe that the Judge of all the earth, who surely will do right, would acquit me of sin, if I should employ these beings, or any other of human kind, and not make them a just return for their services?—Strangely as you may think of it, sir, I should much fear were I to own a slave, in order to profit by his services, my eternal perdition would be almost certain."

"Then," said he, "you certainly ought not to possess one. But should you remain in the country a few years more, and obtain slaves by marriage, I doubt not, but, you would think quite differently." "Well," I replied, "suppose that I do think differently—what then? Is not truth always the same, whatever men may think of it? And moreover, my dear sir, your infidel neighbors know very well, that if slavery is not injustice and oppression, the Christian religion is a fable. They say, if you believe what you profess, and preach the gospel, that you ought not to make wealth from slave-labor. I do not charge you with insincerity; far be it from me to utter a word to wound your feelings; I believe slavery is contrary to the spirit of Christianity; but I would not pretend to say that every master will be consigned to the world of wo. Our Savior is great in mercy; and pardon may be extended to the greatest oppressor, should he repent of his iniquities.

But, sir, if you hope for mercy in that day, when the heavens and the earth shall pass away—and if you are sent by your heavenly father, to preach deliverance to the captives; ought you not, together with every preacher of the gospel, and together with every disciple of the Lord Jesus, to cry aloud and spare not; until the oppressed shall be permitted to go free ?"

This man may be a fair example of many who do evil that good may come. They may all be sincere for aught I can tell; but what may not good men do at length, if they fall in with the first temptation !

On the next day I was invited to a dinner-party. And as it was rather late when I arrived, the dinner was already on the table. So sumptuously was the table spread that I cannot stop to give any particular description, in short half the world seemed to have been plundered and heaped up before us. Various kinds of soup began the feast. Then came a dozen kinds of meats, and from the turkey down to the pigeon. After we had wandered over these numerous dainties—then appeared the dessert of sweetmeats, nuts, and almost every variety of West India fruits. After all came the Champaigne with many other species of wines. Such is the hospitality that turns the heads and hearts of so many grateful strangers. Few I believe have in the term of four years experienced more of southern hospitality than I have. And I duly appreciate the kindness of these generous men. But my gratitude ought never to be weighed against truth and justice. I never sit down to these tables, without reflecting, that all these good things have been purchased at the expense of the groans and blood of human beings. While we eat and drink, the slave bleeds. While we are fanned by cool breezes in the pleasant galleries; the slave is wasting his life under an intense sun, or writhing under the merciless lash. While our eyes are delighted with elegant furniture and rich clothing, the slave is in rags, exposed to fevers, and raising his weary eyes to the slowly moving sun,—longing for the night, that he may lose in the forgetfulness of sleep, the remembrance of wrongs that will soon end his days. O give me rough and barren New-England and poverty with it, rather than wealth and luxury at such a price. Scarcely a night has passed these three years, but the beautiful hills of my own dear native place have occurred to me in my dreams. And now I look anxiously towards the land of the free, with the ardent hope of reaching it again, if it only be, that I may be buried in the land of my fathers.   X. Y. Z.

THE DIPLOMACY OF THE U. STATES IN REGARD TO SLAVERY.

The boasted republics of antiquity, gave the lie to their pretensions to liberty and equality by holding *slaves*,—and they have passed away. In a republic the crime is aggravated by the addition of HYPOCRISY to ROBBERY. While the oppressor blows the trumpet of freedom to the notes " liberty"—" equal rights"—" death to tyrants"— he is compelled to hold the throat of his victim with a stronger grasp, to load his limbs with heavier chains, to shroud his mind in darker night, lest he too should be awakened by the thrilling sound. It is to this remark, as exemplified in the history of our country, that we would call the special attention of our readers. With shame and bitter regret we ask them to inquire, WHETHER ANY NATION, IN ITS FOREIGN RELATIONS, HAS EXERTED A MORE MALIGNANT INFLUENCE AGAINST THE FREEDOM OF ANY PORTION OF THEIR FELLOW MEN, THAN OURS HAS AGAINST THAT OF THE DESCENDANTS OF AFRICA? It was not enough to legalize the slave trade for twenty years, and to retain all the living victims of it—them and their children forever; but we have frowned upon the freedom of colored men wherever it has shown itself.

The island of Hayti has been in point of fact under an independent government for a series of years. That its government has been liberal and highly favorable to the industry, good order, and happiness of its rapidly increasing population is evident from its history. Why have we not by recognising the independence of Hayti greeted her to a stand among the nations of the earth? Did no passage in our own history remind us of it? Did not our own strength, render it as safe to us, as her weakness and the bitterness of her enemies rendered it desirable to her? Yet on one pretence or another this act of mere good neighborhood has been refused! The real reason has been because the people of Hayti are guilty of a peculiar

---

* For the origin of this independence, see Clarkson's Thoughts :—Anti-Slavery Reporter, No. 3.

complexion; their skins, by which we christian republicans judge of men, are of an "*unchristian color!*" Their recognition would have drawn into the neighborhood of our immaculate congress *black ambassadors!* An intolerable outrage upon that nice sense of propriety in such matters, which is essential to the security of our *slaves!*

The history of the discussion in our congress in regard to the " Panama mission," throws a broad light upon this subject. That mission was most strenuously opposed on the ground that the congress to be assembled at Panama, from the well known tendency of the southern republics to universal emancipation, would result in the recognition of Hayti and the emancipation of the slaves of Cuba and Porto Rico. The mission was in fact only carried by a vote of 24 to 20, the majority being gained by the concurrence of some, who voted for the avowed purpose of preventing the dreaded result by a representation in that congress. The following specimens, give a fair view of what has hitherto proved the ruling sentiment in this nation in regard to this subject. Mr. Berrien of Georgia, said in the debate on the Panama question,

" Sir, under such circumstances the question to be determined is this ; with a due regard to the safety of the southern states, can you suffer these islands (Cuba and Porto Rico) to pass into the hands of *buccaniers drunk with their new-born liberty?*"

Again, in the same speech he said, " we must hold language equally decisive to the Spanish Am. states. We cannot allow their principle of universal emancipation to be called into activity in a situation where its contagion from our neighborhood, would be dangerous to our quiet and safety." Language every way worthy of the " holy alliance."

Mr. Hayne of S. Carolina, in the same debate, said, " I consider our rights in that species of property [native born American men and women!] as not even open to discussion, either here or *elsewhere*, and in respect to our duties, (imposed by our situation) we are not to be taught them by fanatics, either religious or political."

The instructions of the executive, to the envoys, Messrs. Anderson and Sergeant, adorned with many noble sentiments on other points, contain the following passage in relation to Hayti.

" The President does not think it would be proper at this time to recognise it as a new state." The reasons assigned for this are three. 1. The nature and manner of the establishment of the governing power in that island. 2 The little respect paid there to any other race than the Africans. 3. The commercial arrangement by which Hayti had yielded advantages to France. In regard to the first of these reasons it may be remarked that however the government of Hayti might have been established, it was then popular and highly conducive to the prosperity of the island. The form of government was not analogous to our own, it is true. But what good reason had we ever given the Haytiens to imitate our form of government? Was it to be found in the fact that we hold two millions of slaves, or in the compact by which the security of slavery is supposed to be guaranteed? Secondly, it is not true that the Haytien government has showed disrespect to any foreigners, much less to the Americans. It is said, on high authority, that Boyer, from the commencement of his administration over the whole island, paid special respect to American citizens * Besides, what claim could we, as *white* Americans, set up to the hospitality of the colored Haytiens? Was it founded on our universal exclusion of their *color* and some of *themselves* from our *tables?* If a reciprocity of respect is called for, it would be perfectly in place for us to take the first step. But the third reason is the " unkindest cut" of all. We will not trust ourselves to express the feelings which it excites within us. The suppliant debtor importuned us to give him the countenance of our name against his hard-hearted creditor. We turned away. He was obliged at length to drive the best bargain he could without regard to our interest. *Now,* we say, because you have given advantages in the way of business to our rival, we will not recognise you as *an honest man!* It was the refusal of our government to countenance the Haytiens that drove them to give commercial advantages to France. Is it for us now to taunt them with having compromised their sovereignty,—made themselves a " colony," and lost their claim to a recognition as an independent state? By what name would such conduct be called in a private citizen?

In the speech at the opening of the Congress of Panama, the sentiment is contain-

* North American Review.

ed which was so much dreaded by our republicans who have out-lived the intoxication attending the birth of their own liberty. It is as follows:

" Let the sad and abject countenance of the poor African bending beneath the chains of rapacity and oppression, no longer be seen in these climes. Let him be endowed with equal privileges with the white man, whose color he has been taught to regard as a badge of superiority, let him in learning that he is not distinct from other men, learn that he is a rational being."

We blush for the disgrace brought upon his country by our minister then residing at Mexico, who labored to have this sentiment disclaimed by the parties to the Congress.

While slavery is thus regarded, what avails our diplomacy in relation to the *slave-trade,* but to protect the domestic traffic which is now in full vigor? With honest shame we ask, what could our government have done, that it has not, to rivet the fetters of the African, under whatever clime he may send up his bitter groans?

ABOLITION OF SLAVERY IN THE BRITISH DOMINIONS.

It is with joy that we are able to announce that the liberation of 800,000 British slaves is likely to take place not only without violence but much sooner than was anticipated. The necessity of emancipation and the offer of 20,000,000 pounds sterling, have annihilated the prospective mischiefs of the " turning loose" from despotism to law. The colonies, for the purpose of the sooner getting at the splendid compensation, are taking measures to substitute acts of IMMEDIATE EMANCIPATION for the apprenticeship system proposed by the mother country. We are informed that such an act has been already passed in Bermuda, where the slave population equals the free, by which slavery, there, will be totally abolished the first of next August. If such an act is safe on an islet of the ocean, will some wise man tell us, why it would be unsafe in the District of Columbia? why it would be unsafe throughout this vast continent?

From the British "Anti-Slavery Reporter" of Dec. 26, we quote the following:

" By far the most predominant feeling in our minds, in reviewing these transactions, and contemplating the present position of our great cause, is that of exultation, and of the deepest gratitude to the Great Disposer of all events, who has put it into the hearts of the rulers and of the people of this nation to send forth the irresistible decree, that the crime of Slavery shall cease throughout the dominions of the British crown. Nor is our satisfaction materially abated by a consideration of the large sum which we have to pay for its final extinction. * * * * * * We also lamented, and still lament, that the emancipation of the slaves should have been clogged with the unnatural and monstrous appendage of an universal apprenticeship, tending to no good, and pregnant with much evil, and bringing with it, among other evils, that of requiring a variety of multitudinous provisions, to be framed by the colonial legislatures, for regulating this anomalous and unwieldy institution. The term of that apprenticeship has, however, most happily been greatly reduced, even by the Act which we have here transcribed; and we rejoice to perceive symptoms of a general feeling in the colonists themselves to get entirely rid, if possible, of this injurious incumbrance. It would be premature to enter upon this part of our subject. The Act had only reached the Colonies at the date of our latest intelligence from that quarter, but we are happy to say that it appears to have been received without any general expression of dissatisfaction on the part of any of the classes affected by it, and that the colonial legislatures have hitherto professed a strong solicitude to meet the wishes of the parent state. We learn from the Jamaica Watchman, of the 9th of October, that it is the Editor's belief, if his information be well grounded, that the apprenticeship system is regarded by the legislature there 'as a fallacy which must be abandoned; and that emancipation, the full and complete emancipation of the slaves, is the only safe, satisfactory, and economical plan, and the one which must be adopted.' 'It is most gratifying,' adds the editor, 'to observe such a oneness of feeling, such a unity of sentiment, in those who are especially called upon, on their own behalf, and that of the inhabitants generally, and of the slave-owners particularly to decide upon it.

'If ever,' he then proceeds, 'there was a period when we felt our souls warmed at the contemplation of the successful, peaceful, and happy termination of a question with which our very existence was at one time bound up, this is! If ever there was a period when we felt disposed to give the rein to fancy, and enjoy to the full (in

anticipation) that exquisite delight which flows from a knowledge that all around us are happy, peaceful, and contented, this is that period. From full emancipation, and the just and impartial administration of equal laws, that happiness, that peace, and that contentment must assuredly flow. Who then, at this eventful period, would not be a legislator? Where is the man so bereft of feeling, so void of sensibility, so great a stranger to that delight which results from an ability to make others happy, who does not covet a seat in that house— who would not be one of that favored band who are to extend the blessings of liberty to three hundred thousand of their fellow men?

'Surely the prospect is most cheering. The heart of the sincere philanthropist warms and dilates, whilst he contemplates it; and we would not exchange our feelings at the present moment, heightened as they are by the reflection of the part we have taken in the arduous struggle, for all the filthy lucre possessed by all the enemies of liberty in this and every other portion of the habitable globe. Some there are who support the plan of immediately emancipating the slaves, from a conviction that such an act is not only consistent with a feeling of the purest humanity and benevolence, but necessary, in order to secure the peace, happiness, and tranquillity of the island in which they reside, and in which their all is situated. Others support such a proposition, as being the most likely to insure the payment, by the government, of the compensation awarded by Parliament, and the obtaining, through the instrumentality of that government, of a loan to enable them to put the new system into active operation, when they shall become, by means of the former, free from the trammels of their mortgage and other debts; and many because the apprenticeship will place them in a much worse condition than emancipation. It will not work, say they; it is surrounded by difficulties; it will ruin our properties and ourselves if attempted, and therefore we oppose it. Of two evils (for freedom by such is regarded as an evil), we choose the least. Give us the compensation—free the slaves, and we shall then employ such and as many as we desire, and have the whole of their time and services. If they misbehave we can discharge them and employ others, without being bothered with stipendiary or any other description of magistrates. Labor will then be a marketable commodity, obtainable by those who will give the highest price for it. Competition will be the result, and both those who desire to employ and be employed will be benefited.

'Thus, although all do not reject the apprenticeship for the same reason, all do not support the proposition to emancipate at once from the same motive : still it is probable that all will agree to carry it ; and if this is done (we care not what the motives or inducements are which lead to it), the grand object will be attained. We anxiously look forward to the proceedings of the House on this subject. Our anxiety is participated in by every slave-holder, and every lover of peace and good order in the country. We trust we shall not be disappointed in our expectations —To conclude, in the language of the Executive to the Assembly : 'Your task now commences, and I have no doubt, that, postponing all minor considerations from a sense of the paramount importance of this great question,you will enter upon it in a true spirit of conciliation, and with that; thorough understanding of the actual state of the case, which can alone lead to a satisfactory decision.' "

From the same pamphlet we extract the following noble Proclamation of Sir James Carmichael Smith, governor of British Guiana, to the enslaved population within his jurisdiction. It will explain to our readers the apprenticeship system as well as could be done by the Act itself under which it was issued.

" In a proclamation which I addressed to you, about three months ago, I told you that whatever orders I received from the King about you I would immediately communicate them to you, and that you might depend upon my carrying them punctually into execution. I warned you of the necessity of your continuing to conduct yourselves quietly; of steadily performing your work; and of yielding to your masters a cheerful and a ready obedience. I am happy to say that you have followed my advice; you have conducted yourselves as well as could have been wished. This country never was happier or quieter. You have shown to the world that you are worthy of the great sacrifice of money the people of England have agreed to give to your masters for your freedom. I thank you for

your good conduct. Listen now to the orders which our great and good King has sent to me about you. You will find that every thing that could be thought of to render you happy and industrious has been attended to.

" 1. You are to continue as you are until the 1st of August next. This delay is necessary to enable the Justices of the Peace (under whose care and superintendence you are to be more particularly placed) to be selected, and to be sent here from England. On the 1st of August next you are no longer slaves, but apprenticed laborers. The difference between a slave and an apprenticed laborer is very much in your favor. A master is, by law, entitled to require his slave to work nine hours per day, or fifty-four hours per week, an apprenticed laborer can only be called upon to work at the rate of seven and a-half hours per day, or forty-five hours per week. You gain, consequently, as soon as you are apprenticed laborers, at once nine hours per week, in which you can work or do any thing for yourselves. The master of a slave can order his slave to be punished. The master of an apprenticed laborer will have no such power over his apprentice ; but if he has any fault to find, he will have to complain to a justice of the peace, whose duty it will be to listen patiently, to examine witnesses, and to write down carefully all the particulars of the story, as related both by the master and the apprenticed laborer, before he gives judgment. These judgments must, moreover, be laid from time to time before me; and if any justice of the peace abuses his authority, or acts with partiality, or under the influence of passion, or in any other way shows himself unworthy of the high trust committed to his charge, you may depend upon his being immediately removed. You see, therefore, the great advantages you will derive from being apprenticed laborers instead of slaves.

" 2. However much your situation will be improved, and your happiness and comforts augmented, by being made apprenticed laborers instead of slaves, yet it is further intended that in a few years you shall be perfectly free, and at liberty to engage yourselves with any master, or gain your livelihood in any way you may think proper. The King has ordered that you are to be apprenticed laborers only, from the 1st of next August until the 1st of August of the year 1840, which is but six years of apprenticeship. On the 1st of August, 1840, you will be as free as any white men.

"3. I have said to you that the master is by law entitled to fifty-four hours per week of labor from his slave, and that from the apprenticed laborer he will only be entitled to forty-five hours per week. There are, however, many domestic slaves employed about a house, and many mechanics and artificers, who do not work in the field, but who are required to give up more of their time to their master. A list of these people will be carefully made; and it is the King's orders that, as they give up a greater portion of their time for the use and advantage of their masters than the slave who merely works at his lawful hours in the field, so they should receive a recompense, by being entitled to their freedom at an earlier period. A list of all slaves employed as I have described will be made out, and on the 1st of August next they are to be called non-predial apprenticed laborers; and they will receive their complete freedom on the 1st of August, 1838, that is, two years before their comrades."

"THE AMERICAN COLONIZATION SOCIETY FURTHER UNRAVELLED."

We have just received a refreshing pamphlet, of the above title, from the pen of that devoted British philanthropist Charles Stuart. In his usual happy style he shows the absurdity of the many arguments by which that moral and intellectual Babel endeavors to support itself. We have time, at present, only to quote his handling of the pretence that colonies on the coast of Africa will put an end to the slave-trade, —that is, aid us in accomplishing our beautiful project of *hanging* all those who bring their wares to sell, to a *market* which we have established *and keep open*.

"In the 14th Annual Report, page 19, Mr. Frelinghuysen, one of the first men of the United States, says, 'We must enlighten the Africans themselves on the nature of this evil. We must raise in their minds a fixed abhorrence of its enormities. We must by our settlements point the African kidnapper to a more profitable commerce, than that in the blood and heart-strings of his fellow men.'

But where is the magic by which this is to be done?

The Americans themselves are surely enlightened to the nature of the evil. If a fixed abhorrence of its enormities could be awakened in the minds of any people, it ought to burn in the bosoms *of the free*. *They* have unquestionably a more profitable commerce, and yet do *they* cease from trading in the blood and heartstrings of their fellow men? No; they themselves proclaim, that that nefarious traffic is less invincible in Africa than in the United States. They find the power of love and reason so ineffectual with themselves, that with respect to themselves, they despair of success: but they *sanely* expect, that the *barbarous* Africans may *easily* be reformed. With all *their* light and liberty and glorious means of independence, they cling with a death-grasp to *their* home slave trade, and to their atrocious system of slavery, and to their insane prejudices; and yet they expect that the untutored Africans will, at a word, abandon similar crimes.

What reason have they to expect it?

The Africans are men as they are. They have the same proud, selfish, and short-sighted views of interest as other men. The same motives induce them to crime. Being men, why should they give up their slave trade, under the tuition of a nation of slave traders? Why should *they* cease from slavery when their teachers are slave masters? Why should they prove as candid and liberal as angels of light, while their patrons are the slaves, or the victims of the most insane and cruel prejudices? Yes, as Mr. Frelinghuysen says, we must enlighten the Africans to the nature of the evils of the slave trade; but we must cease to be slave traders, and companions of slave traders, before we can expect to do so with any blessing. We must raise in their minds a fixed abhorrence of its enormities; but if we would do so, we must shew them that we ourselves abhor those enormities. We must point the African kidnapper to a more profitable commerce than that in the blood and heart-strings of his fellow men. But would we succeed. we must ourselves cease from that detestable commerce.

There is something dreadfully ludicrous in the Liberian procedure.

A nation of slave traders and slave dealers, though endowed with every means of independence, and of wisdom; flourishing, highly cultivated, mighty; a terror to many, in fear of none; overflowing with bibles and with revivals, are yet so desperate and so insane in their wickedness, that if you believe themselves, not even the gospel of

Christ can move them from slave-holding, slave-trading, and the most insane and cruel prejudices. Yet another nation of men like themselves, in circumstances vastly more unfavorable; feeble, uncultivated, uncivilized; a terror to none, in fear of almost all; without bibles and without a gospel ministry, need but a word as it were, to free them from the same crimes; while a class of people, too corrupt and abominable to be allowed to live or die in their native country, by transportation across the Atlantic shall effect all this."

[*From an English Tract.*]

COMPENSATION,

AN EASTERN TALE VERSIFIED.

It was far hence, in eastern climes,
Near where imperial Bagdad shines,
Amidst the spicy groves, and skies,
Which form an earthly paradise,
Mustapha liv'd,—for kindness known;
The small domain was all his own.
Among his treasures was a steed,
Sprung from a prime Arabian breed;
Even as a child, the beauteous mare
Was cherish'd with paternal care;
Oft would he pat her neck with glee,
And say, "I'll never part with thee."
But oft, even to the good and wise,
It comes,—that things they too much prize,
However beautiful and gay,
Pass from their firmest grasp away;
To bid them seek beyond the sky,
Treasures which ne'er decay or die.
So 'twas with Mustapha,—his mare,
So valued, so beloved, so rare,
One morn was missing from the field;
The earliest dawn the theft reveal'd.
With fond solicitude of course,
Half frantic too, he sought his horse;
To stranger, or to friend, in vain
He told his loss, or told his pain;
Made too inquiries far and near,
But could not of his favorite hear.
When seven long years had pass'd away,
(To him, O memorable day!)
A horse went by, at evening's fall,
'Twas near fair Bagdad's stately wall,
And neigh'd—for he his master knew—
And well his Master kenn'd him too;
Up at that dear, known sound he sprung,
And on her neck with rapture hung.
"This horse," said Mustapha, " is mine:
The creature instantly resign."
"I will not," said proud Ibrahim,
"For she is mine, her every limb !"
So Mustapha the Cadi sought,
And to his bar the robber brought:
"O Sir," said he, "I come to claim
My horse; I swear it is the same,
Which from my field was stol'n away,—
'Tis seven years since, this very day."
The Cadi said. "He shall restore
Thy horse, good Mustapha, and more !"
"But hear me too," cried Ibrahim,
"I cannot, will not part with him ;
The horse is his—I can't deny
I took him, time long since gone by ;
But as I've had him now so long,
O righteous Cadi, 'tis not wrong

For me to keep him still. Again,
O righteous Cadi, best of men,
Shouldst thou my humble claim refuse,
I pray thee think,—*how much I lose !*
The horse has earn'd me, it is clear,
At least ten dinas every year ;
Then shouldst thou take the horse away,
Bid him a compensation pay ;
But O let me retain him now,—
Allah is gracious—so be thou !"
Soon as the righteous Cadi heard,
"O wretch !" said he, "by this my beard,
Thou shalt give up the horse; and more,
The dinas he has earn'd, restore,
Nor shalt thou thus escape thy due;
Know, wretch, thou shalt be punished too !
How dar'st thou, villain, Allah name,
To justify so vile a claim !"
The application of the tale,
O hear,—and let the right prevail.
Seest thou yon female, sad, alone,
Flesh of thy flesh, bone of thy bone,
Her feet in cruel thraldom bound,
Her back with many a bloody wound
All cover'd o'er ? The burning tears
Still wet upon her cheek ? For years
She toil'd more than Mustapha's horse,
To fill her Master's store and purse,
Though worn with dreadful bondage, lo,
He says he will not let her go.
But is she his ? O yes, his claim
Is Ibrahim's to the horse,—the same.
"But did he steal her ? Tell the whole"—
He bought her of the man who stole;
"No, no—the slave was will'd to him,—
Who left the horse to Ibrahim ?"
But tell us, by what law of heaven,
A right to will the slave was given ;
And may he that as his dare name,
To which his father had no claim ?
Come show us plainly, if you can,
Your right to buy or sell a man.
"The Parliament has given the right,"—
Should their voice say, that black is white,
Would their decision make it so ?
Plain common sense must answer, No.
Vote as they may, to them belong
No power to alter right and wrong.
Who gave them power to make a slave ?
Nor can they give but what they have.
Know, then, O planter, that thy claim
Is Ibrahim's to the mare—the same.
"What ! must I then the captive free ?
No, no—it must not, shall not be;
Unless you compensation give,
In bondage still the slave shall live;
See, from my books the case is clear,
She earns me fifty pounds a year.
Think what I lose,—I'll be repaid;
Pray let your justice be display'd."
"Then listen," would the Cadi say,
"Know thou, that I decree this day,
That thou this wretched slave shall free,
And give her all she's earn'd for thee.
I will give justice to a slave,
For she should compensation have ;
To her the recompense belongs,
For years of toil, for years of wrongs;
The recompense to Ibrahim due,
THIS, ONLY THIS, BELONGS TO YOU !"

TERMS.

This periodical will be furnished to subscribers at $1 00 per annum, done up in a neat cover ; or 50 cents, without the cover. To those who take several copies a discount will be made as follows : 15 per cent. for 10 copies, 25 per cent, for 25 copies, and 33 per cent. for 100 copies.

AMERICAN

ANTI - SLAVERY REPORTER.

VOL. I.] APRIL, 1834. [NO. 4.

THE DEBT OF THE AMERICAN COLONIZATION SOCIETY.

We had hoped to have little more to do in exposing the false doctrines and injurious tendencies of the American Colonization Society. But there has recently issued a report from its managers, so deceptive and so "highly satisfactory" to many of the doubting friends, that we feel called upon for a few remarks. We regard the Colonization scheme under whatever modifications, and by whomsoever advocated, as but the outbreaking of that spirit of slavery which rivets the chains of two millions of our brethren. In saying this, we do not as a matter of course, impeach the motives of all those who advocate it. Some there are who may be permitted to save their benevolence at the expense of their wisdom. A plan which contemplates the expatriation of a class of our population for their benefit and ours, simply because we indulge a prejudice against them, cannot be saved from our reprobation by any *modus operandi*, however gentle and soothing. Heretofore the Colonization Society has spirited on the public to undertake the removal of the entire colored race : now their design is, to make the colony so attractive that the colored people shall crowd into it of their own accord. But if they could make Liberia a paradise, the plan would be liable to two fatal objections. 1. It would involve a despair of gaining the victory over prejudice here. 2. It would involve an immense waste of labor in doing that at a distance which could be done more easily at home. We shall never cease to oppose this plan, till it is explicitly given up and the flag of *Colonization* struck from the mast. Americans

will be better off if white and black will treat each other as brethren on this continent, and Africans will be better off if we attempt to Christianize them only by the simple and scriptural process of the Boards of Foreign Missions.

The debt of the Society demonstrates, in spite of all explanations, that a colony is not a thing to be managed by a charitable association. The managers, however, have put forth a most elaborate explanation, on which we remark,

1. It would seem to be a very simple thing to give "a detailed statement of the origin, rise, and present condition" of a debt. But the Managers make it far otherwise. They commence by setting forth their own disinterestedness and benevolence, and proceed to state their statistics very much in the lump, buried in an ocean of apologies. It is sufficient to say that instead of explaining any thing, this report is a piece of genuine colonizationism.

2. The Managers profess to "have no concealments." The resolution under which they drew up the report was as follows ;

"*Resolved,* That the Board of Managers be directed to lay before the public, through the African Repository, a full and detailed statement of the origin, rise, and present condition of the society's debt, having particular reference to the causes and manner of its rise and increase ; the times at which it has been incurred ; the individuals to whom it was originally and is now due, and for what in every case ; together with every circumstance within the reach of their inquiries, here and in Africa, which can throw any light on this subject."

If the Managers have honestly exposed

all that they could discover, according to this resolution, they have been eminently unsuccessful, They do not give a particle of information as to "the individuals" to which the debt "was originally and is now due;" and as to the "*for what*, in every case," "they do not deem it important in this communication to give in detail all the distinct objects of expenditure."

They give a detailed statement of the ordinary expenditures for which the receipts were sufficient, but the expenditures which have brought the Society in debt are thrown into the *lump*. They talk largely about expenditures for schools, fortifications, purchase of territory, arms, surgical instruments, warlike stores, and armed vessels; but we are not told *how much for each*. Is this strange and unbusiness-like course pursued in deference to the resolution; or for the purpose of hiding from the donors how "*dearly*" they have paid for the whistle?" We need only extract from this document that part which relates directly to the debt to show to every man who unites *honesty* with a moderate share of intelligence, that the Society is still conducted, as it has been, with a *total want of principle*.

From the year 1820, the receipts and expenditures, and the number of emigrants. in each year, have been as follows:

Years:	Receipts.	Expenditures.	Emig'ts.
1820-2	$5,627 66	$3,785 79	
" '23	4,798 02	6,766 17	390
" '24	4,379 98	3,851 42	
" '25	10,125 85	7,543 88	
" '26	14,799 24	17,316 94	
" '27	13,294 94	13,901 74	781
" '28	13,458 17	17,077 12	
" '29	19,795 61	18,487 34	
" '30	26,583 51	17,637 32	259
" '31	27,999 15	28,068 15	441
" '32	40,365 08	51,644 22	790
" '33	39,242 46	35,637 54	108
		Total,	2,769

It is not deemed important in this communication to give in detail all the distinct objects of expenditure; but it is necessary to a clear and satisfatory exposition that the leading items of expense should be specifically stated.

In the United States, these have consisted of

Salary of the Secretary,	$1,250
Assistant Secretary, (for last year,)	1,000
Treasurer and Clerk,	750
Postage of letters,	150
Office rent,	200
Printing and stationary, (average,)	1,890
Agents in different states, do.	1,356
Fuel and other contingencies,	120
	$6,716

In Liberia.

Colonial agent,	$2,400	
Paid by the U. S. Government,	1,600	
		$800
Colonial physician,		1,500
Secretary,		600
All other salaried officers,		4,220
		$7,120

The agent and physicians receive also subsistence from the colonial stores.

This may be called the expense of the civil list, in the administration of the colony in the United States and in Liberia.

Here it may be proper to remark, that most of these colonial salaries were not created by the Board, and whatever may have been the necessity heretofore, when the colony was in an infant state, the managers now consider most of the salary officers in the colony to be unnecessary. The measures which they have adopted on this branch of the subject, will be found in another part of this communication.

The expenditures in the United States, besides those for the civil list, have been, for collecting emigrants for their embarkation—for subsistence till their arrival—for provisions, subsistence and colonial stores, sent from the United States for their support for six months after their arrival in Liberia—for charter of vessels, freight and transportation—for medicines, surgical instruments, arms, warlike stores, and armed vessels; and also for the maintenance of three medical students.

The expenditures of the colony, besides those for the civil list, have been, for the support of public schools, for buildings, presents to native kings, fortifications, purchase of territory, expense of court house and jail, opening roads, and the founding of new settlements.

It was at all times the desire of the Board, that all the expenses at the colony should be paid by the agent, either from the sale of articles from the colonial stores, or by cash in his hand. The ruinous practice of purchasing provisions from the merchants in Liberia on credit, and paying for them from time to time by drafts on the Board, was never for one moment contemplated, except in cases of peculiar and rare contingency; and yet, owing to adverse circumstances of the last two years, this very practice has been the principal cause of the present embarrassment in the finances of the society.

It will be seen that the number of emigrants sent out during the years 1830, '1, '2, '3, was 1598, and, to meet their expenses at the colony, it appears from the society's books, supplies were furnished and sent out amounting to $40,946 63. In addition to this amount, the drafts on the Board have been $32,939 15, making the entire charge on the funds of the institution $73,885 78, for these four years, exclusive of the civil list in the United States, support of medical students, collecting emigrants, charter of vessels, freight and transportation.

The sum of $40,946 63, vested as it was in colonial stores and provisions, was deemed sufficient for all the expenses of the colony. The highest estimate made by the colonial agent, was at all times less than twenty dollars for the support of

THE DEBT OF THE AMERICAN COLONIZATION SOCIETY.

each emigrant after his arrival. Estimating that sum for each, the 1598 emigrants would require for their support $31,960, leaving a balance of $8,986 63 for the civil list and the other expenditures at the colony. This balance was in colonial stores, and worth, in Liberia, at least $12,000. This sum was evidently too small for the payment of the civil list in the colony for four years, and for the other expenditures, for objects of a permanent character. The purchase of additional territory, the founding the colony at Grand Bassa, and the purchase of the agency house from the United States, were objects of a permanent nature, and, taken together, tended much to increase the debt against the society. As a matter of course, drafts from the colony to some extent were necessary to meet this deficit. In the purchase of the supplies sent to the colony, the Board had incurred a debt in the United States of $11,708 97.

In thus extending the operations of the society, in advance of their means, the Board, it is believed, fell into an error. But it arose, in a great measure, from the want of full and precise information. Additional light would have prevented the outfit of so many expeditions in 1832. The object of the Board was undoubtedly praiseworthy; their accounts from the colony, throughout 1832, were most encouraging. Emigrants offered themselves, and liberated slaves were offered in greater numbers than the means of the Board would enable them to send to the colony. Many friends of the cause urged the Board to give more vigor to their operations, and expressed the opinion that the public liberality would sustain them in their efforts to increase the numbers of the colony. This desire to extend and enlarge the beneficial operations of the society, the number who were waiting and anxious to go to Liberia, induced the Board to incur responsibilities, both in the United States and at the colony, which, in the most favorable circumstances, would have left a heavy balance against them.

Although a resort to drafts, to some extent, was foreseen by the Board, yet from the general and favorable information received from the agent, they could not have anticipated such frequent and heavy drafts as were made upon them. The agent, though frequently written to, did not always furnish them with the necessary details. Hence, the Board were not aware of the ruinous debts that were accumulating against them at the colony. When the drafts were presented, they were at a loss to know whether to accept them for payment or refuse. Fearing, however, the effect of the return of the drafts to the colony, the Board did accept them in the absence of the accounts and estimates. In this, also, the Board may have erred, although, under all the circumstances, it is not clear that it was an error: they were reduced, as in several other instances, to a choice of evils, under circumstances that rendered it extremely difficult to determine how the balance of evils turned. In future, however, it is their determination, so to arrange the business that a resort to drafts shall be unnecessary, unless under special circumstances.

Since the annual meeting of the society, the Board have, with great care, examined the expenditures at the colony, for the last four years; but this examination has not been satisfactory in

its result. The loose state of the accounts, their want of system, the long period in which accounts with the merchants at the colony have been accumulating, without knowledge on the part of the Board—the absence, to some extent, of vouchers, or suitable explanations, for many items, and the general want of care and economy, are painful results to which their examinations have led them. To this must also be added the secondary attention bestowed on the encouragement of education and agriculture at the colony; both of which the friends of the society have so much at heart. It is due, however, to the agent, to state, that a great part of the time he was laboring under the want of health, that his duties were at all times laborious; that his services, in many respects, have been of great value; and that he has returned to the bosom of his friends in a weak state of health. It is due to him also to state, which the Board do with pleasure, that in no one instance does it appear, that any improper considerations of personal emolument for one moment influenced his conduct, on the contrary, he is now a creditor of the Board for a part of his compensation.

In the examination of the accounts for articles purchased in Liberia, at a large advance upon the original cost, there is no evidence that either shipmasters or colonial merchants asked or received more than the current market price of such articles.

Other causes, however, and those which no human foresight could have provided for, tended greatly to increase the debt against the society. The failure, to a great extent, of the rice crops, the vast demand for it from the Cape de Verd Islands, and the dependence on the society, beyond the usual time, of many families afflicted with sickness, all tended greatly to increase the expense. In these visitations of Divine Providence, the Board would desire to feel how much the blessing of God is needed in all their affairs; and without that blessing, how vain are all their efforts.

The amount of such debts of the society as have been accepted or settled by the Board, including the sum of $5,705 41, falling due in March and May next, is $36,635 40

To which must be added various claims before the Board, not yet settled, and which may be subject to some deduction,   2,955 00

In addition to this, various evidences of debt, held by individuals in the colony, have been purchased by another individual, and presented for payment. These claims have not been passed upon by the Board; they are payable at the colony, are not transferred by any assignment to the present holder, and may be subject to deduction. They amount to   6,055 32

        $45,645 72

Now let any man tell us, if he can, the "individuals" to whom the debt "was originally and is now due, and for what in every case." But the "accounts" from the colony are in a loose and unsatisfactory state. What then? The committee either had some " accounts" in their hands or they had none. If they had some, why did they not honestly state the *how much*, and the *what for*, so far as those accounts extended? If they had none, on what authority do they state that the money is owed for the erection of schools, the purchase of territory, &c.? We say confidently that it is impossible for the Managers to know so much as they profess to, without knowing more than they communicate.

3. The Managers, though "they have no concealments," still hold up the colony as excellent in *morals*—as tending to " elevate the *moral* and physical condition" of the free colored men. Did not this part of their subject remind them of some "horrifying" facts? We appeal to Gerrit Smith, Esq., whether the true state of morals in the colony has not been concealed. We ask him whether it is not well known to the Managers that Mechlin, Todsen and Ruswurm, by their own testimony have been guilty of the most flagitious conduct? Why is this hid from the American public? Shall the Managers be allowed to pretend that this experiment has been successful—that its tendencies are to elevate the *morals* of the subjects of it, when they hold in their hands a letter from the editor of the Liberia Herald, in which he confesses the crime of seduction, and apologizes for it on the ground of *the low state of morals in the colony?* We have full confidence in the benevolence and the frankness of Mr. Smith, and we put it to him, whether it is not time that the public should know the worst, on more weighty authority than ours If there are any such facts as we have alluded to, it will be difficult to see how the Managers are clear of *concealing* them.

4. The Managers by no means give up the darling scheme of removing the colored population. They are compelled to stop for the present. But they propose to pay off their debt by the creation of a stock of $50,000, and then they will be ready to proceed in the expatriating process. In the mean time by attention to " education, " agriculture," and "temperance," the colony will have become so *attractive* that the poor abused colored man will be glad to go. On this point they hold the following singular language, " To this class we address no *arguments* to induce them to leave the

United States. We have no entreaties to offer. We trust, that in a short time, *facts* will supersede the use of *arguments*, (!) and an enlightened self-interest render all entreaties unnecessary. We say distinctly we want none to go there but men and women of good morals and industrious, and friends and members of the temperance cause. As far as we have the power [and how far is that?] we will permit none of a different character to go." What insanity, when the managers know perfectly, that the best portion of the colored people abhor their whole plan, and, what is more, are well acquainted with the state of the colony which they are vainly endeavoring to conceal. Even the poor slaves of the South accept Liberia only as a miserable alternative to their more miserable bondage. Were the colored people free and equal here, this plan would be nothing worse than folly, but when they are oppressed and despised and treated as a nuisance from one end of the land to the other, for no cause but their color, to talk about making a Paradise for them, whither they may flee at their own expense, is cruel and wicked in the extreme.

ANTI-SLAVERY IN THE GREAT VALLEY.

We feel a special pleasure in presenting the following letter to our readers. It was addressed to the editor of the New-York Evangelist.

                            LANE SEMINARY, WALNUT HILLS,
                            near Cincinnati, Ohio, March 10, 1834.

Brother Leavitt—Many of your readers are undoubtedly interested in whatever concerns this rising institution. Therefore, I send you the following. Slavery and its proposed remedies—immediate abolition and colonization, have been subjects of occasional remark among the students, since the last term (June.) A flourishing Colonization Society has existed among us almost from the foundation of the institution. Our interest in these topics increased gradually until about the first of February, when it was resolved that we discuss publicly the merits of the colonization and abolition schemes. At this time, there were but few decided abolitionists in the seminary. The two following questions were discussed, separately: "*Ought the people of the slave-holding states to abolish slavery immediately?*" 2nd, "*Are the doctrines, tendencies and measures of the American Colonization*

Society, and the influence of its principal supporters, such as render it worthy of the patronage of the Christian public?"

Our respected Faculty, fearing the effect the discussion would have upon the prosperity of the seminary, formally *advised* that it be postponed indefinitely. But the students, feeling great anxiety that it should proceed, and being persuaded from the state of feeling among them, that it would be conducted in a manner becoming young men looking forward to the ministry of the gospel of reconciliation, resolved to go on. The president, and the members of the faculty, with one exception, were present during parts of the discussion.

Each question was debated nine evenings of two hours and a half each—making 45 hours of solid debate. We possessed some facilities for discussing both these questions intelligently. We are situated within one mile of a slave-holding state: eleven of our number were born and brought up in slave states, seven of whom were the sons of slave-holders, and one of them was himself a slave-holder till recently: one of us had been a slave, and had bought his freedom "with a great sum," which his own hands had earned: ten others had lived more or less in slave states, besides several who had traveled in the midst of slavery, making inquiries and searching after truth. We possessed all the numbers of the African Repository from its commencement, nearly all the Annual Reports of the Colonization Society, and the prominent documents of the Anti-Slavery Society. In addition to the above, our kind friends in the city furnished us with Colonization pamphlets in profusion. Dr. Shane, a young gentleman of Cincinnati, who had been out to Liberia with a load of emigrants, as an Agent of the Colonization Society, furnished us with a long statement concerning the colony; and a distinguished instructress, recently of Hartford, Connecticut, now at Cincinnati, sent us a communication from her hand, which attempted to prove that Colonizationists and Abolitionists ought to unite their efforts, and not contend against one another. These were our materials. And, sir, it was emphatically a discussion of *facts,* FACTS, FACTS.

The first speaker occupied nearly two evenings in presenting facts concerning slavery and immediate emancipation, gathered from various authentic documents.

Conclusions and inferences were then drawn from these facts, and arguments founded upon them favorable to immediate abolition, during the two next evenings. Nearly four of the remaining five evenings were devoted to the recital of facts in regard to slavery, slaves, and slave-holders, gathered, not from written documents, but from careful personal observation and experience. Nearly half of the seventeen speakers, on the evening last alluded to, were the sons of slave-holders; one had been a slave-holder himself; one had till recently been a slave; and the residue were residents of, or had recently traveled or lived in slave states. From their testimony, the following facts and premises were established, to wit: That slaves long for freedom; that it is a subject of very frequent conversation among them; that they know their masters have no right to hold them in slavery; that they keenly feel the wrong, the insult and the degradation which are heaped upon them by the whites; they feel no interest comparatively in their master's affairs, because they know he is their oppressor; they are indolent, because nothing they can earn is their own; they pretend to be more ignorant and stupid than they really are, so as to avoid responsibility, and to shun the lash for any real or alleged disobedience to orders; when inspired with a promise of freedom, they will toil with incredible alacrity and faithfulness; they tell their masters and drivers they are contented with their lot, merely through fear of greater cruelty if they tell the truth; no matter how kind their master is, they are dissatisfied, and would rather be his hired servants than his slaves: the slave-drivers are generally low, brutal, debauched men, distinguished only for their cruelty and licentiousness; they generally have the despotic control of the slaves: the best side of slavery is seen—its darker features being known only to slaves, masters and drivers; [upon this point, horrid facts, in regard to the whipping and *murdering* of slaves, were developed. God sparing my life, they shall be given to the public.] The state of morals among slaves, especially in regard to licentiousness, is sickening! This condition is attributable to the treatment they receive from their masters—they being huddled together from their infancy in small apartments without discrimination of sex; and oftentimes being compelled to steal or starve; the influence of slavery upon the physical condition, and mental and moral character of the whites, is decidedly and lamentably pernicious; the internal slave trade is increasing, and is carried on by men distinguished even among slave-drivers, for their cruelty and brutality! No class in the country have stronger social affections than slaves; nevertheless, the ties of parent and child, husband and wife, brother and sister, are torn asunder by this bloody traffic! A husband has been known to cut his throat deliberately, because this damnable traffic was about to separate him from a wife whom he tenderly loved. The horrid character of Louisiana slavery was developed in some degree by one who had resided there. The planters in that state, when sugar commands a high price, do not hesitate to kill a few of their negroes by overworking, if by that means they can bring more sugar into a favorable market: in consequence of this, one of the usual prayers of the poor negro is, *that sugar may be cheap.* Multitudes of slaves are being carried into that state from other slave states: blacks are kidnapped from this state (Ohio,) and sold into slavery; slaves are decidedly hostile to Liberia, and only consent to go there to escape from slavery; masters are generally opposed to their negroes being educated; *that the blacks are abundantly able to take care of and provide for themselves; and that they would be kind and docile if immediately emancipated.* These points, with many others equally important, were established, so far as a multitude of facts could establish them. On the two last points, the following was interesting and decisive.

James Bradley, the emancipated slave above alluded to, addressed us nearly two hours; and I wish his speech could have been heard by every opponent of immediate emancipation, to wit: first, that it would be unsafe to the community;" second, that "the condition of the emancipated negroes would be worse than it now is—that they are incompetent to provide for themselves—that they would become paupers and vagrants, and would rather steal than work for wages." This shrewd and intelligent black cut up these *white objections* by the roots, and withered and scorched them under a sun of sarcastic argumentation for nearly an hour, to which the assembly re-

sponded in repeated and spontaneous roars of laughter, which were heartily joined in by both Colonizationists and Abolitionists. Do not understand me as saying, that his speech was devoid of *argument.* No. It contained sound logic, enforced by apt illustrations. I wish the slanderers of negro intellect could have witnessed this unpremeditated effort. I will give you a sketch of this man's history. He was stolen from Africa when an infant, and sold into slavery. His master, who resided in Arkansas, died, leaving him to his widow. He was then about 18 years of age. For some years, *he managed the plantation of his mistress.* Finally, he purchased his time by the year, and began to earn money to buy his freedom. After five years of toil, having paid his owners $655 besides supporting himself during the time, he received his "free papers," and emigrated to a free state with more than $200 in his pocket. Every cent of this money ($855) he earned by labor and trading. He is now a beloved and respected member of this institution. Now, Mr. Editor, can slaves take care of themselves if emancipated? I answer the question in the language employed by brother Bradley on the above occasion. "They have to take care of, and support themselves *now, and their master, and his family into the bargain;* and this being so, it would be strange if they could not provide for themselves, *when disencumbered from this load."* He said the great desire of the slave was, *"liberty and education."* And shall this heaven-born desire be trampled in the dust by a free and Christian nation?

At the close of the ninth evening, the vote was taken on the first question, *when every individual voted in the affirmative, except four or five,* who excused themselves from voting at all on the ground that they had not made up their opinion. Every friend of the cause rendered a hearty tribute of thanksgiving to God for the glorious issue.

At the next evening, we entered upon the discussion of the second question. Here, there was much greater diversity of sentiment. But we entered upon the debate not like blinded partizans, but like men whose polar star was facts and truth, whose needle was conscience, whose chart the Bible. The witnesses summoned to the stand, were the documents of the Colonization

Society. They were examined at great length and in great numbers. We judged it out of its own mouth. There was no paucity of testimony; for, as I before observed, we had all its "Repositories," and nearly all its Reports and Addresses, in addition to which, we were benevolently furnished by friends with numerous collated witnesses, whom we of course had the privilege of cross-examining. Notwithstanding the length of this part of the discussion, but two individuals spoke, one on each side, and another read some testimony in favor of the Colony. Several individuals at the opening of the debate, intended to speak on the affirmative, but before it was closed they became warmly attached to the other side. Others were induced to espouse the cause of Anti-Colonizationism, by examining documents of Colonization Society, for the purpose of preparing to speak in the affirmative. *Most of the Colonizationists who expressed any opinion on the subject, declared their ignorance of the doctrines and measures of the Society until this debate.* They cannot find words to express their astonishment that they should have been so duped into the support of this Society, as a scheme of benevolence towards the free blacks, and a remedy for slavery. They now repudiate it with all their hearts. Is it not a fact that the great majority of the supporters of this Society, *have never examined* its doctrines, its tendencies and its measures? Do not nine-tenths of the colonizationists with whom you come in contact, express incredulous surprize at the announcement of almost any one of its prominent doctrines, and meet you with the reply, "This cannot be so?" Is it not the "immediate" duty of such men (benevolent, and scrupulously honest no doubt,) to examine this subject?

I will state a fact. A member of this institution was a member of the Oneida Institute, during the Colonization debate held there last summer, and took an active part in that discussion. An Anti-Slavery, and a Colonization Society, were the offspring of this debate. My worthy brother was placed at the head of the latter Society. He was a sincere friend of the negro, and what is quite as rare, was a consistent and practical man. About five months since, he left Oneida and came to Lane Seminary. On his way hither, he took great pains to converse with every negro he could find

about emigrating to Liberia. He talked with some thirty or forty, all of whom except one, were incorrigible in their preference to remain in their native land, rather than to emigrate "home" to a foreign shore. This shook his faith in the entire practicability of the scheme. Still he arrived here, the warm friend of the Society; and so continued until this debate, in which he intended to have taken an active part. But before he had an opportunity to take the floor, facts pressed upon him, (he was always open to conviction,) he changed his views, became the decided opponent of the Society, has left the institution for the purpose of commencing a school for the education of the people of color in Cincinnati, and has devoted himself to the elevation of the free blacks on our own soil, and to the making up of a public sentiment favorable to the abolition of slavery without expatriation. I would give you his name were it not that he is about to present to the public some interesting facts bearing upon slavery and emancipation, which he has collected within a few weeks among the free people of color in Cincinnati, in the course of which he will probably allude to the facts stated above by me. This, sir, is what I call *practical* anti-colonizationism.

At the close of the debate, the question was taken by ayes and noes, and decided in the negative with only one dissenting voice. Four or five who did not regularly attend the discussion, declined voting. Two or three others were absent from the Seminary. When the debate commenced, I had fears that there might be some unpleasant excitement, particularly as slave-holders, and the prospective heirs to slave property, were to participate in it. But the kindest feeling prevailed. There was no crimination, no denunciation, no impeachment of motives. And the result has convinced me that prejudice is vincible, that colonization is vulnerable, and that immediate emancipation is not only right, and practicable, but is "*expedient.*"

The result has convinced me of another thing, which I hail as the bright bow of promise to this holy cause. It is that southern minds, trained and educated amidst all the prejudices of a slave-holding community, can, with the blessing of God, be reached and influenced by *facts and arguments, as easily as any other class of our citizens.* To be sure, they will not endure *blind* and *un-*

intelligible denunciation; and what *rational being* will? But after being thoroughly a-roused by facts, they will receive rebuke, remonstrance, and entreaty, if kindly offer-ed, with that frankness and honesty which have ever marked the southern character. And when thoroughly converted, they man-ifest an ardor in behalf of the deeply injur-ed black, which astonishes while it delights. Almost all of our southern brethren are engaged in colored Sabbath schools and Bible classes. Some of them have devo-ted their lives to doing good to that op-pressed race. Let me state one or two facts on this point. The son of a slave-holder has just left the institution on ac-count of ill health, with a determination that he will not cease his efforts until his parent is induced to liberate his slaves. Another said, until this debate, he had ever considered slave-holding right, but now, being convinced it was wrong, he should exert an influence accordingly. Another entered this institution last spring the own-er of two slaves. Having been taught to look upon slavery as a necessary evil and not a sin, he hired out his slaves where they would receive kind treatment, intend-ing that the proceeds of their labor should aid him in his preparation for the ministry. Towards the close of the last session, facts were pressed upon his conscience, his duty was pointed out, he saw it, returned home to Kentucky, liberated his slaves, and now, instead of their working to educate *him*, he is working and studying and educating *them*. I need not add, that, on this occa-sion, he took the side of immediate aboli-tion, and anti-colonization. This, Sir, is what I call a *practical* "immediate eman-cipation."

It is the decided opinion of our brethren from the slave states, that if the plan of abolition proposed by the friends of that measure, could be kindly spread out before the southern community, and the entire practicability of the scheme illustra-ted and enforced by existing facts, slave-holders would embrace it as the only ra-tional remedy for slavery, and would come over to the cause of immediate emancipa-tion in crowds. They have somehow got the opinion that *abolitionism* is an infuria-ted monster, with a thousand heads and ten thousand horns, panting after blood, and ready to gore to death every slave-holder in the Union. And is it wonderful that they

should receive this impression, when we consider the tone of the colonization journ-als of the north? Our southern fellow-citi-zens should be disabused on this vitally interesting subject. Depend upon it the *people*, (I speak not of *politicians*,) the peo-ple of the south are not devoid of rea-son. *I know* that facts and reasoning *have* prevailed with them: and until truth loses its power, they *will continue* to prevail, overcoming prejudice, reaching the con-science, and changing the mind. I am ac-quainted with intelligent gentlemen resi-ding in this country, not professing Chris-tians, who are intimately acquainted with slavery in all its details, having lived many years in slave holding states, who *on prin-ciples of political economy*, are the decided advocates of immediate emancipation. Look at the facts as they exist in this seminary. Every member of this institution who was born and brought up in the midst of slave-ry, or who now resides in a slave-state, with one exception, is the advocate of im-mediate abolitition without expatriation. [The opinion of one who was absent from the seminary during the debate, I do not know.] There has been no necromancy employed in this work. *Prayer, the Bible, the condition of the slave, and the documents of the Colonization Society*, have been the instruments. When a brother resolved to use these means faithfully, we had no anx-iety as to the result. Would not the use of these measures by every Christian in the land, work wonders in the American church? Alas! how few Christians have prayed over, and talked about, and examin-ed a system which crushes into the dust two millions of their brethren and sisters, and consigns them over to oppression, to caprice, to lust, to brutality, to ignorance, to degradation, to death, to damnation. I thank God that the night of torpor is past in this institution; that prejudice has been buried in a dishonored grave, and that the persecuted blacks, bond and free, have a place in our sympathies, our prayers, and our labors.

Some important facts in regard to the character of emancipated negroes, and their ability to provide for themselves, have re-cently fallen under my observation in the city of Cincinnati. A large majority of the adult blacks in that city, are liberated slaves. Many of them earned with their own hands and paid six hundred, nine hundred, and some nearly fourteen hundred dollars for themselves individually, or for themselves and families. The majority of these have likewise acquired considerable property since their liberation. Many of them have already purchased their friends out of slavery!—and it is probable that at least one-third of the adult blacks in this city, are employed in earning money to buy their friends and relatives now in slavery. And this too is accomplished under peculiar embarrassments, heaped upon them by the oppressive laws of this state. They hold a debating society for mutual improvement every week. A lyceum in which lectures will be delivered two or three times a week, and male and female schools, are being established among them by abolitionists of the institution. Many of them meet in Bible classes, and Sabbath schools. And yet, these industrious people, have to be constantly on the alert to avoid being kidnapped, and sold into slavery, to supply the New-Orleans market! It has several times happened to these persecuted people, *after partly paying the ransom* of their relatives, that the master has sold the objects of their toil to slave-traders, who have carried them into hopeless bondage.—This was the case recently in regard to a wife, whose husband had paid in part for her freedom, and was laboring in this county to earn the residue. The master sold her for the New-Orleans market! A grand-mother had redeemed her daughter, and several grand-children out of slavery. Only one little girl remained, and the stipulated sum for her liberation had nearly all been paid. Disregarding his solemn pledges, the master sold the child to a man who was about to remove out of the state (Kentucky.) Distracted, the grand-mother went to the former master and entreated him with tears, either to re-purchase the little girl, or refund the money she had paid him. He would do neither. With much effort she succeeded in borrowing a sum sufficient to purchase her at full price of the latter master, while the former retained his ill gotten lucre. This transpired within three weeks. But why need I go on? Who will heed the cry of the oppressed? My soul sickens as I ponder over these *legalized* cruelties. Is it surprising that these persons do not rise higher in the scale of wealth, intelligence and respectability? Pressed down as they are by the whites, under such a

load of prejudice, and civil and educational disabilities—and liable to be kidnapped and sold into slavery, is it not surprising that they rise at all? It is literally true, that they stint themselves in food and clothing, and go bare-headed and bare-footed, so that they may appropriate their earnings to the purchase of their relatives in bondage. Noble spirits! An emancipated slave said to me to-day, " *Even freedom is bitter to us, while our friends are in slavery.*" And shall we make the *present* degradation of the free blacks, *which is the work of our own hands,* the premises from which to draw the conclusion, that "they can never rise in this country," and *therefore*, " it is benevolent in *us* to transport them to a foreign shore where they can escape" *our* "persecutions?" It is easier to estimate the *benevolence* of the argument, than to discover its *soundness.*

This evening, we formed an Anti Slavery Society.

Yours in the gospel,

H. B. STANTON.

———

LETTER IV.

LETTERS FROM THE SOUTH-WEST TO A. TAPPAN.

During my residence here, I have frequently diverted myself with collecting together and comparing the various reasons assigned by the slave party, why the slaves should not be emancipated. The following are some of them. 'The state of the slaves is better than that of the free blacks at the North.' 'They are treated so well that many of them are so attached to their masters they would not be free, if they had the opportunity, and most of them are contented and happy.' 'The slaves hate their masters so much, that were they set at liberty they would in all probability murder them and their families.' 'The slaves are naturally so indolent that, had they not masters to compel them to labor, they would soon starve to death.' 'They were not made slaves by us, hence we are not bound to make them free.' 'If we lose our slaves, which are our property, we shall be reduced to poverty.'

Whatever these unreasonable and contradictory statements may convey to your mind, they appear to me to evince a disposition to evade the main question—that of doing justice to the wronged. I do not believe that there is one in a hundred among those, with whom I have conversed on the subject, who is willing to do any thing to benefit the slave, if he must in consequence forego the profits of his labor. Masters talk of their own rights, as though the slave had none. They talk of being reduced to poverty—but do not hesitate to impoverish hundreds, in order that their own comforts and luxuries may be supplied.

And who has been so discerning as to discover that the free blacks at the north are in a worse state than the slaves at the South? I have had some acquaintance with both. And I know, as well as I know any thing, that such an assertion is not true. There may, indeed, be a greater proportion of blacks in the prisons in Massachusetts than in Virginia. But before the question of comparative vice is settled, it ought to be considered, that masters punish almost all crimes themselves; and that the prisons of Virginia are filled with profligate outcasts from the North.

In regard to the slaves being happy and contented—take the facts stated in my former letters and then judge of their happiness. But suppose that they were contented in their present state. What would that show? It would show, sir, that slavery in this country is a most degrading and brutalizing system.

And do these men undertake to say, that slaves, so happy, so contented, so attached to their masters that they would not be free if they had an opportunity; do they undertake to say that these slaves on becoming free would murder those they love so well?

Or, would they say that their slaves hate them now for their oppressions, and would do no injury—but, should they do them justice; these same slaves would take vengeance on them, and put them to death?

Again, we are told that white men cannot labor in the field in such a climate; and that laborers must be had or the country would suffer great loss. Then laying aside all equivocation, tell me by what rule of equity you conclude, that white men should have all the profits, if they cannot labor here. Ought not those that do the labor to have at least a share of the avails? Let the capitalist then pay colored laborers what is their due, if he must have them. But it is true that we do want the services of the black to make sugar and cotton, and it would be next to impossible to supply their place with white laborers. And we may lawfully have them, if we will pay honestly for their labor and not misuse them.

And this is all that the friends of the blacks seek for. Not to send them all out of the country—not to turn them wild into the woods—not to encourage them to plunder and murder—nor do they seek to make them judges of the supreme court—nor to send them as ambassadors to foreign courts. But they do seek that they may be made free—that they may be taken out of the absolute power of their masters, and permitted to serve as free laborers, under proper restrictive laws.

But suppose the present masters should say that they would not give them employment. Nevertheless I think they would, inasmuch as they would find it profitable; though less so than under the existing state of things. But if they would not, others would. There are in Mississippi, Louisiana, Alabama, and Florida, 130 millions acres; of which only one-seventh has yet been brought under cultivation. The remainder is government land. Now it would not require one-tenth the amount of capital, to engage in planting with free laborers, that it does under the present system. And I doubt not, but, thousands from the North would willingly employ their capital in making sugar and cotton.

Under the free labor system, it is not likely many would soon amass great fortunes, on account of the competition, which by the way would be all the better for the laborers; but they would make greater profits than are now made in the cultivation of any thing except sugar and cotton.

If in the British West India islands, where less than two hogsheads of sugar are made to the hand, the planters find the cultivation profitable; it might be supposed that in Louisiana where five hogsheads are made to the hand, even under a free labor system, the making of sugar would not, at least, be unprofitable. In Mississippi, a slave worth five or six hundred dollars, will make from five to seven bales of cotton, worth from two to three hundred dollars. This is a great profit; but in Mexico, with free labor, one hand, according to Mr.

Ward, the British envoy, produces nearly seven hogsheads of sugar with an equal weight of molasses,—all worth there seven hundred and thirty dollars. Now the bottom lands of the Mississippi valley are as fertile as any part of Mexico, and under the same cultivation certainly ought to produce as much. Then with proper laws for regulating their laborers, the planters would make sufficient profits. But considering the question in regard to justice, it matters not whether slaves are profitable or unprofitable, whether the masters are enriched or impoverished, or whether the country meet with loss or gain; Justice will ever remain pure justice, whatever names men are pleased to call it.

Now, let us suppose that the slaves are in such a state that the masters could not live with them if made free. Then most certainly some mode of instruction ought to be immediately instituted to prepare them for freedom. If they knew that they soon were to be at liberty, no danger could arise from giving them any amount of knowledge. And it is not true, that the laws effectually prohibit their owners from bettering their condition. As individuals they cannot, indeed, do any thing; but were the majority in favor of any system of amelioration, surely they might effect their wishes, inasmuch as the majority determine the laws.

But if they could not live with free blacks at all, then it would be better to give up a part of the South to them, than to continue them as slaves. It would be better to permit them to wrong one another, if such an event should ensue, rather than to wrong them ourselves. The laws of God do not allow us to deprive men of their freedom, merely because there is a chance that they may abuse it. And if these men are in such fear of poverty, let them take their axes, clear away the forest, and plant their own corn, as the inhabitants of Ohio, Indiana and Illinois have done. There is room enough in 'the far west,' for hundreds of millions. Industry and economy only will be necessary to ensure all the comforts of life.

After all, notwithstanding all the objections, and all the evasions that have been used to obscure the subject, a free labor system, appears to me, so far from bringing danger to the masters, to be the best mode of securing their safety.

A spirit of inquiry has gone forth among the slaves. They have heard of the Southampton affair; they only need another Nat Turner to lead them on to murder. And the masters are aware of this danger.— Hence they parade their military forces to intimidate them; and speak in whispers of all that relates to the subject of freedom and slavery. I remember well that the signs of fear were but too plainly manifested, at two different periods, when it was reported that an insurrection was about to break out at Natchez. It happened on one of these nights that a menagerie of wild beasts entered the town with a tumultuous noise of horns and drums. And so terrified were some of the females, being under the impression that the insurrection had begun, that their screams were heard in various parts of the town. Plots were also formed at Baton Rouge, St. Francisville, and in many other places, though they were never carried into execution. And one family of my acquaintance actually hid themselves in the woods on the night that they thought the massacre of the neighborhood was to happen.

That was another indication of fear.— Many, at the time of these rumors, armed themselves with dirks and pistols; and such was the demand for these weapons that they were sold in Natchez at an enormous profit.

Such have been the real or imaginary dangers in years that are past; and when the British West India islands shall have become free, these dangers are likely to be greatly augmented.

Therefore, in conclusion, I affirm, justice cannot be done, nor safety secured, without letting the oppressed go free.

Now, considering the present state of things, what ought to be done? Surely we have the right of discussion—and if we can do nothing more, we ought to raise our voices against the crying sins of the nation. Instead of asking the blessing of God on unrighteous deeds and their products, we ought to pray, that we may be delivered from temptation. And have we none among us who are willing to make a small sacrifice, to save men from temporal and eternal death? I know we have many who are willing to go to the ends of the earth in the cause of humanity and religion. But who is willing to spend a single year to do a service for the negro race, that has served for centuries to contribute to the luxuries of all civilized white men? Where is the humane Sharp? Where is the persevering Wilberforce? And the enterprizing Clarkson who traveled more than thirty thousand miles, and exposed himself to all dangers and hardships to save his nation from sin and the innocent from oppression?

Shall the weak longer hold up their hands, and cry in their distress to the followers of Him who came to deliver the captives, and find none to help? What, at our dying day, will be half so consoling to our departing spirits, as to reflect that we have endeavored to imitate the example, and to follow the precepts of the Lord of life! The slave of heathen Athens, and cruel Egypt, had an asylum to which he might fly in distress. But in Christian America there is no temple of Hercules to which he can go. Shall he appeal to the laws? They are all made against him. Shall he appeal to the humanity of his master? His interest outweighs the rights of the slave. Shall he, with tears of blood, appeal to the land of the pilgrims, to those men whose fathers gave up all for freedom? He is told that there must be no interference. To whom shall he go? To his God? Alas! he may never have been taught the consolations of religion.

May God grant that this question may be settled without blood. No swords or bayonets are now wanted, and if every man will do his duty they never will be wanted. Let us not wait then until some great calamity shall compel us to act. Let us not wait until like the waters of Egypt, our streams flow with blood, and the dead are found in every house, before we attend to the commands of the Almighty.

X. Y. Z.

TO SOUTHERN CHRISTIANS.

" *Whatsoever thy hand findeth to do, do it with thy might.*"

Brethren—The Bible is a book, not of explicit statutes, but of general principles, to be applied by individual conscience to every case of moral action. In regard to human rights its grand law is: " Love thy neighbor as thyself." " Whatsoever ye would that men should do unto you; do ye

even so to them." Oppression under various forms is exhibited in Scripture as drawing down the special curse of God upon those nations that practised it. Liberty is everywhere held up as a great blessing, for it is made the type of those scriptural blessings which the blood of Christ has purchased for the immortal soul. We need not say to you that there is a system of servitude in our country, which grossly violates the holy principles of the Bible, as illustrated and enforced by its history. You are familiar with it. You have wept over its enormities. You have seen it prostrating all that is fair, and lovely, and of good report. A thousand times has the question pressed upon you, " Lord, what wilt thou have me to do with this system?" Our purpose, brethren, is to throw before you some suggestions which will enable you to come to a right decision on this important question. Whatever others may do, we trust that you will not treat this appeal, as an unwarrantable interference. Slaveholding as a system, sanctioned by general practice and long usage, possesses such deceivableness—is so wonderfully adapted to enlist all the bad passions of our corrupt hearts, that those most intimately connected with it, however upright their intentions, are the least qualified to judge of their duty in regard to it. We have examined the subject in the light of facts drawn from all quarters, and in the light of the laws by which the system is protected, and we trust, in the light of conscience, and the word of God. The result has been the overwhelming conviction that, *we*, though not slave-holders, nor living in a slave-holding state, have a duty to perform in behalf of the slaves, and of their masters. This duty is not, to appeal to the slaves to assert their rights and maintain them by physical force ; for the Bible, without any proviso as to the justness of the tenure, enjoins upon servants to obey their masters, for the Gospel's sake ; but it is to appeal to the masters to " give unto their slaves that which is *just and equal.*" We do not see what other remedy is provided in Scripture, except such an appeal : we do not see how slavery can ever be peaceably overthrown, unless this appeal is powerfully and uncompromisingly made.

Let us look, then, calmly, attentively and prayerfully upon American Slavery, as it exists. We will not refer you to individual instances of outrageous cruelty, or shameful lust, nor will we be turned aside from our purpose by listening to individual instances of commendable kindness. Kindness you will readily acknowledge is not the apropriate fruit of the system. We appeal to you, whether the following characteristics do not belong to Slavery as a whole :

1. It gives up a man for life, for no crime, to the arbitrary control of another, subjecting him to the liability of cruel treatment, which he very often receives.

2. It places the female slaves within the control of the masters, and thus directly induces the practice of unbounded licentiousness.

3. It virtually destroys the family relation, and as a matter of fact, the slaves pay little regard to that relation.

4. It induces a traffic in the persons of men, which is always marked by outrageous cruelty.

You cannot fail to see then, that slavery is directly theft, and indirectly a violation of all the other commandments.

How can this charge be evaded? Can it be set aside on the ground that public opinion sanctions it ? What is the standard? Is it the will of the multitude, or the will of God ? Can all the men on earth alter the will of God ? But you had no intention of disobeying God, you say. How can this be ? How can you have usurped the rights of another man without intending it ? Is this the testimony of your conscience? The most that can possibly be said in palliation, is that you have sinned *ignorantly*. But still, remember that you have SINNED. The ignorance is comparative. But another plea is that you are not voluntary. This, of course, can be offered only by a minority of slaveholders. The laws forbid emancipation. Are those laws *righteous*, or not ? If slavery is a violation of God's law, your liberty of *conscience*, requires that you be permitted to emancipate. Do you submit to a law which compels you to violate the Divine law ? which sets aside the dictates of conscience ? As the laws are, you reply, you would do more injury to the slave by emancipating than by retaining. For his own good you retain him. Now, who has made *you* judge in the case ? The Divine law secures to every man *his own*. Many men are ignorant and vicious, and do not use their own, so much to their own advantage as you could do it for them.

But, if you have used the property of your neighbor without his consent, whatever may have been your intentions, you have violated a principle, the observance of which is necessary to the very existence of Society. The only reason why the social system is not totally wrecked under your violation of this principle, is, that it is confined to a particular caste ; in regard to that caste, the benefits of the social system are annihilated. But look at the action of your supposed humanity, in retaining your slaves, upon the system as a whole. For the sake of the argument, we will grant that *your* slaves are more comfortable, physically, than if liberated. Does not your admission, that they are so, and your tame acquiescence in the laws against emancipation, without protest or remonstrance, confirm in their iniquity, the majority that enacted the law ? Throughout all the slave states, we have heard no serious opposition to these cruel laws. We have good right to suppose that the minority has acquiesced in their *expediency*, to the entire prostration of justice. But again, suppose you were to remonstrate against these laws, would it not be your duty *also* to say to your slaves that *you* do not feel bound by them ; that so far as *you* are concerned they are free ? Are laws that violate the rights of conscience to be set aside by obeying them ? Will the unjust law-makers learn to respect a conscience that is so pliable ? What case ever called men to resist the laws of their country, not to violence, but to martyrdom, if this does not? If injury comes to your slaves by your non-compliance with the law, the guilt will not rest upon you. In consistency with human rights, you must in no case even *pretend* to hold a man in slavery for his own good, unless *he*, of his own free choice, requests it. In this case, he is plainly a slave only in name. Against those so called slave-holders, who only receive *voluntary* service, provided, they openly protest against slavery, we have nothing to say. How shall this baleful system of legalized violation of human rights be overthrown, except by insurrection, while even its opposers *practically* acquiesce in it ? If there be, south of the Potomac, any Christianity of the Apostolic school, will it not show itself by a vigorous, uncompromising opposition to slavery, even in the face of fire and faggot ?

We trust you will not so much disparage

the sacred volume as to pretend, as many do, that this unjust system derives any countenance from that quarter. Those who are entangled by such Jesuitism would do well to consider, first, for what reason slavery was permitted at all to the Israelites; and whether either the permission or the reasons of it now exist: And, secondly, what sort of slavery it was that was then permitted. Clearly it will be as wrong for *us* to transcend the permission as it was for the Israelites; and you will remember that the vengeance of God repeatedly came upon them because they did so.* The whole sacred history confirms the remark; but read the prophet Jeremiah especially. The seventh year put an end to the slavery of every Hebrew, and the heathen slave had the right to become such. The year of Jubilee gave liberty to *all* the inhabitants of the land. At no time was it lawful to give up to his master a fugitive slave. Let the advocates of slavery from Scripture, advocate merely Scripture slavery, and we have nothing to say to them, except that they mistake the dispensation under which they live! The wall which God had built around his peculiar people has been leveled by the bringing in of the glorious gospel. The form under which the gospel recognizes the rights of man, cuts up slavery root and branch. "Whatsoever ye would that men should do to you, do ye even so to them." The pæans to "liberty" that ring through all the South show the conscious but unblushing violation of this holy maxim. The servants that were recognized in the New Testament as justly such, were plainly not slaves. For we have the explicit injunction, "Masters give unto your servants that which is JUST and EQUAL." Does *he* obey this who holds a man as *property?* who exacts the unpaid services of another according to a system that turns into *property* entire races of men—from the cradle to the grave, generation after generation? That makes *beasts* of *men*, to the complete prostration of their immortal interests? No. If there is *justice* here, it is that of the robber who takes the whole, and then restores an insignificant pittance. If there is *equality;* it is that which exists between the rider and his horse! The whole scope of Scripture in regard to slavery is, "Come out of her,

* Jeremiah chap. 34.

my people, that ye be not partakers of her sins, and that ye receive not of her plagues." Understand us, brethren. We do not seek to exasperate the slaves against you. We do not forget that the gospel enjoins the sufferance of injuries; that it forbids us to take vengeance out of the hands of Him to whom it belongeth. If we had access to your slaves, we would earnestly counsel them to wait on God for deliverance. *Your* lives and souls are as precious in our sight as theirs. And it is for this very reason that we hold up your sin faithfully before you and entreat you to repent before the coming of the terrible retribution.

Do not think to wait for the removal of the slaves, and emancipate only on condition of such removal. The scheme is delusive. The majority of slave-holders are not willing to emancipate upon the soil, in which case they could employ the emancipated as free laborers for an expense, surely not much greater than that which it now costs to support them as slaves. Will they be willing then, not only to emancipate, but to have their laborers transported; thus inducing a scarcity of labor utterly destructive of their agriculture? Will increasing the value of slaves, the inevitable result of deporting a measurable portion of Southern laborers, render the masters more willing to emancipate? That masters, generally, fear and tremble, amidst their unrighteous gains, and wish for some change for safety, if it do not cost too much, is certain? But which alternative will they choose; to give up the 500,000,000 of dollars, the estimated value of the slaves—principal and interest, a dead loss, to say nothing of the expense of deportation, *or,* sink the principal only, while they retain the interest, for this is the worst that can happen, in case they exchange the slave system for one of free labor. Indeed the slightest acquaintance with political economy will show that the principal will not be sunk, but transferred in the aggregate to the value of the land. Every body knows that the land alone, when it is cultivated by free hired labor, is worth as much as the land and the slaves together, when the laborers are articles of property or capital, to be paid for. Look then at the comparative practicability of the two schemes, if colonization may be said to be practicable at all. In one case we endeavor to persuade men to purchase personal safety by a total sacrifice of their wealth; in the other we plead with them, with all the facts and arguments in the world in our favor, to secure both their persons and their just wealth by an act of justice and humanity. The scheme of colonization to be *effectual* must contemplate the deportation at once of 2,000,000 of laborers and the importation of at least 1,000,000 to take their place: to be *just* it must do the whole with the free and intelligent consent of all the laborers. But colonization as it exists, and as it always must, is an insignificant drain to the inexhaustible fountain of slave population, leaving justice and humanity out of sight. And it can have no other tendency than to abate nature's remedy for slavery, viz. redundancy of slaves. To the business of colonizing Africa with suitable emigrants, who go of their own free choice, we do not object. But when the scheme swells into a remedy for American slavery, we must regard it as a delusion almost equally disastrous to the slave, to the emigrants and to Africa. It turns all the sympathy for the slave into an inoperative channel; it throws together an ill-qualified, ill-assorted population upon the coast of Africa, there to perish under complicated evils, or to subsist by a traffic which ministers directly to that abominable one in slaves; it holds up before the nations of Africa a specimen that must excite their abhorrence of the very name of Christianity.

The evil of slavery is a moral one, and must be met by a moral remedy. There is no such thing as putting the wrath of God away from us, except by repentance, and by treating our abused brothers justly and mercifully. That crushing pride of caste, must be abandoned: we must no longer make the hue of man's skin the test, according to which he is to receive the treatment of a *man* or of a *brute*.

We are speaking to sincere christian men. We trust therefore, that we need not, after proving the *justice* of immediate emancipation, stop to prove to *you* its safety. It is always safe to obey God, whatever man may do to us. But, upon this point, of the safety of emancipating, we beg you candidly and carefully to examine the history of past experiment. In the abolition contest, in England, this matter has been most thoroughly brought to light. If the facts, showing the safety of unprepared-for emancipation, could have been set aside,

the powerful West India body had all the means in the world of doing it. *But there they stand.* And what is more, the planters themselves, now that emancipation is inevitable, prefer to make it *immediate* instead of *gradual.* They throw the *preparation* for the enjoyment of *inalienable rights* to the winds, without the least fear of the consequences.

Even the "horrors of St. Domingo" do not appal them. For they know that all the bloodshed in that injured island, occurred before the act of emancipation, while the masters refused to liberate, or, after they attempted to re-enslave. For years, subsequent to the general act of emancipation, all was tranquillity, and the agriculture of the island never flourished more.[*] Emancipation has been tried in numerous instances, in large districts of country. The result has uniformly been happy and safe. Indeed, how could it be otherwise, in consistency with the well known laws of human nature? Men are not exasperated by kindness. A single act of generous magnanimity has often made a friend of the bitterest foe. The advocates of slavery in exciting the alarm against immediate emancipation, confound two cases which are widely different: the case where liberty is freely granted by the master, with that where the slave vindicates it by his own arm, or is rescued by the physical force of another. When an ignorant and degraded populace have thrown off the yoke of a tyrant king, they have committed horrible excesses, and fallen at length under more grievous despotism. When, by the prowess of some desperado, the slaves of a district have thrown down the hoe and got clear of the whip, they have committed deeds of violence, at which humanity stands aghast. But these are the dangers of tyranny and oppression, not of mild government and equal rights. Insurrections do not occur among freemen—they do not occur without motive.

It is not less insane to plead that the slaves will die of starvation, if set at liberty —that they will be incorrigibly idle. This is contrary to all history. It supposes that those, to whom labor is a habit, will not work when starvation is the only alternative. As it regards vagrancy and plunder-

[*] See Clarkson's Thoughts, No. 3, Anti-Slavery Reporter.

ing, they can be as easily prevented after emancipation as now. The law will wield the combined power of all the white men, and can any thing more be done now? Besides, the motives to vagrancy and plunder are incomparably greater under a system of forced labor.

If it be objected that they will not labor twelve or fifteen hours a day for a *peck of corn* a week, we grant it. We do not believe that labor forced beyond the powers of the constitution on stinted food, is any more profitable to the master in the long run, than it is agreeable to the dictates of humanity.

But these, brethren, are not the arguments on which our appeal rests. Depraved human nature never fails to bring such objections against any reformation. And we thought it worth while to show you, that, in this case, they can be triumphantly refuted. Honesty *is* the best policy. True *expediency* is always in the same scale with *justice*. But were it not so, we plant ourselves on the firm ground of changeless *right*, and to *you* we make our appeal in the unfaltering tone of self-evident truth. If you do not wish to see the bolts of divine vengeance descend upon our guilty land; if you do not wish to answer at the bar of God for the blood of murdered souls, take up the *martyr's* testimony against *slavery.* When we attempt to speak on this subject, we are rudely repulsed as impertinent intermeddlers. This implies that *you* have a better right to speak. Avail yourselves of this advantage. The *moral force* of the Universe is on the side of the oppressed. The crisis is approaching; slavery must be annihilated by pouring down upon it the moral indignation of a renovated world, so long due to its dark abominations, or nothing remains to us but the sure expectation of overwhelming wrath. Let man say what he will, God will not endure that millions of his rational creatures shall to all ages be the victims of our foul hypocrisy—shutting from them both the comforts of this life and the hopes of the next!

A FRIEND TO THE SOUTH.

The Treasurer of the American Anti-Slavery Society acknowledges the receipt of the following donations:

From a Friend,	$50 00
From the Aux. Soc. of Oneida Institute,	34 40

WILLIAM GREEN, Jr. Treasurer.

OFFICE OF THE ANTI-SLAVERY REPORTER,
130 Nassau street, New York.

☞ The following admirable lines contain more *truth* in regard to the Colonization scheme than we recollect to have seen any where else within the same compass. They ought to be set to music and sung in the ears of the "hunters" till they are ashamed of themselves.☜

From the Liberator.
THE HUNTERS OF MEN.

Have ye heard of our hunting, o'er mountain and glen,
Through cane-brake and forest—the hunting of men?
The lords of our land to this hunting have gone,
As the fox-hunter follows the sound of the horn:
Hark—the cheer and the hallo!—the crack of the
    whip,
And the yell of the hound as he fastens his grip!—
All blithe are our hunters, and noble their match—
Though *hundreds* are caught, there are *millions* to
    catch:
So speed their hunting, o'er mountain and glen,
Through cane-brake and forest—the hunting of men!

Gay luck to our hunters!—how nobly they ride
In the glow of their zeal, and the strength of their
    pride!—
The Priest with his cassock flung back on the wind,
Just screening the politic Statesman behind—
The saint and the sinner, with cursing and prayer—
The drunk and the sober, ride merrily there.
And woman—kind woman—wife, widow, and maid—
For *the good of the hunted*—is lending her aid:
Her foot's in the stirrup—her hand on the rein—
How blithely she rides to the hunting of men!

Oh! goodly and grand is our hunting to see,
In this "land of the brave and this home of the free."
Priest, warrior, and statesman, from Georgia to Maine,
All mounting the saddle—all grasping the rein—
Right merrily hunting the black man, whose sin
Is the curl of his hair and the hue of his skin!—
Wo, now to the hunted who turns him at bay!—
Will our hunters be turned from their purpose and
    prey?—
Will their hearts fail within them?—their nerves trem-
    ble, when
All roughly they ride to the hunting of men?

Ho—ALMS for our hunters!—all weary and faint
Wax the curse of the sinner and prayer of the saint.
The horn is wound faintly—the echoes are still
Over cane-brake and river, and forest and hill.
Haste—alms for our hunters!—the hunted once more
Have turned from their flight with their backs to the
    shore;
What right have *they* here in the home of the white,
Shadowed o'er by *our* banner of Freedom and Right?
Ho—alms for the hunters!—or never again
Will they ride in their pomp to the hunting of men!

ALMS—ALMS for our hunters!—why *will* ye delay,
When their pride and their glory are melting away?
The parson has turned; for, on charge of his own,
Who goeth to warfare, or hunting alone?
There is doubt in his heart—there is fear in his eye.
Oh! haste—lest that doubting and fear shall prevail,
And the head of his steed take the place of his tail.
Oh! haste ere he leave us!—for who will ride then,
For pleasure or gain, to the hunting of men!
                                        NIMROD.

TERMS.

☞ This periodical will be furnished to subscribers at $1 00 per annum, done up in a neat cover; or 50 cents, without the cover. To those who take several copies a discount will be made as follows: 15 per cent. for 10 copies, 25 per cent. for 25 copies, and 33 per cent. for 100 copies.

AMERICAN

ANTI - SLAVERY REPORTER.

| VOL. I.] | MAY, 1834. | [NO. 5. |

REVIEW OFA COLONIZATION ARTICLE IN "THE LITERARY AND THEOLO-GICAL REVIEW," AND A DEFENCE OF ABOLITION.

Review of Anti-Slavery Publications and defence of the Colonization Society. By the HON. THEODORE FRELINGHUYSEN, *Senator in the United States Congress.*

That a distinguished champion of human rights, conspicuous for his able and eloquent defence of the Indians against the unconstitutional encroachments of Georgia avarice, should be found urging on the feelings ot national intolerance against a portion of his own countrymen even more injured and oppressed than the Aborigines of our soil themselves, is truly cause of grief, if not of indignation.

We freely admit that the writer may think himself actuated by the principles of Christianity and benevolence, and though with the motives of an individual we may have little to do, yet upon great principles of action, upon results and facts, it is our undoubted right to be heard, especially in defence of principles, which however they may be stigmatized as "abstract," are of undeniable truth, and of such practical importance that our fathers hesitated not to stake their " lives, fortunes and sacred honor" in their vindication.

We are struck at once in reading the review with this remarkable concession " yielding to the opposers *all which they urge against the unchristian spirit* that estranges from us our colored brethren," &c. and we wonder how the honorable gentleman after yielding so much would venture a conflict in which, to us it appears, the most important ground of all is in the outset conceded.

The most serious charge, this writer has made against the Anti-Slavery Declaration is that of enjoining political action. The implication contained in this charge we confess in our opinion not very creditable to the candor of its author. It is well known both from the professions of that Declaration, and from the character of the Abolitionists, that no idea of political elevation at all influences them; that their aims are solely moral and their measures only such as are employed by the advocates of the gospel of peace itself. But with what consistency the charge of political action can be cast upon abolitionists from this quarter, let the public decide. Since it is well known that the 2d article of the Constitution of the Amercan Colonization Society contains this clause, " and the Society shall act to effect this object (the colonization of the free people of color,) *in co-operation with the general government, and such of the States as may adopt regulations upon the subject.*"

In order more fully to show the foundation of this charge, we transcribe from the Declaration the two sentences whose connexion is necessary to preserve the true sense of either, and one of which only the gentleman has chosen in order to establish his position ; a position, which if established, would put us on precisely the ground assumed by the Colonization Society itself.

But we maintain that Congress has a right, and is solemnly bound, to suppress the domestic slave trade between the several States, and to abolish slavery in those portions of our territory which the Constitution has placed under its exclusive jurisdiction.

☞ *When gratuitous, please to read and hand it to your neighbor.* ☜

We also maintain that there are, at the present time, the highest obligations resting upon the people of the free States, to remove slavery by moral and political action, as prescribed in the Constitution of the United States.

With all due deference to the learning and sagacity of the gentleman, we beg to say that in the first paragraph the particular measures are referred to by which it is competent for Congress, according to the Constitution, to operate upon this great moral and political evil, viz. to interdict the execrable slave trade and to abolish slavery in those portions of the country exclusively under their jurisdiction—and in the second it is maintained that the duty of the people of the whole country is, to promote and support such action, both by moral means and by the constitutional exercise of their political rights.

Will not the American people exercise their political power for good or for evil on this and on every other subject, whether A. S. Societies exist or not? We presume the distinguished gentleman does not mean seriously to propose to the people the abdication of this right. And is it any thing but a moral measure for the A. S. Convention to recommend to their fellow citizens so to exercise their political and moral powers, as to discharge their own consciences of the sin of participating in this enormous iniquity? Now to us it appears quite an unworthy attempt, for this, to implicate A. S. Societies or Conventions in any political projects whatever. We cheerfully concede that a better system of public morals than slavery produces, would improve all our legislation, but this is no more an argument against Anti-Slavery principles and measures than similar results of the Temperance Reform is proof that the Amer. Tem. Society entertains a political project.

The reviewer exclaims, "What the political action is which the Constitution *prescribes* for the removal of slavery, we have yet to learn, nor is it easy to imagine a federal principle adequate to that result, and at the same time compatible with the "sovereignty of each state to legislate exclusively on the subject." Here the quotation from the Declaration is incomplete and its incompleteness perverts its meaning. The sentence reads thus, "We fully and unanimously recognize the sovereignty of each state to legislate exclusively on the subject of the slavery which is tolerated within its limits." Passing over the unfairness of these quotations, it will be recollected that Congress according to the constitution, has power "to regulate commerce among the several states." And having exercised its power to abolish the accursed trade in human beings from without, by denouncing it as PIRACY, it certainly might, according to the express words of the Constitution so "regulate commerce among the several states," as to abolish all traffic in the bodies and souls of native Americans, throughout the Union. It is self-evident that the two measures of interdicting the brutal and revolting trade in human flesh between the states, and destroying slavery in the District and Territories under its control, constitute "the political action which the Constitution prescribes" as referred to in the Declaration. We are therefore at a loss to understand how such action of the General Government to abolish the iniquitous slave trade *between* the several states can at all interefere with "the sovereignty of each state to legislate on the subject of the slavery which is tolerated *within* its own limits." We have special reason to deny the right of any sovereign state to legislate beyond its own limits on this or any other subject.

Shame then that Congress should permit for one moment this accursed trade "among the several states," in native born men, women and children of America? Ever to be lamented that an eloquent Senator and pious man should employ his talents in mystifying this plain and rightous cause.

If it is PIRACY to trade in foreigners, it should be regarded as a higher crime to buy and sell native Americans. Yet the laws of the Union uphold this *piracy.* The power to abolish this nefarious trade is therefore "expressly warranted by the clear terms of the Constitution," and it is a gross error to say that "these terms do not in any case contemplate an inhibition of the transfer of slaves from one territory to another, in both of which slavery is recognized by law."

We confess ourselves horror-struck at this cold-blooded defence of slavery and the slave trade!

Again says the Review, "The first affirmative point in the conclusions at which the Convention arrive from their premises is, " *That there is no difference in principle between the African slave trade and American slavery."* By this it is obviously meant that it is as wicked for an American owner of slaves to retain them, as it is to engage in the African slave trade."

In the Declaration of the Anti-Slavery Society the words *in principle* are in italics but are not printed as emphatic in the quotation. But we are astonished that any one should attempt to show that an identity of *principle* was the same thing as an identity in the degrees of crime. It is a palpable sophism. Indeed, if the Convention had said that American slavery was as bad as the African slave trade, there would have been sufficient defence of the charge in the fact that a single state (Virginia) sells annually to the farther south 6,000* *native victims;* violating all the holy ties of domestic life, masters selling their own sons and daughters, brothers and sisters, into hopeless and perpetual bondage. Is there any feature in the African slave trade as unearthly, as unspeakably revolting as this! We really think that the honorable Senator has become the advocate of a system in all respects *worse* than the proscribed slave trade itself. If in the dark corners of the earth it is piracy to steal or buy and transport human beings into bondage, how aggravated is the crime of perpetrating and perpetuating this enormous outrage *by law,* and all this in the full light of civilization and the gospel.

The article under consideration repeats the favorite pretexts and bugbears of the defenders of slavery. The necessity of "preparatory measures," such as "the cultivation of the intellect to obviate the recurrence of the scenes of St. Domingo." And pray what cultivation of the intellect can ever be afforded in slavery?

And how can a candid man seriously propose such a preparation for liberty, when with one accord all slave-holding legislatures make the instruction of slaves penal and in some states the second offence is punishable with death? As to St. Domingo we could not have supposed the gentleman so utterly unread in the history of occurrences "within the memory of this generation," or so unfair if informed, as to repeat the stale and often refuted slander against the negro, or rather against humanity itself, that the massacres in that Island were "the consequences of premature abolition." Be it remembered that it was the attempt to subjugate the free, and not the emancipation of the slave, which oc-

* Professor Dew.

casioned the massacres of St. Domingo. As well might we regard the overthrow of Pharaoh and his hosts in the Red Sea, as "the consequence of premature abolition," as to make the same charge against a people who had been free six or seven years.

Is it not contrary to all the known laws of human action, for men who have peaceably submitted to be plundered of their labors, to be scourged, to be bought and sold like beasts, and to be robbed of their wives and their children; when emancipated from bondage, rewarded for their toil, made secure in the possession of their domestic relations, treated kindly, instructed in learning, religion and the useful arts, to become on this account suddenly full of turbulence and rebellion, of violence and massacre? The St. Domingo history proves directly the reverse of all this, and so does every other history of emancipation! Witness the half million of free blacks among us—the most peaceable and inoffensive people in the world. Emancipation in Colombia, Mexico, and Guiana proves the same thing, as also the experience of the colony at the Cape of Good Hope.

We did anticipate from the pen of the New Jersey Senator something better than this *poetry of Colonization.** Yet he fondly dotes on the effects of the Colony upon "the native tribes of Africa," "the fountains and streams of salvation" gushing from Liberian sands, while "the native tribes look on and wonder," and many other pretty poetical imaginings. For the truth of these representations, we turn to the unmannerly testimony of facts as recorded in the Af. Repos. The Rev. Mr. Pinney, missionary to Liberia, being on the spot and above all suspicion, by his letter dated Liberia, Feb. 20, 1833, completely overthrows this visionary fabric.

"The colonists are very ignorant of every thing about the interior: except of the tribes along the coast *nothing at all* is known, and of them little but their *manner of traffic.* NOTHING *has been done for the natives,* hitherto, by the colonists, except to educate a few who were in their families in the *capacity of servants.* The *natives* are, as to wealth and intellectual cultivation, *related* to the colonists as the

---

* "The poetry of philanthropy" is the coinage of the Rev. Dr. Hawks. At a large Colonization meeting, he declared that the evils of slavery are but "the poetry of philanthropy," and boasted that "he had drawn his first nourishment at the South!!" It was on this occasion, that the Hon. Mr. Frelinghuysen said that nine-tenths of these evils were imaginary. Mr. F. could not go the whole!

negro in America is to the *white man*—and this fact, added to their mode of dress, which consists of nothing usually but a handkerchief around the loins, leads to the SAME DISTINCTION as exists in America between ' *colors*. A colonist of any dye (and many there are of a darker hue than the Vey, or Dey, or Croo, or Bassoo,) would, if at all respectable, think himself *degraded* by marrying a native. The natives *are* in fact *menials*—I mean those in town—and sorry am I to be obliged to say, that from my limited observation, it is evident, that *as little effort is made by the colonists to elevate them, as is usually made by the higher classes in the United States to better the condition of the lower.* Such I suppose will ever be the case, when men are not actuated by a pure desire to do good."

"It requires no great keenness of observation, to see the cause why the colony is not more prosperous. But two or three hitherto have done any thing scarcely towards agriculture. The *wealthy* find it easier to trade; the *poor* suppose it degrading."

" The native tribes" in the neighborhood of Liberia know little of the reviewer's visions. The Rev. Mr. Ashmun explains in some measure how they " look on and wonder," and gives a true picture of the influence of the Colony upon them. Describing an engagement he had with them, he says,

"Eight hundred men were here pressed shoulder to shoulder in so compact a form that a child might easily walk on their heads, from one end of the mass to the other, presenting in their rear a breadth of rank equal to 20 or 30 men, and all exposed to a gun of great power raised on a platform at only from 30 to 60 yards distance. ☞ Every shot literally spent its force in a solid mass of human flesh! ☜ The fire suddenly terminated. A savage yell was raised which filled the dismal forest with a momentary horror. It gradually died away and the whole host disappeared. At 8 o'clock the well known signal of their dispersion and return to their homes was sounded and many small parties were seen at a distance directly afterwards moving off in a different direction. One large canoe employed in reconveying a party across the Montserado, venturing within the range of the long gun, was struck by a shot and several men killed.* Af. Rep. Vol. 2. page 179.

Very recently a merchant of Philadelphia at Liberia on a visit, came near falling a victim to the hostility of the natives—the boat in which he was, being pursued by a canoe manned with armed savages, he and his party only escaped in consequence of *shooting two of their pursuers.* Otherwise this gentleman and his company might have become very soon "the property" of the savages. From all these sources, and indeed from every other unprejudiced authority, we gather the information that the natives, while they have been awed by the arms, have not been improved by the proximity of the Colony. Tens of thousands of spear-

* Obad. 14. Neither shouldst thou have stood in the crossway to cut off those of his that did escape. How shall we account for the inconsistency of this Rev. Gentleman.

pointed knives, brass blunderbusses, muskets, pistols, and rivers of intoxicating liquors have been poured into this devoted country by the regular trade of the Colony, as is proved by the advertisements in the Liberia Herald. The licentiousness of the colonists, and we have high colonization authority for saying the licentiousness of some, who should have been their guides in virtue is now so notorious, that it is perfectly monstrous to hear colonization melodies chaunted in their praise while we have the evidence of the missionary, the returning emigrant, and confessing and mutually accusing officers, of the universal demoralization which prevails there. " There is not moral energy enough in the colony," says the Rev. L. Bacon, "to replace a flag staff which has rotted away, and signals cannot be made to ships."

The Review, in order to urge the claims of colonization, makes an array of the names of several great men who are understood to be connected with the Society. But what evidence have we that they understood the *real project* with which they have thus unguardedly associated themselves? Clarkson Wilberforce, Cropper and Buxton, and in fine all the British philanthropists, were themselves at first thus misled, and at one time the Af. Rep. sung their praises and claimed the influence of their illustrious names. The slave trade itself, though now regarded as the greatest enormity in the history of crime, had in its origin the approbation of the great Cotton Mather.

" And holy men gave Scripture for the deed."
Campbell.

To us it is not a little astonishing to see the name of Bushrod Washington quoted here to give popularity to the scheme. A man, though the nephew of the Father of his Country, and President of the American Colonization Society, who was the impious owner of about 1,000 human beings whom he claimed as property. His name is familiar to our eye, as subscribed to advertisements of runaway slaves, offering large rewards for their apprehension. On a single occasion, (in his own words,) "a sale was made of 54 negroes" to Louisiana, and in defence of this execrable traffic, in which he had been employed, and for which his name had been held up to scorn by the Baltimore Morning Chronicle, (a southern print) Judge Washington used this language—"I never heard a sigh or a complaint from the parents of the two most valuable servants I ever owned, that their sons had abandoned them and my service and sought new habitations in Northern States, where they now are." And here we have Bushrod Washington, Lafayette, Mills and Finley, in one discordant group to prop up by factitious influence the falling temple!

The pious and devoted Mills supported the Colonization scheme with a single view to missionary effort in Africa. He never contemplated the forcible separation of Americans on account of complexion. He hoped that "a few of the blacks of good character could be settled on the African coast," thus to introduce "civilization and religion among the barbarous tribes already there." His name cannot, with any fairness therefore, be referred to in support of a society which has transported "ship-loads of vagabonds coerced away as really as if it had been done with a cart whip;" and whose publications stigmatize our oppressed though respectable colored brethren as "nuisances," "a degraded caste," "dull as brutish beasts," and "vagabonds," &c. Nor did the pious Mills anticipate the flourishing trade which the colonial merchants have carried on in rum, and in the instruments of murder, constituting at present their chief commerce!

Lafayette has had just as much to do with approving this Society as Clarkson, for they have both been seduced into its support by being made to think it an Anti-Slavery Society.

The Rev. Dr. Finley, one of the earliest and warmest friends of this scheme, himself a native of a slave state, gives his motives in a letter to a friend published in the Af. Rep. page 2, of the 1st vol. In the highest exercise of charity we can only say, that in our opinion, such principles of action are of most questionable humanity. "Could they be sent back to Africa," says he, "a threefold benefit would arise. WE SHOULD BE CLEARED OF THEM, we should send to Africa a population partly civilized and Christianized for their benefit, and our blacks themselves would be put in a better situation."

All the impressions which the reviewer would make on the public mind, of the favorable influence of the colony upon the natives, has been contradicted by the information communicated to the managers at their late annual meeting at Washington,

as reported for the N. Y. Observer (a col. print,) and the Evangelist. We are constrained therefore to suppose that the review was written before its author attended that meeting, and we regret that we are not able to see in its publication so many weeks afterwards the evidence of that ingenuousness of character for which we have always regarded him. From the Report alluded to we find he was very anxious about its probable effect on the public.

"When the fact of our debt was first developed last night, (said Mr. F.) it made my heart feel sick, especially because it will be so effectively employed against us. * * * While we were holding ourselves out to the public as able to transport any number of emigrants for $30 each, and that the colony was prosperous, the emigrants thriving and happy, these disclosures came upon us. In the midst too of our conflict with the Abolitionists, as well as in the midst of this triumph respecting the Colony, we have gone in debt in two years to the amount of $40,000. ☞I trust that when the Secretary comes to publish his report he will prepare a statement on this subject, so that the public may have what I apprehend will be a perfectly satisfactory explanation of this business."

The Review seems in general to content itself with simply denying what the Abolitionists have proved from the authorized journal of the Society, and in that journal the managers of the Colonization Society have underwritten *by the very act of publication, and sometimes by expressed approbation*, some of the most gross and impudent pro-slavery doctrines which have ever disgraced the annals of tyranny.

To consider slavery as a "monstrous incubus never sought, but imposed upon us," to call the oppressor "unfortunate," and to say not one word of sympathy in favor of poor bleeding humanity at home, suffering under the tyrant's scourge and the more cruel violation of those ties which notwithstanding slavery, bind together the tender relations of life, is to show a turpitude of principle and a moral apathy utterly inconceivable in an enlightened and noble mind. It proves how the sin of slaveholding obliterates from a nation that intuitive sense of the injustice of oppression, otherwise universal amongst men. Such language is only another, though a more subtle method of saying with an "unfortunate" ancient afflicted with this "entailed curse," "I know not the Lord, neither will I let Israel go."

It is a consideration of overwhelming power, that God has, in effect, added the title of liberator of the slave to the names of his glory, saying to Israel, "I am the Lord that brought thee out of the land of Egypt, out of the house of bondage."

When Moses sounded through Egypt the command of the Most High to let his oppressed people go, Pharaoh exclaimed, who is the Lord that I should obey his voice? And is not the present time the parallel of that? Is there no analogy between the answer of Pharaoh and the declaration of the Colonization Society with respect to emancipation, that "in the age of nations a century is but a day?" And is not the bold and honest confession of the Egyptian tyrant the more parallel? If a century of bondage is but a day in their eyes, 3,000 years are but a month? Thus would they postpone abolition indefinitely forever. Were your brother, your son, a daughter, or a wife thus suffering bonds, what would be your feelings in respect of every hour's delay? In contrast with the apostle's command that we "remember them that are in bonds as bound with them," how cold-blooded, how like mockery is the pretence that "in the age of nations a century is but a day." This sentiment would consign to hopeless slavery during the next century upwards of 100 millions of our slaves, and their descendants, every one of whom would die in slavery, in intellectual and moral darkness. And what is pretended in extenuation of this gradual scheme of indefinite postponement? An imaginary Expediency! But how blind is the expediency which would usurp the place of everlasting rectitude! Before the lapse of half a day of Colonization mercy, (viz. 50 years,) by the onward progress of population alone, it is more than probable that the just vengeance of offended heaven will cry to them, "Behold the hire of your laborers who have reaped your fields which is of you kept back by fraud, crieth and the cries of them which have reaped are entered into the ears of the Lord of Sabaoth." And before 50 years it is certain that the whole southern region of our country will be in possession of the slaves unless we restore them their rights. This will result from the natural growth of slavery and the necessary emigration of the whites. But in case of war we cannot expect this event and its awful concomitants to be by any means as distant. Thus the boasted expediency of our adversaries shows the unsoundness of their political principles them-selves, and throws a strong light on the perfect safety and expediency of immediate emancipation, by which in case of war two millions of people would become our defenders whom we are now wantonly rendering our enemies.

We are astonished to learn that "the great majority of the colonists are emancipated slaves, liberated by southern owners." This is undoubtedly incorrect—The African Repository speaks only of 3,000 colonists—more than that number have never gone there, and of this number 1,200 were Africans taken from slave ships captured on the ocean, and not "liberated by southern owners"—1,200 free people of color have been enticed or "coerced" away and there remains but 800 liberated slaves to complete the population of the colony. We are credibly informed by returning colonists that of this 3,000 persons not more than 1,700 are to be found, so that the colony has not increased but has actually suffered a diminution of 1,300 persons. Nor is this unlikely when we consider that by the confession of Rev. Mr. Gurley, the Secretary, that of the last 600 and odd emigrants 134 had died within 6 months, and very probably by this time the mortality is as great as 200. At any rate 20 per cent. in 6 months is a most horrible mortality, and no matter whether the expeditions were furnished with men enticed or "coerced," will not the blood of these poor fellow creatures be demanded at the hand of those concerned in their destruction? The mortality of the cholera in New-York in 1832 was sufficiently terrible, and yet amounted only to one and a half per cent. of the whole population; but what picture of death did that scourge present to be at all compared with the carnage of African Colonization!—During the last 6 months the mortality of 20 per cent. which prevailed was as if this city should loose 48,000 of its inhabitants. In the light of these facts how is it possible for us to desire or promote such emigration! "How or on what authority" the honorable writer could have declared that one half the colonists were slaves liberated by southern masters or could call Liberia "that happy community, now gratefully enjoying the fruits of this enterprise on the coast of Africa," "we have yet to learn." It is not, however, strange, with such facts as these before them, that the poor people of color should be in the habit of calling the Colonization Society "that bloody institution."

There is entirely too much "kindred sympathy and cordial co-operation" with oppression in this composition of the U. S. Senator. It is indeed only necessary to read his paper to be convinced of the deadly nature of the Colonization leaven which can thus pervert the good and estrange the virtuous to be the defenders of oppression, and we can the more readily trace the identity of that influence which "hath leavened the whole lump." Nor are we surprised that such an influence should move the mass of profligacy and sin to aid "the benevolent objects of the Colonization Society" by physical force, by scurrilous abuse, by outrageous falsehood, and by mobs—when we see in the intelligent and pious such lamentable effects.

The very desire "to find common ground" with those who trade in sinews, is disgraceful in its own nature. We are not advocates of an impolitic, gratuitous and abusive manner, but we would rather be guilty of all this than find ourselves yielding high moral principles for the sake of harmony. Let us be *first* pure, then peaceable. We protest against any common ground from which our oppressed brethren are to be excluded.

The only common ground acknowledged, is that upon which *all* the inhabitants of this land ought to unite, namely, "Whatsoever ye would that men should do unto you, do ye even so unto them." Now the uniform declaration of the colored people is that they are unwilling to leave this land in which they were born, where they have many dear attachments and where though they have been persecuted, they would rather live than to go to a barbarous and a deadly shore, shut out from the privileges of the gospel and deprived of the countenance, assistance and counsels of many disinterested and kind friends. They hope that the prejudice against them on account of color will be destroyed as Christians learn more and more to realize that God has made of one blood all the nations of men to dwell on the face of the whole earth They feel confident that expatriation is impracticable, and they would rather suffer extermination than leave the land of their fathers, for whose liberty many of them fought both in the war of the revolution and in the last war, and received too the high-

est approbation of the present Chief Magistrate for their valor and patriotism. The single fact that colored Americans so love their country that they will not leave it, settles the whole question and renders it unnecessary to resort to other arguments, equally unanswerable.

A respectable colored man gave the following reason why he did not think he would be better off in Africa than in this country—That as they were Christians here and civilized men, and yet treated colored persons so badly as to wish them to leave the country of their birth, he was sure that the barbarous and heathen nations would be likely to be more cruel still, and instead of desiring them to emigrate to a foreign land would very likely drive them back into the sea, "to be cleared of them."

It seems almost idle to answer the often repeated assertion of the Colonizationists, that Maryland, Virginia, Kentucky, and Tennessee are becoming favorable to abolition: for there is not a particle of evidence that colonization influence which has for seventeen years prevailed among the people of these states has kindled in them the smallest interest in such guilty and "ill-judged measures." On the contrary, the argument of Mr. Cropper has never been answered, and perhaps never will be. We believe that if a change in favor of liberty can be proved to have taken place within the period of the existence of the Colonization Society, its advocates will not be backward to claim the honor of it. We too, cheerfully grant, that *whatever change* of feeling and opinion has taken place in the country, is very much if not entirely the effect of their principles, for during the last 17 years they have occupied "common ground" with the slaveholders, to the virtual exclusion of all genuine Abolitionists.

In the year 1790, says the venerable Mr. Cropper, there were 59,000 free blacks in America. Emancipation was then going on with considerable rapidity, and feelings were cherished then, similar to those entertained in South America, and various other places; so that in 1810, the number had augmented to 186,000. Had emancipation got on in the same ratio, the ensuing 20 years, there ought to have been 594,000 free blacks; but when the census of 1830 was made up, we found the number to be only 319,000; and, consequently, owing to some change of feeling in America, there are 265,000 negroes now left in slavery, who would otherwise have been set free. Now it is a singular fact, that during the last 20 years, the American Colonization Society has been in operation.

We therefore believe that the actual influence of this scheme has been in all respects unfavorable to the cause of human liberty.

We all know what arguments were brought against West India emancipation by the Duke of Wellington and his tory adherents, from the fact that the people of the United States regarded the blacks as inferior and destined to perpetual degradation. Is it not painful to see free America giving lessons on the *necessity* of political tyranny even to the inveterate tories and tyrants of Europe.?

That the boasted law of Maryland (in favor of colonization) is calculated to drive colonization by force, or in other words, to expatriate the free by violence, and that the managers of the American Colonization Society are officially implicated in the cruelty of its provisions, we think the following evidence will fully show.

At the last meeting of the American Colonization Society, on motion of the Hon. Mr. Chambers, it was *Resolved*, That the Society view, with the highest gratification, the continued efforts of the State of Maryland to accomplish her patriotic and benevolent system in regard to her colored population, and that the late appropriation by that State, of two hundred thousand dollars in aid of African colonization, is hailed by the friends of the system, as as a bright example to other states.

In support of this resolution, Mr. C., among other things said,

"Sir, I reside in a slave State, alive to all the jealousies which a consideration of this kind must excite. No other state would be more sensitive at the slightest effort to withdraw from its own peculiar cognizance, the exclusive and entire control of all questions touching this species of property; none will go farther to sustain her right to such exclusive jurisdiction; and no citizen of the State would vindicate that claim with more untiring zeal and firmness, than the individual now before you. But, sir, the apprehension is groundless—your constitution avows, and your whole history proves that no such purpose exists. The Society interferes with the rights and interests of no one. Who has ever claimed for the Society or for the National Government, operating through its agency, the right to interfere with, or control State legislation on the subject of slavery? There may be individuals in this Society, as there are out of it, who intemperately urge the subject of emancipation, and would desire to see it advance quite beyond the limits of prudence and safety. Such enthusiasts may be willing to make any institution, society, or government, auxiliary to their wild and mischievous projects; but the Colonization Society, is not responsible for these intemperate fanatics: nor does it countenance or encourage their schemes:—It interferes in no way with the rights or the interests of owners of slaves. That in the prosecution of its legitimate operations, and by affording the prospect of comfort and respectability to the man of color, it may exert an influence altogether of a moral nature favorable to emancipation, with a view to colonization, may be admitted. It imposes no restraints, makes no demands, assails no man's rights, nor seeks to invade the volition which he indulges, or to disturb the enjoyment of what the laws secure to him. Its sole and single object is the colonization of the free, and with their full consent."

It will be plainly seen by the following extract from the Maryland Act, how the "full consent" of the "*free*" colored people is to be obtained. The most "benevolent" thing in the law appears to be this : it gives the slave the alternative of remaining in bond-

age if he does not *consent* to be an exile from his native land !

———— " or *in case the said person or persons shall refuse to be so removed,* then it shall be the duty of the said board of managers to remove the said person or persons to such other place or places beyond the limits of this state, as the said board shall approve of, and the said person or persons shall be willing to go to, and to provide for their reception and support at such place or places as the said board may think necessary, until they shall be able to provide for themselves out of any money that may be earned by their hire, or may be otherwise provided for that purpose, and in case the said person or persons shall refuse to be removed to any place beyond the limits of this state, and shall persist in remaining therein, then it shall be the duty of the said board to inform the sheriff of the county wherein such person or persons may be, of such refusal, and it shall thereupon be the duty of the said sheriff forthwith to arrest or cause to to be arrested the said person or persons so refusing to emigrate from this state, and transport the said person or persons beyond the limits of this state ; and all slaves shall be capable of receiving manumission, for the purpose of removal as aforesaid, with their consent, of whatever age, any law to the contrary notwithstanding."

Virginia has either driven away or kidnapped and sold into slavery many of her free negroes, and the same malign influence, so active among these states has disgraced Ohio, and stained her statute book with laws passed to expel the unfortunate yet industrious and inoffensive colored people who had fled to her for protection. What infamy ! for a Christian people thus to trample on distressed innocence. Besides the pusilanimity of the persecution, it violates the express injunction of God—" Thou shalt not deliver unto his master the servant which is escaped from his master unto thee : *He shall dwell with thee even among you in that place which he shall choose in one of thy gates, where it liketh him best :* thou shalt not oppress him." Deut. xxiii : 15—16.—The rapid progress of this desire to expatriate the colored people, has originated undeniably in the colonization scheme—It was never heard of before that project was set on foot.

The State of Connecticut, many of whose citizens are an ornament to human nature and the glory of our land, has become conspicuous for her legislation against the instruction of the colored people, and in the chivalrous war recently waged against a devoted and " glorious woman," for daring to teach poor females of the proscribed hue, certain eminent colonizationists, *worthy fellow citizens of Benedict Arnold,* have led the gallant assault.

It is not a little surprising that the Colonizationists think it undoubted that all the manumissions which have taken place during the last 17 years are the legitimate results of their "benevolent operations," while they consider it quite certain that these cruel, disgraceful, and unconstitutional persecutions of the free colored citizens of this land unknown as they were until the colonization era, were the results of other causes and have no relation whatever to any influence exerted by that illustrious Institution.

It is a recorded fact that 300 poor free negroes principally women and children (or as the Sec. of the Col. Soc. elegantly expresses the idea, " families without their male heads") were transported to Liberia by the Managers of the Am. Col. Society, and who were yet "coerced away as truly as if it had been done with a CARTWHIP." One of these individuals, a man, declares that he was several times called out of his bed at midnight in Virginia for no other offence than

" The curl of his hair and the hue of his skin."
Whittier.

and suffered in all the infliction of 300 stripes with the cartwhip before he was made " willing" to leave what *he consider-ed* his native land and all he held dear to go to a dark, inhospitable, and deadly shore.

" *There is an immense aggregate of blame some-where ; and I want to find out where it belongs, and put it there. Two years ago, I warned the managers against this Virginia business. And yet they sent out two ship loads of VAGABONDS not fit to go to such a place, and that were COERCED away as truly as if it had been done with a CARTWHIP. Sir, we are not only embarrassed, but we are BRO-KEN.*" Speech of Rev. J. R. Breckinridge.

It is a fact that this honest and manly speech has been suppressed in the publication made in the African Repository of the proceedings at the annual meeting of the Colonization Society recently held at Washington.

" So I returned and considered all the oppressions that are done under the sun, and 'behold the tears of such as were oppressed and they had no *comforter*, and on the side of the oppressor there was power, and they had no comforter."

We regret to have to remark that the writer of the review has been betrayed by the spirit of Colonization into the use of all the epithets and the gross and unmerited abuse which characterize the tactics of his party. We will not hesitate to say boldly, while we particularly regret that the censure falls where it does that his

language is decidedly censurable as un-gentlemanly and unkind. Was it argument, manners, Christian decorum, or even manliness, toward his adversaries in this discussion to use such epithets as the following ;

" Downright madness,"
" Regardless of consequences,"
" Rash and dangerous spirit,"
" Threatens ruin and destruction,"
" Wild on rushing of fanaticism."

We can freely forgive Mr. F. for the public abuse of the Abolitionists which won him the applause of the thousands at the Colonization meeting at the Masonic Hall, but we suspect that it did not win him the peace of his own conscience. That gentleman well knew that the excitement which was got up on that occasion by the vilest press in this city or the land, had gone so far that dirks were drawn and pistols cocked to seek the heart's blood of men who had often sat with him at the table of their common Redeemer. Yet at this moment were terms of abuse poured forth from his mouth calculated to incense the already inflamed and ignorant multitude. Thus adding coals to the fire of a persecution which he may yet live to regret he did not strive to quench.

Oh! it is a bad augury when the sympathies are on the wrong side ! It were better " to have allowed something to the spirit of liberty," than thus to have set on the dogs of persecution and lighted the flames of discord, against brethren !

But the holy cause of liberty is worth the contest. Let none join the battle of the free whose hearts do not welcome the shock. It is the cause of God—it is the sacrifice of the Highest—" to undo the heavy burdens, to let the oppressed go free, and to break every yoke." The consciences of men are with us, the indications of Divine Providence are favorable, the cause is onward. The Declaration of Independence furnishes us our " abstractions."— The word of God teaches us our duties, marks out our paths, and puts the words into our mouths, " Let my people go." The Constitution of our Union is framed with a view to liberty and not to slavery, and the hearts of freemen cannot forever slumber over the wrongs of the bleeding, the destitute and the oppressed.

Indeed we are disposed to entreat our " respected friends " the Colonizationists no longer "to stand in the breach for the slaveholder to keep off the Abolitionists,"* but take the great lesson on "abstract rights" which the word of God teaches, the voice of conscience reiterates, and which the thunders of Divine vengeance will yet vindicate, unless we repent and forsake our sins.

We rejoice at the protestation of the Reviewer, that if the Colonization Society "soothed the conscience of the slaveholder and contented him in the enjoyment of slaves as property," he would be among the first to forsake it. While we have great confidence in the sincerity of this declaration, we are not disposed to admit that the gentleman is altogether an unprejudiced judge. He is to some extent committed. All his writings and speeches on the subject betray a spirit of excited personal feeling amounting even to intolerance which indicates too strong an interest in the cause of the Society, to favor a dispassionate and sound judgment. The native of a slave state, and having for a number of years been accustomed to occupy "common ground" with the slaveholder, we sincerely think that it is expecting too much of humanity to anticipate from this gentleman a perfectly unprejudiced mind.

If, however, we shall succeed in establishing the charge that the American Colonization Society "soothes the conscience of the slaveholder, &c." we call on the magnanimity of the New-Jersey Senator, for the sake of the most holy cause of freedom, to make the sacrifice of his personal feelings and to put the weight of his name and character, his talents and his purse on the side of bleeding humanity. Instead of saying that "nine-tenths of the evils of slavery are imaginary," a sentiment highly derogatory to a Christian and a republican, and untrue in fact, let his voice ring through the halls of his country's legislature and jurisprudence, with the praises of liberty and the high duties and destinies of American Christians.

Abolitionists in general regard the person more highly and more kindly than they do the sentiments of this eminent individual. They do not charge him with intending a conspiracy against the poor and needy, but they do believe him to have been

misled by the craftiness and double intentions of men of a different spirit from himself. Let him not, however, regard these concessions to his motives as an attempt to fawn upon his person or to compromise the glorious and heavenly principles of Abolition. The truth is immutable! if we are not on that rock—it will not be moved for our convenience—if we are there, we will *in principles* be uncompromising.— Truth holds no parley with error, nor can she. But while *uncompromising in* principle we desire to be *courteous in manner.* Our aim has been not to be overawed by greatness, by influence, or by talents, but to speak the truth in love. Relying with unaffected and unshaken confidence on the word of God, we wait with happy anticipations its destined triumph. We have aimed not to return railing for railing while we have attempted fearlessly to discuss principles most dear to our hearts. With what success we shall not however presume to judge.

While we hope that the evidence already laid before the public, and the facts constantly developing which can be no longer so ungraciously attributed to slander, may turn the minds of all good men in the Colonization cause we fear that party spirit and self-love may deter many from the manly acknowledgement of error—the ingenuousness of honorable confession. We have indeed sometimes thought that some persons whom we regard as good men, when actuated by party spirit and pride of opinion, would rather fight against God than publicly to confess an error or abandon a wrong enterprise once undertaken.

The African Repository and Colonial Journal, published by order of the Managers of the American Colonization Society, is the only source from which we desire the privilege of bringing our proofs. The Repository contains the addresses of auxiliaries, the speeches of distinguished members, editorial notices, and original matters. But that the chief moral influence of the Journal resides in the speeches, we have no hesitation whatever to declare. If the speeches exert no moral influence why are they published? If they do, the publishers are liable for the character of that influence. The correctness of this principle they have practically acknowledged by accompanying the publication of an abolitionist member with a disclaimer

* Rev. Mr. Breckinridge's col. speech.

of its doctrines; and by actually suppressing the publication of abolition speeches, while their open and ready page is unhesitatingly and unblushingly given to the defenders of oppression. To what end do they protest that they are not liable for the opinions of individual members? No one ever held them so. But they *are* liable for what they publish, be it what it may, no matter who its author is. The very apology is a tacit admission that their publications are of evil tendency. While they profess to be a benevolent society and the friends of the black man, they print and circulate vilifications of his character, call him a "vagabond," "dull as a brutish beast," "abandoned," and "a nuisance." Blessed be the God of the oppressed—their defender is mighty, and he hears the groans of the poor, and will avenge them who are trodden under foot.

Suppose the "Literary and Theological Review," for instance, to publish this very article, would the hon. Senator hold it irresponsible? Surely not,—and therefore its Editor has already refused to admit any thing in answer to the Reviewer. Or suppose it to publish the vile tirades of Atheists against Christianity for the sake of finding "common ground" with these enemies of God, and then hold itself irresponsible, saying that it was a matter of individual opinion only—the writer solely accountable, would not the common sense of men protest against them as false or mad? Hear then the proofs!—

"Slavery is an evil entailed upon the slave holders which they must suffer whether they will or not." Af. Rep. vol. v. p. 179.

"There is no ground for fear on the part of our southern friends, we hold slaves as we hold their other property, SACRED. Let not this slander be repeated." Af. Rep. vol. 1. p. 283.

But now Abolitionists are slandered for charging them on their own authority with soothing the conscience of the slaveholder by calling the wrongs which they inflict on the helpless, rights. "Wo unto them that call evil good and good evil; that put darkness for light and light for darkness; that put bitter for sweet and sweet for bitter!"

"And the slave holder so far from having just cause to complain of the colonization society has reason to congratulate himself that in this institution a channel is opened up in which the public feeling and public action can flow on without doing violence to his rights. The closing of this channel might be calamitous to the slave holder

beyond his conceptions, for the stream of benevolence which now flows so innocently in it might then break out in forms even far more disastrous than Abolition Societies and all their kindred and ill-judged measures." Af. Rep. vol. vi. p. 363.

"To the slave holder who had charged upon them the wicked design of interferring with the rights of property under the specious pretext of removing a vicious and dangerous free population, they address themselves in a tone of conciliation and sympathy. We know your rights, say they, and we respect them." Af. Rep. vol. vii. p. 100.

These publications speaking to the slaveholder in tones of "sympathy and conciliation," and acknowledging the right "of enacting iniquity by law," of retaining in bondage men originally stolen, plundering the laborer of his hire, of carrying on the nefarious trade "in the bodies and souls of men," aye, and holding these rights "SACRED," without doubt must tend to quiet the conscience of the oppressor and to perpetuate oppression.

Thus to denounce as "ill-judged" abolition ocieties and their measures, to call God's oppressed people vagabonds and nuisances, to declare beings purchased by the blood of Christ, property, while professing to be their friends, to consider slavery a curse entailed upon the master "which he must suffer whether he will or not," to fawn on the haughty tyrant, to pander to his base passions, is not this enough to disgust any human being with their professions of benevolence? Is it not enough to establish beyond dispute that the tendency of the American Colonization Society "is to soothe the conscience of the slaveholder, to content him with the enjoyment of slaves as property, and thus to retard the advance of free principles?"

We pray God that one like the writer of the review whose very instincts have heretofore always been on the side of virtue and holiness may be saved from the ruin and infamy of this moral whirlpool, whose outer edies, though serene as the undimpled lake, conduct only to the more certain ruin the hapless bark that trusts its deceitful edge. A Society of whose principles we must be permitted to exclaim, "O my soul come not thou into their secret; unto their assembly mine honor be not thou united!" **A. L. C.**

New-York, April 9, 1834.

THE AMERICAN SLAVE-TRADE.

We have heard it stated that about 2,000 slaves are to be sold in New-Orleans during the present month! Yet good people celebrate the abolition of the slave-trade, and flatter themselves that slavery is dying away quite as fast as is, on the whole, desirable!—*Emancipator.*

We extract the following from the spirited preamble of the Constitution of the Anti-Slavery Society of Lane Seminary. The whole should appear if our limits would permit.

PREAMBLE TO THE CONSTITUTION
OF THE ANTI-SLAVERY SOCIETY
OF LANE SEMINARY.

Believing it incumbent upon all, who associate for the advancement of the general good, to state explicitly their *object,* their *reasons* for seeking it, the *means* proposed for its accomplishment, and the *principles* which are to control their action ; we make the following exposition.

I. *Object.* Our object is the immediate emancipation of the whole colored race, within the United States; the emancipation of the slave from the oppression of the master, the emancipation of the free colored man from the oppression of public sentiment, and the elevation of both to an intellectual, moral, and political equality with the whites.

II. *Reasons.* We advocate the immediate emancipation of the slaves for the following reasons.

1. He is constituted, by God, a moral agent, the keeper of his own happiness, the executive of his own powers, the accountable arbiter of his own choice ; personal ownership, his birthright, unforfeited and inalienable ; liberty and the pursuit of happiness, chartered rights, inherited from his Maker and guarantied by all the laws of his being.

Slavery robs him of himself, body and soul ; and though he is immortal, created in God's image, the purchase of a Savior's blood, visited by the Holy Ghost, and invited to citizenship with angels, and to fellowship with God, it drags him to the shambles, and sells him like a beast ; goads him to incessant and unrequited toil— withholds from him legal protection in all his personal rights and social relations, and abandons to caprice, cupidity, passion, and lust all that is dear in human well-being. It crushes the upward tendencies of intellect, makes the acquisition of knowledge a crime, and consigns the mind to famine.

It stifles the moral affections, represses the innate longings of the spirit, paralyzes conscience, turns hope to despair, and kills the soul.

As a *system,* slavery annihilates the marriage relation, exposes to pollution a million of fe-

males, and makes stripes or death the penalty of resistance. It tears asunder parents and children, husbands and wives, sisters and brothers, and consigns them to distant and hopeless bondage—desolate and heart-broken.

2. It excites the enmity of the oppressed against the oppressors, goads to desperation and revenge, provokes insurrection, and perils public safety.

3. It *tends* to blunt the sensibilities of all who exercise authority over the slave, and to transform them into tyrants. The whole process is drawn to the life by President Jefferson, who lived and died a slave-holder.

"The parent storms : the child looks on, catches the lineaments of wrath, puts on the same airs in the circle of smaller slaves, gives loose to the worst of passions, and thus nursed, educated, and daily exercised in tyranny, cannot fail to be stamped with odious peculiarities. The man must be a prodigy, who can retain his morals and manners undepraved in such circumstances."

4. It is the occasion of deep moral pollution to the families of slave-holders—a pollution mingling with the first thoughts, spreading wider and wider with the increase of years, and naturally resulting from contact with those whom legalized oppression renders liable to prostitution.

5. It cripples the energies of the whole nation, entails poverty and decay upon the states which uphold it, foments division and alienation in our public councils, and puts in jeopardy the existence of the union.

6. It is opposed to the genius of our government, makes our constitution a mockery, converts our national declaration into a rhapsody of sentimentalism, convicts us of hypocrisy at the bar of the world, neutralizes the power of our example as a nation, and checks the progress of republican principles.

7. It opposes an insuperable barrier to the conversion of the world, is a standing libel upon the avowed influence of the Christian religion, and heathen nations will not be slow to read the disgraceful commentary. It sanctions as a principle, the absurd and wicked prejudice against color ; and thus not only dooms to despair the unfortunate millions of colored people in our own country, but would, if carried out, paralyze all missionary effort, and shut the bowels of mercy forever against the world.

8. Slavery exposes the nation to the judgments of God. We adopt and reiterate the memorable sentiment of Jefferson : "I tremble when I reflect that God is just, and that his justice cannot sleep forever ;" and we urge an immediate repentance of the sin which provokes his wrath, and an immediate breaking off from it by righteousness.

We advocate the emancipation of the free colored man from the oppression of public sentiment and civil disabilities :

Because color, condition of birth, poverty,

calamity, and complicated wo, deserve no punishment. It is the part of a tyrant to inflict penalties upon the innocent; and when the victim is powerless, friendless, long-oppressed, and already heart-broken, it is the part of a fiend. The colored race in this country are the objects of scorn and persecution. Impoverished, disfranchised, and trodden into the dust, they faint under the inflictions of a public sentiment, "which exalteth itself above all that is called God."

We cannot hold our peace, while these, our brethren, are immolated upon the altar of prejudice and pride. They need our sympathies and our aid, *and they shall have them.*

We repudiate the doctrine that they cannot be elevated in this country. We believe they *can* be elevated, we believe they *will* be, and that "their redemption draweth nigh."

We invite public attention to the following letter from a student in the Lane Theological Seminary, recently published in the Western Recorder. Humanity sleeps over the wrongs of TWO MILLIONS OF STOLEN MEN, because the FACTS are hid. We hear not the slaves, because they are *slaves!*—And the smooth tongue of the manstealer—the wealthy, polite, and *generous* manstealer—has silvered over the abominable system till we, gentle and easy souls, suppose its horrors are "*imaginary.*"— Let us peruse and weigh these penitential confessions.

LANE SEMINARY, MARCH 6, 1834.

MR. EDITOR—We have just closed one of the most interesting debates that I have ever attended. For eighteen evenings we have discussed the subject of abolition and colonization; and what is very remarkable, not the least unkind or even unpleasant feeling has been excited. There has been no shuffling, no quibbling, no striving to evade the truth; but, on the other hand, candor, fairness and manhood, have characterized the whole debate. Every argument has been fairly weighed; every objection duly considered. Neither side finds any fault with the other. All are satisfied that justice has been done.

The subject was divided into two questions. First—Ought the people of the slave-holding states to abolish slavery immediately?

Second—Are the doctrines, tendencies and measures of the American Colonization Society, and the influence of its principal supporters, such as to render it worthy of the patronage of the Christian public?

The speakers were from Virginia, Alabama, Kentucky, Louisiana, Arkansas Territory, Ohio, Pennsylvania, New-York and Connecticut; most of them the sons of slave-holders.

The debate was opened by Mr. ——, of Alabama. He commenced by asking this question—"What is slavery?" "Before we can prescribe a remedy," said he, "we must understand the disease. We must know what we are attempting to cure before we give the medicine." I was rejoiced to hear such a beginning from the son of a slave-holder; for I had longed to learn the true condition of the slave. And I had no doubt but that the feeling of the abolitionists on the subject of slavery, "was the poetry of philanthropy,"* and that "nine-tenths of the horrors of slavery were imaginary."†

Mr. —— proceeded to give us facts illustrating slavery, and its effects on the social and political relations; facts illustrating the kind disposition of the slaves, and their gratitude for favors. He ridiculed the idea of its being dangerous to emancipate them immediately; then referred us to facts in point, and closed by giving us his hearty assent to the doctrines of immediate emancipation, as defined by the Emancipator, viz :—

" By immediate emancipation, we do not mean, that the slaves shall be turned loose upon the nation, to roam as vagabonds or aliens; nor, that they shall be instantly invested with all political rights and privileges; nor, that they shall be expelled from their native clime, as the price and condition of their freedom. But we mean, that instead of being under the unlimited control of a few irresponsible masters, they shall really receive the protection of law : That the power which is now vested in every slave-holder to rob them of their just dues, to drive them into the fields like beasts, to lacerate their bodies, to sell the husband from the wife, the wife from the husband, and children from their parents, shall instantly cease : That the slaves shall be employed as free laborers, fairly compensated, and protected in their earnings : That they shall be placed under a benevolent and disinterested supervision, which shall secure to them the right to obtain secular and religious knowledge, to worship God according to the dictates of their consciences, to accumulate wealth, and to seek an intellectual and moral elevation."

He occupied nearly three evenings. When speaking of the cruelties practised upon the slave, he said—"At our house it is so common to hear their screams from a neighboring plantation, that we think nothing of it. The overseer of this plantation told me one day, he laid a young woman over a log, and beat her so severely that she was soon after delivered of a dead child. A bricklayer, a neighbor of ours, owned a very smart young negro man, who ran away; but was caught. When his master got him home, he stripped him naked, tied him up by his hands, in plain sight and hearing of the academy and the public green, so high that his feet could not touch the ground; then tied them together, and put a long board between his legs to keep him steady. After preparing him in this way, he took a paddle, bored it full of holes, and commenced beating him with it. He continued it leisurely all day. At night his flesh was literally pounded to a jelly. It was two weeks before he was able to walk. No one took any notice of it. No one thought any wrong was done."

He stated many more facts of a similar kind. It will be recollected that he was attempting to give a fair *expose* of slavery. "And (said he) lest any one should think that *in general* the slaves are well treated, and these are the exceptions, let me be distinctly understood:— *Cruelty* is the *rule*, and *kindness* the *exception.*"

This was assented to and corroborated by all from the slave-holding states. And to show its truth, I will here introduce a few facts, as related by individuals from different parts of the country.

Mr. ——, from Kentucky, who came here a colonizationist and a slave-holder, but has since turned abolitionist and emancipated his slaves, said—"Cruelties are so common, I hardly know what to relate. But one fact occurs to me just at this time that happened in the village where I live. The circumstances are these. A colored man, a slave, ran away. As he was crossing Kentucky river, a white man, who suspected him, attempted to stop him. The negro resisted. The white man procured help, and finally succeeded in securing him. He then wreaked his vengeance on him for resisting—flogging him till he was not able to walk. They then put him on a horse, and came on with him ten miles to Nicholasville. When they entered the village, it was noticed that he sat upon his horse like a drunken man. It was a very hot day; and whilst they were taking some refreshment, the negro sat down upon the ground under the shade. When they ordered him to go, he made several efforts before he could get up; and when he attempted to mount the horse, his strength was entirely insufficient. One of the men struck him, and with an oath ordered him to get on the horse without any more fuss. The negro staggered back a few steps, fell down, and died. I do not know as any notice was ever taken of it."

Mr. ——, of Virginia, amongst others, related the following :—"I frequently saw the mistress of the family beat the woman who performed the kitchen work, with a stick two feet and a half long, and nearly as thick as my wrist; striking her over the head, and across the small of the back, as she was bent over at her work, with as much spite as you would a snake, and for what I should consider no offence at all. There lived in this same family a young man, a slave, who was in the habit of running away. He returned one time after a week's absence. The master took him into the barn, stripped him entirely naked, tied him up by his hands so high that he could not reach the floor, tied his feet together, and put a small rail between his legs, so that he could not avoid the blows, and commenced whipping him. He told me that he gave him five hundred lashes. At any rate, he was covered with wounds from head to foot. Not a place as big as my hand but what was cut. Such things as these are perfectly common all over Virginia; at least so far as I am acquainted. Generally, planters avoid punishing their slaves before strangers."

Mr. ——, of Missouri, amongst others, related the following :—"A young woman who was generally very badly treated, after receiving a more severe whipping than usual, ran away. In a few days she came back, and was sent into the field to work. At this time the garment next her skin was stiff like a scab, from the running of the sores made by the whipping. Towards night, she told her master that she was sick, and wished to go to the house. She went; and as soon as she reached it laid down on the floor exhausted. The mistress asked her what the matter was? She made no reply. She asked again; but received no answer. 'I'll see,' said she, 'if I can't make you speak.' So taking the tongs, she heated them red hot, and put them upon the bottoms of her feet; then upon her legs and body; and, finally, in a rage, took hold of her throat. This had the desired effect. The poor girl faintly whispered, 'Oh, misse, don't—I am most gone;' and expired."

We want no other commentary on the state of feeling in that community than this. The woman yet lives there, and owns slaves.

I am aware that it will be said, this is not a fair picture of slavery. But, sir, if I can judge from the conversation of gentlemen who have lived and been brought up amongst it, or from the testimony of respectable emancipated negroes, I know the picture has never yet been presented to the public, in all its ugliness. Such facts as *these* are as common to them as household affairs; and so common are they in the community where they occur, that little notice is taken of them. They produce no effect upon the public heart. They enlist no sympathy. They call up no pity. I do not mean to say, that every individual slave-holder treats his slaves cruelly. I know that there are exceptions. But it will be readily admitted by all, that the system of slavery tolerates it, and that the slave has no security, and can have no redress.

But to be short. As the debate progressed, objection after objection was cleared up; argument after argument overthrown; and on the ninth evening, when the question was taken, every individual who had heard the debate voted in the affirmative, except three or four from non-slave-holding states, who declined voting.

After listening nine evenings to this discussion, and most of the time to those who were from the bosom of slavery, and who understood well its genius, I was irresistibly driven to this conclusion:—That there is no subject before the American people, so little understood at the north, as the subject of slavery—particularly its horrors, its miseries, and its cruelties. These are not dreamed of there. And so much pains has been taken to varnish over the truth, that the general impression is, that the slave is better off than the free black. An opinion more inconsistent with truth could not well be entertained.

Another equally erroneous and as generally received opinion is, that the slaves could not take care of themselves, if they were set free. As fact is better than theory to answer such an objection, I will here state one as related by Mr. ——, of Virginia. "Several years ago," said he, "I knew a slave who bought himself, and paid twelve hundred dollars. Some time after this, when coming up from Lynchburg, I happened to stay at the same place with this colored man. I found on inquiry, that by his industry and honesty he had secured quite a respectable property; that he was then driving a team of five horses, that belonged to himself; and that he was esteemed and employed as much as any man in the town in his line of business."

This is not a solitary case. Many of a similar kind have come under my own observation. I am acquainted with nearly fifty colored gentlemen in the city of Cincinnati, who have paid from $200 to $1200 for themselves or families, and are now living in a style that would not disgrace any man. They are as honest, as upright, and as industrious, as any community of men with whom I am acquainted. Beside, it may be safely said, that two-thirds of the colored families in this city are laying up money to buy their friends who are in slavery.

But suppose the slaves cannot take care of themselves, if set free; what is the argument? Is it perpetual servitude? If not, then slavery is the school to prepare them for freedom, and their masters and overseers are the tutors. And pray how long will it be before they can graduate with all the honors and learning that can be obtained in such an institution? Will another century roll away, and find them still incompetent? No doubt it will, sir; for their tutors, kind souls! are quite unwilling to crowd them in their studies. But, Mr. Editor, what distinguishes our happy country from heathen lands? Is it not our Christian, our benevolent and our charitable institutions? Is it not, that for our unfortunate deaf and dumb we have asylums? for our halt and lame and sick and insane we have hospitals? for our poor and helpless we have alms-houses? What provision, then, should be made for our more unfortunate and doubly miserable colored brethren, who have not mind enough to take care of themselves,

and whose very weakness and ignorance render them still more the objects of our pity? What provision has been made? O, tell it not in Gath—America has provided for her poor and powerless, chains and slavery!

The second question was also debated nine evenings; and when the ayes and nays were taken, only one said aye, and he was from a non-slave-holding state. It is hardly necessary for me to add, though it is a part of the object for which I write, that I have altered my opinion both in regard to the Abolition and Colonization Societies. And as I have a large number of friends who take your paper, and in it have seen my endorsement to the colonization scheme, as President of the Colonization Society of Oneida Institute, and who know that I have talked upon the subject both in public and in private; and that I have written letters to promote its interests, and given and begged money to help forward its operations; I wish them to know that I disclaim all connection with it; that I believe its doctrines, tendencies and measures are calculated to subvert the best interests of the colored people, to strengthen prejudice, to quiet the conscience of the slave-holder, and put far off the day of emancipation. I can abundantly prove all this, and much more. But the length of this communication forbids. I will only state one or two facts, illustrating the effects of the two societies.

Conversing with a slave holder a few weeks since, he said—"I always knew that slavery was wrong in the abstract; but I think it is right under existing circumstances. At any rate the Colonization Society says so; and its agents preach it where I live; and all my neighbors believe it. We all belong to the Society, and give money to it. I have regularly given ten dollars per year to help remove slavery." So far his views were formed by colonization influence; and no doubt he was truly benevolent in giving his money to remove slavery in this way; for he thought it was the only way. He says now, "That the $10 a year which I gave to the Colonization Society, was but a quietus to my conscience; and I thought I had a right to hold slaves indefinitely. But I find that the blacks have rights, as well as the whites, and we are invading them. I can give no more money to the Colonization Society, for I believe it is doing a vast deal of harm."

One individual, a student, came here a slave-holder and a colonizationist. He depended upon his slaves for support while obtaining his education. But as soon as he was convinced that it was wrong to hold slaves under existing circumstances, he went home and set them all free, and put them in a course of education, and now applies all their wages to their own benefit. This fact, politic, wise, and benevolent, developes the principles of abolition, and exhibits the genuine philanthropy of the system of immediate emancipation. Your's, &c.

AUGUSTUS WATTLES.

☞ We are much gratified to be able to lay before the readers of the Reporter, the following interesting communication. Who would believe that a serious attempt is now making to deprive every alleged fugitive from slavery, arrested in this state, of a TRIAL BY JURY ? Such is the fact. ☞

Bedford, N. Y. 19th April, 1834.

Dear Sir—Incessant occupation since I returned from New-York, has prevented me from complying before this, with your request to furnish you with certain particulars relative to slavery in the District of Columbia. In the enclosed paper, you will find some interesting facts. With much respect, I remain your obedient servant,   WILLIAM JAY.
Elizur Wright, Jr.

FACTS RELATIVE TO SLAVERY IN THE DISTRICT OF COLUMBIA.

On the 1st August, 1826, a notice appeared in the National Intelligencer at Washington, from the Marshall of the D. of C., that a negro named Gilbert Horton, and claiming to be free, had been committed to jail in Washington city as a *runaway*, and unless his *owner* proved property, and took him away by a certain time, the negro would be sold *"for his jail fees and other expenses, as the law directs."* Horton was a native of Westchester Co. N. Y., and known there to be free. A public meeting of the inhabitants of the county was called, to take measures for his liberation. The meeting was held 30th August, 1826, and a series of resolutions were unanimously adopted ; one of them calling on the Governor to demand the instant liberation of Horton as a *free citizen* of the State of New-York. Two of the resolutions were as follows :

"Resolved, That the law under which Horton has been imprisoned, and by which a free citizen without evidence of crime, and without trial by jury, may be condemned to servitude for life, is repugnant to our republican institutions, and revolting to justice and humanity ; and that the representatives from this State in Congress are requested to use their endeavors to procure its repeal."

"Resolved, That a committee be appointed to prepare and present to the citizens of this county for their signatures, a petition to Congress for the immediate abolition of Slavery in the District of Columbia."

Governor De Witt Clinton in compliance with the request of the meeting, wrote to the President of the United States, forwarding evidence of Horton's freedom, and requiring his immediate liberation " as a free man and a *citizen*." Horton was released before the receipt of the Governor's letter. The Westchester petition was signed by 800, and presented to the House of Representatives.

In Dec. 1826, Mr. Ward, representative in Congress from Westchester, introduced a resolution calling on the committee for the D. of C. to inquire whether there was any law in the district authorizing the imprisonment of a free person of color, and his sale as an unclaimed slave for his *jail fees.* The resolution was adopted after much opposition by the Southern members. The committee reported that there *was such a law, vir.dicated* its general policy, but recommended that when the arrested negro was unclaimed he should not be sold, but that the *county* should pay the cost of imprisonment. The people of Georgetown presented *a remonstrance* against this proposition of the committee. The law remained unchanged, and *so remains,* it is believed, to this day.

On the 12th Feb. 1827, Mr. Nelson, of the New-York Senate, introduced the following resolutions, which were referred to the committee of the whole, but were not finally acted upon.

"Resolved, As the sense of this legislature, (if the assembly concur therein,) that the existence of slavery at the seat of the government of the U. States, and in a district under its exclusive control, is derogatory to the national character, and inconsistent with the great principles of liberty, justice and humanity, on which the institutions of our republic are founded."

"Resolved, That in the opinion of this legislature,

Congress ought to take such measures as in their wisdom may be deemed advisable for the final abolition of slavery in the District of Columbia, and for the immediate prohibition of the further introduction of slaves into that District."

"Resolved, That his excellency the Governor, be requested to transmit a copy of these resolutions to the President of the United States, and to each of the senators and representatives in Congress from this State."

On the 27th March, 1827, a petition was presented to Congress from 1,000 citizens of the D. of C., praying for a revisal of the slave laws, and an act declaring that all children of slaves to be born in the District after the 4th July, 1828, should be free at the age of 25, and that the importation of slaves into the District might be prohibited. From this petition, the following is an extract : viz.

"A colored man last summer, who stated that he was entitled to freedom, was taken up as a runaway slave and lodged within the jail of Washington city. He was advertised, but no one appearing to claim him, he *was according to law* put up at public auction *for payment of his jail fees, and sold as a slave for life!* He was purchased by a slave trader, who was not required to give security for his remaining in the District, and he was soon after shipped from Alexandria for one of the southern states. Thus was a human being sold into perpetual bondage, at the capital of the freest government on earth, without even a pretence of a trial, or the allegation of a crime."

In 1828, both houses of the Pennsylvania Legislature passed the following resolution by an almost unanimous vote : viz.

"Resolved, That the Senators of this state, in the Senate of the United States, are hereby requested to procure, if practicable, the passage of a law to abolish slavery in the District of Columbia, in such a manner as they may consider consistent with the rights of individuals and the Constitution of the United States."

On the 9th Jan. 1829, the House of Representatives "Resolved, That the committee for the District of Columbia, be instructed to inquire into the expediency of providing by law for the gradual abolition of slavery in the District, in such manner that no individual shall be injured thereby." Ayes 141—Noes 59.

On the 28th Jan. 1829, a committee of the N. York Assembly, to whom had been referred various memorials relating to slavery in the District of Columbia, made a report, in which they remarked, " Your committee cannot but view with astonishment, that in the capital of this free and enlightened country, laws should exist, by which the free CITIZENS of a state are liable, even without trial, and even without the imputation of a crime, to be seized while prosecuting their lawful business, immured in prison, and though free, unless claimed as a slave, to be sold as such for the payment of *jail fees.*" The committee recommended the following resolution : viz.

"Resolved, (if the Senate concur herein,) That the senators of this state, in the Congress of the United States be, and are hereby instructed, and the Repre sentatives of this state are requested, to make every possible exertion to effect the passage of a law for the abolition of slavery in the District of Columbia. The resolution *passed* the Assembly but was not acted upon in the Senate.

In 1831, the corporation of Georgetown passed a law making it penal for a *free negro to receive from the Post-office,* have in his possession, or circulate, any publication or writing of whatever description, of a *seditious* character, and particularly the newspaper called the Liberator, published at Boston. The punishment for each offence to be a fine not exceeding $20, or imprisonment for not more than 30 days. In case of inability to pay the fine and prison fees, the offender to be *sold* as a servant for four months.

AMERICAN

ANTI - SLAVERY REPORTER.

VOL. I.]   JUNE, 1834.   [NO. 6.

ANNIVERSARY OF THE AMERICAN ANTI-SLAVERY SOCIETY.

The week of the anniversaries in New-York is so fully occupied by the public meetings of numerous long established societies, that any new ones must have a strong hold upon the public interest to gain a hearing. Our readers will know how to estimate the excitement in regard to the American Anti-Slavery Society, when they are informed that it absorbed the thought and feeling of the week so largely, that on every occasion, where decorum would permit, it furnished the topic of conversation. It may fairly be said to have swallowed up all the other subjects. Bible and Tract and Missionary Anniversaries were well sustained, as usual, but no one could witness the gathering and dispersing of those assemblies without perceiving that the long neglected cause of the slave was pressing upon the consciences of men, that it was beginning to be felt that all our parade about Bibles and Tracts, Missionaries and Sabbath schools, while no voice is raised in behalf of the oppressed, is in danger of becoming the seal of our hypocrisy instead of our crown of glory.

The limits of this periodical will allow us only to give a few extracts from the interesting speeches and proceedings of the anniversary, and the meetings connected with it.

Among the important measures considered at the business meetings were the following.

THE BIBLE TO BE SENT TO THE SLAVES.

It was proposed to the American Bible Society to raise $20,000 to supply every colored family in the United States with a copy of the Holy Scriptures. The American Anti-Slavery Society pledged itself to contribute $5,000, provided the Bible Society would undertake to carry the measure into effect in two years. This proposal was kindly received by the Bible Society, and referred to a committee which has not yet reported.

It is difficult to see, why in distributing the scriptures we should treat with any more delicacy the wicked prejudices and anti-Christian laws which stand in our way in our own country, than those in Spanish America or in China. Yet in the general effort to supply every family in the United States with the word of God, very little has been said of the appalling fact that the book has been excluded from one sixth of the families in the land. Had a caste been discovered in India so carefully hedged in from all access of saving truth, should we not have heard more of it? Would not our prayers and our sympathies have been invoked in their behalf? Have our missionaries in Syria treated with great delicacy those laws which forbid the people to receive the sacred volume, or hold any intercourse with its teachers?

This measure will bring to the test those who say that the slaves are generally held not as property—not in the spirit of the original kidnappers—but in trust, till they can be *prepared for freedom.* Let the philanthropists of the north say to the people of the south through the American Bible Society, "If as you pretend, you really desire to fit the slave for liberty, here are the means. We do not say, teach them to read and *then* we will give Bibles ; but here are Bibles which they may have to read." If the slaves need "*a preparation for freedom*," what can be a better and safer one than instruction in the word of God?

Let every auxiliary of the Bible Society at the south be proffered Bibles enough to put one in the hands of every five slaves, and then at length we shall see how much regard they have to the command of the Savior to carry the gospel to every creature.

This measure will also bring to the test the confidence of the slave-holders in their own assertion that the Bible sanctions or allows slavery. Are they afraid to put into the hands of the enslaved the authoritative charter of the masters' rights? Have they a virtual "BILL OF SALE FROM THE ALMIGHTY ;" and are they afraid to show it to the party concerned? If ever a falsehood was made palpable, the slave-holders have made theirs so, in refusing the Bible to the slaves, while they pretend to derive their *right* from it. Let those who still believe that the slave-holders really wish to get rid of the system " as soon as it can be done *safely*," take hold of this enterprise.

ABOLITION OF SLAVERY IN THE DISTRICT OF COLUMBIA.

This subject engaged the attention of the Society, and we trust will not be suffered to rest till the object is attained. It was

" Resolved, That the Executive Committee be requested to issue circulars calling on the friends of abolition to petition the state legislatures to pass resolutions, requesting their representatives and instructing their senators in Congress to use their influence in favor of the immediate abolition of slavery in the District of Columbia, and the Territories of the United States, and the entire suppression of the domestic slave-trade."

Let it be remembered that for the continuance of slavery at the seat of the national government *the whole people are responsible*. We have not only a natural right but a legal and constitutional right to say whether, in mockery of our Declaration of Independence, *men* shall be made property of under the windows of the Capitol,— whether the red flag of the slave-trade shall float under the stars and stripes, and the din of the auction of souls, the clank of chains and the wailing of the captives shall mingle forever with the voices of our republican orators.

Most earnestly we entreat all who value justice and the rights of man, to pour in upon the next Congress such notes of remonstrance as shall break the seal which our national hypocrisy has placed upon their ears as well as their lips.

$20,000 TO BE RAISED THIS YEAR.

" Resolved, That the great objects of this Society require funds during the current year to the amount of at least $20,000."

A reformation of manners so surely follows a thorough dissemination of light in regard to truth and duty, that a man might safely guarantee the extinction of slavery within a given short time, provided the pecuniary means were put in his hands of bringing information to all the individuals that make up the community. It would certainly be safe to undertake to set the whole mass of the slaves free at the rate of *one dollar* a piece, for $2,000,000 would saturate the nation with arguments, demonstrating beyond the reach of a doubt, the perfect safety and profitableness, as well as the *duty* of immediate abolition. We believe a far smaller sum will do it : and shall it not be raised? Who is there that would not glory to make himself poor to give freedom and manhood to 2,000,000 of brethren? to relieve his country, in the spring tide freshness of her hopes, from a curse that is bringing her down to a dishonored grave?

The men who have given to this cause have been hitherto few, but we believe this year will make them many. We hope to see an Anti-Slavery Society starting up in every hamlet, which shall pour in its contributions to the cause with unceasing activity. Let one be formed wherever there are three abolitionists of the right sort.— And let them adopt an efficient system of means to aid in disseminating our victorious principles.

We would venture to recommend that every society should open a subscription, in which every person shall name the sum that he will pay monthly, or weekly, and that a sufficient number of collectors be appointed to gather the subscriptions with promptness and ease. Let the name of every man, woman and child that can give even a cent a month be on this subscription, and let the proceeds be at short intervals remitted to the parent society. By thus combining the strength of the feeble a mighty result may be produced. Such a system will not only give the means of propagating the true doctrine of human rights, but it will give life and permanence to the Anti-Slavery spirit, and will kindle up something better than a barren sympathy for the enslaved.

EXTRACTS FROM THE SPEECHES AT THE ANNIVERSARY OF THE AMERICAN ANTI-SLAVERY SOCIETY.

Rev. Amos A. Phelps, late of Boston' moved the following resolution :

Resolved, That inasmuch as foreign slave trading has been justly decreed by civilized nations to be piracy, slave-holding is a sin of no less atrocity; and that, existing as it does in our country, it brings the Declaration of American Independence and our republican institutions into contempt, and gives just occasion to apprehend the judgments of a righteous God, if it be not speedily abolished.

He proceeded to support this position by a very lucid train of logic, and closed with the following touching *facts*.

The U. S. have just paid $5000 for repairing it, [the jail of the D. C.] The debtors and criminals are located in rooms above, and below are 16 solitary cells, used and constantly occupied for the confinement of slaves and persons taken up on suspicion of being slaves. On inquiring of one and another, My lad, what are you here for? it was affecting to hear the reply, " For my freedom, sir." Just down the hill in the other direction, and like the jail within sight of the Capitol, is the slave tavern of William Robie, a depot for the American slave trade. And seven miles distant, in Alexandria, and under the exclusive jurisdiction of Congress, is the larger establishment of Franklin & Armfield. One of the partners told me he had probably sold a thousand slaves already this year. And he told a gentleman, who told me, that he had made not less than $30,000 by his operations. According to the city laws of Washington, every slave trader pays $400 for a license, and this goes to support the city government.

Need I ask whether such things bring us and our declaration of independence into contempt? Sir, look at Europe. The Christians—the infidels—the supporters of tyranny—the friends of liberty—point the finger of scorn at our inconsistency. We boast that our country is the home of the oppressed, and yet there is not a nation on earth that holds so many slaves. We cheer on the Greeks to break the Turkish yoke,

and we make contributions in aid of the Poles, and yet hold greater numbers in more cruel and crushing bondage. We boast of our freedom of speech and of the press. And yet, in the District of Columbia, a free citizen, if he has a colored skin, is liable to a fine of $20 for taking the Emancipator. And we have seen the legislature of a sovereign state at the south, offering a reward of $5000 for the head of a citizen at the north, who undertook to awaken public attention to the enormities of this system.

Mr. JAMES A. THOME, of Kentucky, a delegate from the Anti-Slavery Society of Lane Seminary, moved the following resolution :

Resolved, That the principles of the American A. S. Society commend themselves to the consciences and interests of slave-holders; and that recent developments indicate the speedy triumph of our cause.

Of the truth of the first proposition contained in this resolution, that our principles commend themselves to the consciences and interest of slave-holders, I have the honor to stand before you a living witness. I am from Kentucky. There I was born and wholly educated. The associations of youth and the attachments of growing years ; prejudices, opinions and habits forming and fixing during my whole life, conspire to make me a Kentuckian indeed. More than this ; I breathed my first breath in the atmosphere of slavery—I was suckled at its breast and dandled on its knee. Black, black, black was before me at every step— the sure badge of infamy. The sympathies of nature, even in their spring tide, were dried up ; compassion was deadened, and the heart was steeled by repeated scenes of cruelty, and oft taught lessons of the colored man's inferiority.

What I shall say, is the result either of experience or of personal observation.

Abolition principles do take strong hold of the conscience and of interest too. Permit me to say, sir, I was for several years a member of the colonization society. I contributed to its funds, and eulogized its measures; and now, though I would not leave my path to attack this institution, yet duty bids me state, solemnly and deliberately, that its direct influence upon my mind was to lessen my conviction of the evil of slavery, and to deepen and sanctify my prejudice against the colored race.

But, sir, far otherwise with abolition.—

Within a few months' residence at Lane Seminary, and by means of a discussion unparalleled in the brotherly feeling and fairness which characterized it, and the results which it brought out, the great principles of duty stood forth, sin revived, and I died. And, sir, though I am at this moment the heir to a slave inheritance, and though, forsooth, I am one of those *unfortunate* beings upon whom slavery is by force ENTAILED, yet I am bold to denounce the whole system as an outrage, a complication of crimes and wrongs and cruelties that make angels weep. This is the spirit which your principles inspire. Indeed, I know of no subject which takes such strong hold of the man, as does abolition. It seizes the conscience with an authoritative grasp—it runs across every path of the guilty, haunts him, goads him, and rings in his ear the cry of blood. It builds a wall up to heaven before him and around him ; it goes with the eye of God, and searches his heart with a scrutiny too strict to be eluded. It writes a "thou art the man" upon the forehead of every oppressor.

It also commands the avenues to the human heart, and rushes up through them all to take the citadel of feeling. All the sympathies are its advocates, and every susceptibility to compassionate outraged humanity, stands pledged to do its work.

Will you permit me to state some of the vantage grounds upon which we stand in the public discussion of this question?

1. The duty of the slave-holder. The duty of the slave-holder—what a weapon! a host in itself! sure as the throne of God, and strong as the arm of God. It is untrue that this consideration loses its force in slave states. It is the power of God there and on this subject, as it is elsewhere and on every other. Facts are daily occurring, which show that when every other motive fails, this is efficient. It is a libel upon the western character, to say that duty there must bow before *expediency ;* and this miserable policy will soon be visited with a just rebuke from the people it has slandered.

2. Again—The sufferings of the slaves. It is well known that in Kentucky slavery wears its mildest features. Kentucky slaveholders are generally ignorant of the cruelties which are practised further south, and on this score are little aware of the bearings of the system. Those good matter-of-fact patriots, who call such recitals "the poetry of philanthropy," and who in the south have the control of the press, have studiously refrained from instructing the public on this point. A noble expedient this, to close the ear of the oppressor against the wail of the oppressed. But it will not avail. The voice of their lamentations is waxing louder, and *it will be heard.* Sir, is it not unquestionable that slavery is the parent of more suffering than has flowed from any one source since the date of its existence? Such sufferings too! Sufferings inconceivable and innumerable—anguish from mind degraded—hopelessness from violated chastity—bitterness from character, reputation, and honor annihilated—unmingled wretchedness from the ties of nature rudely broken and destroyed, the acutest bodily torture in every muscle and joint—groans, tears and blood—lying forever "in perils among robbers, in perils in the city, in perils in the wilderness, in perils among false brethren, in weariness and painfulness, in watchings often, in hunger and thirst, in fasting often, in cold and nakedness."

What! are these our brethren? And have we fattened like jackalls, upon their living flesh? Sir, when once the great proposition, that negroes are *human beings*— a proposition now scouted by many with contempt——is clearly demonstrated and drawn out on the southern sky, and when underneath it is written the bloody corollary—the sufferings of the negro race—the seared conscience will again sting, and the stony heart will melt.

But, brethren of the north, be not deceived. These sufferings still exist ; and despite the efforts of their cruel authors to hush them down, and confine them within the precincts of their own plantations, they will, ever and anon, struggle up and reach the ear of humanity.

A general fact ; though I would by no means intimate that Kentucky slave-holders are themselves free from cruelty—far from it !—yet I have found, in narrating particular cases to them, as evident expressions of horror and indignation, as men ordinarily feel in other sections of our country. Such facts have their effect upon them.

3. Licentiousness. I shall not speak of the far south, whose sons are fast melting away under the unblushing profligacy which prevails. I allude to the slave-holding west. It is well known that the slave-lodgings—I refer now to village slaves—are

exposed to the entrance of strangers every hour of the night, and that the sleeping apartments of both sexes are common.

It is also a fact, that there is no allowed intercourse between the families and servants after the work of the day is over. The family, assembled for the evening, enjoy a conversation elevating and instructive. But the poor slaves are thrust out. No ties of sacred home thrown around them—no moral instruction to compensate for the toils of the day—no intercourse as of man with man ; and should one of the younger members of the family, led by curiosity, steal out into the filthy kitchen, the child is speedily called back, thinking itself happy if it escape an angry rebuke. Why this ? The dread of moral contamination. Most excellent reason; but it reveals a horrid picture. The slaves, thus cut off from all community of feeling with their masters, roam over the village streets, shocking the ear with their vulgar jestings and voluptuous songs, or opening their kitchens to the reception of the neighboring blacks, they pass the evening in gambling, dancing, drinking, and the most obscene conversation, kept up until the night is far spent, then crown the scene with indiscriminate debauchery. Where do these things occur ? In the kitchens of church members and elders !

But another general fact. After all the care of parents, to hide these things from their children, the young inquisitors pry them out, and they are apt scholars truly. It's a short sighted parent who does not perceive that his domestics influence, very materially, the early education of his children. Between the female slaves and the misses, there is an unrestrained communication.—As they come in contact through the day, the courtesan feats of the over night are whispered into the ear of the unsuspecting girl, to poison her youthful mind.

Bring together these three facts—1st, that slave lodgings are exposed, and both sexes fare promiscuously—2d, that the slaves are excluded from the social, moral and intellectual advantages of the family, and left to seek such enjoyments as a debased appetite suggests—and 3d, that the slaves have free interchange of thought with the younger members of the family ; and ask yourselves what must be the results of their combined operation.

Yet these are only *some* of the ingredi-

ents in this great system of licentiousness. Pollution, pollution! Young men of talents and respectability, fathers, professors of religion, ministers—all classes ! Overwhelming pollution ! I have facts—but I forbear to state them—facts which have fallen under my own observation, startling enough to arouse the moral indignation of the community.

I would not have you fail to understand that this is a general evil. Sir, what I now say, I say from deliberate conviction of its truth ; let it be felt in the north, and rolled back upon the south, that the slave states are Sodoms, and almost every village family is a brothel. (In this, I refer to the inmates of the kitchens, and not to the whites.) And it is well ! God be blessed for the evils which this cursed sin entails. They only show that whatever is to be feared from the abolition of slavery, horrors, a hundred fold greater, cluster about its existence. Heap them up, all hideous as they are, and crowd them home ; they will prove an effectual medicine. Let me be understood here. This pollution is the offspring of slavery : it springs not from the character of the negro, but from the *condition* of the *slave*.

I have time merely to allude to several other considerations.

4. The fears of slave-holders. These afford strong evidence that conscience is at work. In the most peaceful villages of Kentucky, masters at this time sleep with muskets in their bedrooms, or a brace of pistols at their head.

5. Their acknowledgments. The very admissions which they make, for the purpose of silencing their growing convictions of duty, may be successfully turned upon them. They almost unanimously say that slavery is a great evil—that it is abstractly wrong ; yet there is no help for it—or their slaves are better off than they are—or, or, or.

Now be they sincere or insincere, out of their own mouth we can condemn them. I met, the other day, in traveling a short distance on the Ohio river, with a good illustration of the manner in which these admissions are made. It is also a pretty faithful exhibition of the uneasy, conscience-struck spirit which is beginning to pervade Kentucky. The individual was a citizen of that state, and a slave-holder in it. He was free in conversation on the subject of slavery. He declared in the outset that slavery was wrong—a most iniquitous system, and ought to be abolished. Quite a point gained, thought I, and I proceeded very confidently to the application. But I soon found that my friend had deserted his position. "The old dispensation, sir, what d'ye think of that? Didn't Abraham hold slaves? and what does Paul say?"

You perceive he was a *Christian*, sir—quite orthodox withal.

Soon again he returned to his post, and asserted as roundly as before, the wickedness of slavery. "Wrong—totally wrong! I would free all my slaves if—but—O tell me, sir, were not the Jews permitted to hold slaves, because they were a favored people; and are not WE a favored people? Abraham, Paul, the old dispensation"—and thus he rung the changes, stung on the one hand by a guilty conscience, and met on the other by opposing selfishness. It may be said, this man was not intelligent. He was unusually so *on every other subject.*

6. Safety of emancipation. On this point, the slave-holder is more than ignorant—he is deplorably misinformed. Who have been his counsellors, judge ye. It is remarkable what a unanimity of sentiment prevails on this subject.

You would suppose that they had long been plied with stories of butchered parents, murdered children, and plundered houses. This might be discouraging if the short history of emancipation did not furnish us with so many conclusive facts. With these facts you are quite familiar; and yet there is no objection more common, than the dangers, the dangers of emancipation. Travel in slave-holding states, and talk with masters, and you will find, in a great majority of cases, they will point to St. Domingo, and exultingly say, "Behold the consequences of your measures."

7. Slave-holders are not so inaccessible as they are thought to be in the north. There is a strong degree of excitability in the character of our southern brethren, it is true; but this is not all. There is reason too, and common sense, and conscience.

I, for one, beg leave to enter my decided protest against those *friendly* representations of southern character, which have been made to scare away abolitionists, and prolong a guilty repose. Unless I read amiss, assertions are repeatedly made to this effect; that argument, in the south, has no weight; that truth, facts, experience are all inefficacious; that slave-holders have no conscience, no heart, no soul, no principle, nothing but selfishness, that they are boisterous and passionate when you speak of the rights of man, and you must beware—soft! delicate matter! Sir, I repudiate these sentiments. They are as groundless as they are insulting. Let them strike with all their force against certain wordy orators of the south, whose arguments are powder and ball, but they illy fit those worthy citizens whose voice constitutes public sentiment.

The slave-holder, if rightly approached, exhibits all the courtesy for which the south is noted. I have conversed with many, and scarcely know an instance to the contrary. No indignation—no rage—no fierce indications of hostility. I lately had opportunity to converse with several intelligent families in a small village of Kentucky. The state of feeling was truly gratifying. Many inquiries were made concerning the principles of abolitionists. Some were anxious to know the plans of operation, others expressed themselves in very unexpected terms. Said one, "I am decidedly opposed to the spirit of the Colonization Society." Said another, "I am determined to emancipate my slaves just so soon as circumstances, now without my control, will permit."

8. Kentucky. I have already made frequent allusions to Kentucky. The spirit which is beginning to prevail there, though not a fair representative of the state of the public mind in other slave states, is to be hailed, on other grounds, as constituting no small item in our account. Colonization—which, like the Hindoo goddess, with smiling face and winning air, grasps in her wide embrace, the zeal of the church and the benevolence of the world, and, pressing them to her bosom, thrusts them through with the hidden steel, colonization has indeed done its mournful work in Kentucky.

Sir, perhaps I owe an apology to this house for such frequent allusions to the Colonization Society. This is my apology; I *know* its evils, and can lay my finger on them, one by one. I *know* the individual slaves who are now in bondage by its influence *alone.* I *know* the masters whose *only* plea for continuing in the sin, is drawn from its doctrines. I know, and therefore have I spoken. Many of its friends I reverence; they are worthy men. But the tendencies of the system I *know* to be pernicious in the extreme,

But the State is rising above this influence. Conscientious citizens are forming themselves into other associations. Many hold this language: "Slavery stands in opposition to the spirit of the age, to the progress of human improvement—it cannot abide the light of the nineteenth century." The legislature has taken up the subject. The spirit of inquiry is abroad, "Kentucky is rapidly awakening." She should now fill up the eye of abolitionists; for if she were induced to take a stand with you, her example would be of incalculable worth.

These are some of the results of a life thus far spent in the midst of slavery; less than this I could not prevail upon myself to say. The design of these statements has been, to encourage you in your holy enterprise, inasmuch as they show that your principles do take strong hold of the consciences and interest of slave-holders.

Now, sir, the great object of my presence here, is to urge upon you an appeal for renewed effort on the behalf of the slave. The question has been asked here, and repeated in the south, "What has the north to do with slavery?" At present she has every thing to do with it—every thing. Will you please to bear in mind three considerations: 1st, We have no abolition paper in the west or south! 2d, Your principles have been grossly misrepresented, and misunderstood. 3d, You have effected incredible things already.

With regard to the first fact I only say, with shame, there is no editor in the Valley who is willing to hazard his living, by establishing an abolition press.

2d. I can give you but a faint idea of the notions which are entertained of abolition principles and men. Recklessness, false estimate of right, fanaticism, Quixotism, sublimated austere bigots, incessantly harping upon abstract principles, incendiaries, officious intermeddlers, arrant knaves who would break up all well ordered society, set every slave at his master's throat, and enjoy the massacre with infinite delight; outlawed renegades who, having themselves no interest at stake, would bankrupt the honest planter, and most horrifying of all, introduce a general system of amalgamation. Notions so monstrously perverted, have not been caught up at hap-hazard, but most faithfully instilled by the timorous cautionists of our day. But from what source soever they may have come, they clamor for correction, immediate correction. It is of immense importance that the public mind should be disabused by a faithful presentation of facts.

Under all these disadvantages you are doing much. The very little leaven which you have been enabled to introduce, is now working with tremendous power. One instance has lately occurred within my acquaintance, of an heir to slave property—a young man of growing influence, who was first awakened by reading a single number of the Anti-Slavery Reporter, sent to him by some unknown hand. He is now a whole-hearted abolitionist. I have facts to show that cases of this kind are by no means rare. A family of slaves in Arkansas Territory, another in Tennessee, and a third, consisting of 88, in Virginia, were successively emancipated, through the influence of one abolition periodical.

Then do not hesitate as to duty. Do not pause to consider the propriety of interference. It is as unquestionably the province of the north to labor in this cause, as it is the duty of the church to convert the world. The call is urgent—it is imperative. We want light. The ungodly are saying, "the church will not enlighten us." The church is saying, "the ministry will not enlighten us." The ministry is crying "Peace—take care." We are altogether covered in gross darkness. We appeal to you for light. Send us facts—send us kind remonstrance and manly reasoning. We are perishing for lack of truth. We have been lulled to sleep by the guilty apologist. O *tell* us, if it be true, that our bed is a volcano. O roll off the Colonization incubus, which is crushing us down, and binding us hand and foot. Show us that "prejudice is vincible," that slavery is *unqualifiedly* wrong, and strip us of every excuse. Come and tell us what shocking scenes are transpiring in our own families, under the cover of night. Go with us into our kitchens and lift the horrid veil—show us the contamination, as it issues thence, and wraps its loathsome folds about our sons and daughters.

Nay, tell us if indeed these miserable beings are *themselves* our sisters and brothers, whom we have buried *alive*, with our own hands, in corruption. Point us, with painful exactness, to the forehead, from which God's image is well nigh effaced, to the soul-less eye, to the beast-like features, the leaden countenance and the cowering air, and tell us, "That is the immortal mind in ruins." Repeat the sufferings of the slave, the stripes, the cruel separation, the forlornness of the friendless slave, and flash upon us the truth, "thy brother, thy brother!"

Sir, we have sympathies yet alive within us, we have feeling. The great deep of our hearts, though it has long been calm, may be moved, and it will be broken up by such stirring facts.

You hear the appeal of the south—can you resist it? You will not. The work is yours—your heart is in it. Move onward, and soon the triumph will be yours.

None but God *can* stay your course, and God is with you.

Rev. BERIAH GREEN, president of the Oneida Institute, presented the following resolution.

Resolved, That the claims of the colored people of the United States upon our fraternal sympathy, and effective aid, are not only manifestly just, but peculiarly impressive, imperative and powerful.

Mr. Green said he felt himself thrown into an awkward predicament, in attempting to arrest and retain the attention of the audience, after the agonizing interest which had been excited. In his view, the prominent point in the resolution was in the word *peculiar*, as expressing the claims of the colored people on our commiseration. We are enjoined to keep still, for this matter does not belong to us : or in plain words, they mean, it is none of our business. Suppose we listen to this exhortation, or rather, this temptation; and stubbornly refuse to give attention to these claims and appeals of our suffering brethren,—would our own interests be safe in a single department? What effect would our silence have upon our poor oppressed brethren? Let no person imagine they are unacquainted with what takes place. Sir, there is not a pulse of sympathy for them in the north, which is not felt by the slave at the south. God will see to it that they are not left strangers to it. But suppose the slaves were to look around, and the soul-freezing report should come home that in all our borders there was not a friend who would sympathize with his bonds, or plead his rights, —would he not be driven to desperation, and violence because his situation could not be made worse? And we should

be called upon, and legally compelled to imbrue our hands in his blood, to shield the oppressor from the horrors of servile war.

Our brother has told us that not an editor in the Western Valley dares advocate the rights of the slave. What, sir, has this tyranny already laid its hand on the palladium of liberty, the free press? All the world seems to be alarmed if but a word be said to illustrate the great elementary principles of society, in their bearing upon human rights. I look into our Reviews and our Quarterlies, and see confusion worse confounded in their ideas. We have seen two brethren thrown into prison unlawfully, and a single state bid defiance to the Union, and there was not to be found a power that could bring them out—all because of slavery. A noble hearted brother of our own rose up and attempted to defend the oppressed, and lo, a price is set on his head. And do our editors, the guardians of liberty, magnanimously rebuke such arrogant pretensions? No, sir, they are ready to give him up as a victim on the altar of slavery. Sir, if this spirit is allowed to proceed, unchecked by public sentiment, it will soon reduce us all to servitude.

Again—What is this *prejudice*, that lays its iron grasp on our brother? Is that a *harmless* sentiment, that may touch the fibres of the heart without polluting it. The moral agent who yields to this loathsome prejudice, welcomes a corrupt principle to his soul, and how shall he escape its influence? I shall not attempt to be metaphysical, but the very child knows that every wrong desire, and every sinful affection grows stronger by indulgence. If we could take up our colored brethren, because we despise their color, and throw them into paradise—into the very bosom of God, it would be our destruction; for the sinful prejudice, indulged—not repented of, would fasten on some new object. Prejudice is not killed, when its victim is removed. There is no way for us to escape from guilt and corruption of heart, but by cordially and joyfully yielding to our colored brethren the sympathies of our common humanity.

We are called together to hear about our being a benevolent people, awake to the strong ties of brotherhood with nations the most distant and the most degraded. And we shall be made to feel for China and Hindostan, and all that. And very likely we shall be told too, that our colored brethren cannot, in this land, be made the Lord's freemen. Have you ever thought of the influence of this doctrine on Christian benevolence? You say Christianity itself cannot elevate the blacks in this land. This must be said, or what becomes of those PENS into which we thrust those of them who choose to visit our houses of worship. If the gospel cannot destroy the cords of caste in this country, why go to attempt it in Hindostan? Perhaps some shrewd Brahmin may find out, that Christianity is not able to make an American believer receive his brother as his own mother's son. And he will say to your missionary, "Go home and break the cords of caste in your own CHURCHES, before you come here to make the Brahmin and the Soodra mingle together in the charities of life."

I have heard many people say they want to do something for the heathen—they can give but little money—they are not fitted to go on a foreign mission. Why, Sir, to meet the case, and test the sincerity of such, God has taken up a nation of our poor heathen brethren, and brought them to our coasts, and scattered them among us. Here they are, scattered and degraded, at your doors. And what is the result? Why, we have formed a great national society, and employed eloquent agents to traverse the country, and make appeals to the public heart throughout the length and breadth of the land, to provide the means to take up these perishing heathen, and throw them back upon a barbarous coast, and into the deep shades of a savage forest. If infidelity ever curls its lip in scorn at the claims of Christianity, it must be when we vaunt the power of the gospel to break the proudest heart, and subdue every thing contrary to the law of God, and then, in the same breath confess that our colored brethren cannot be raised in this country.

But the resolution says, that the "peculiar" condition of our colored brethren, calls for our sympathy and efforts. Is not their claim peculiar? Let any individual put himself in their condition for an hour. This is what the Bible requires. Let him have his family broken up, and his sons and his daughters wrested from his arms and carried into bondage, where he can never hope to set his eyes on them again, while the stricken parent must not give utterance to a single expression of his feelings; must not shed a tear nor utter a groan, without the penalty of the lash. Is there not something peculiar, when we think of our brethren in such a situation. So our Savior seemed to think, when he uttered the beautiful discourses in the 15th of Luke. The kind shepherd leaves his ninety and nine, while the *one sheep* that is lost absorbs his feelings and occupies his cares and labors until it is restored. The tender mother bends over the couch of one child that is sick and dying. She has other children, and she loves them, but she hardly thinks of them; the peculiarity of the sick one absorbs her whole soul for the time. Sir, this is nature. It is nature on earth, and nature in heaven—in the bosom of man, and in the great heart of God. The condition of our colored brethren calls for the most decisive and vigorous exertions for their relief. Ask your own hearts what they felt when our beloved brother from Kentucky described the condition of the slave. Did not your souls echo back his feelings, and cry "Hurry, hurry, to relieve such fearful misery. It cannot be endured." Sir, this is nature's voice, coming from the deep recesses of the soul; nature, as God made man's nature. And shall our very nature cry, and we stifle the sound, or refuse to listen?

God said to the cold-hearted Cain,— "Where is Abel thy brother?" He presents us the past generations of slaves, multitudes of whom have gone to the grave literally weltering in their blood, and says to us, "Where are those colored brethren?" The fraticide was impudent enough to reply, "Am I my brother's keeper?" Shame on the murderer! But what do *we* say? One man replies, "Consider my situation, I am president of a college, a professor in a theological seminary, surrounded with great responsibilities, I pray thee, have me excused." Another says, "I occupy the pulpit of a large congregation, and depend on public sentiment for my comfortable support, and there is a strong prejudice among my people. I don't keep public sentiment. I must wait till some bold innovator shall strike out a path and wear the cornet, and then you will hear my voice in behalf of our suffering brethren." Another says, "I am an editor of a newspaper, and my subscription list—you know—!" I say, sir, take care, lest the curse of the fraticide come upon you.

For, one, I cannot escape from the coviction that our Savior has presented to us this very case of our colored brethren, in the 25th of Matthew, and pointed them out as his appropriate representatives. It seems to have been his design to refer to those who were most distressed and degraded and despised, as the test by which our destiny shall be determined. And when we are called to give an account for not relieving these poor brethren, the plea of ignorance will be of little avail. "Inasmuch as ye did it not unto one of the least of these, ye did it not unto ME." He will not hear our plea, "I did not know that poor, distressed and abject slave was my Judge in disguise."

Rev. Dr. Cox offered a resolution, that those ministers of the gospel, and editors of newspapers, who have exposed the sin of slavery, deserve the thanks of this society. He said if he did not hold in his heart, he should go beyond the proper limit in what he wished to say ; but the lateness of the hour constrained him to confine himself. As to those who thought it strange that he should alter his views respecting the people of color, by going to Europe, he would only say, he wished they could themselves go to Europe, and see how the wise and good look with amazement upon our preposterous and wicked feelings towards the people of color. When convinced that he had been wrong, he considered it a privilege to get right. On this subject he had erred, he was convinced of it, he was sorry, and he was willing to say it before the world. He saw there was an analogy between this and the temperance cause. Both are practical, and in principle opposed to visionary theories and dreamy extravagances. The evil attacked in both cases is defended by the cry of "Let us alone." He was prepared to maintain the ground that it was a duty instantly to recognize the colored man as the Lord Jesus Christ recognized him. The Rev. Dr. Ritchie, of Edinburgh, in giving his farewell in an ecclesiastical assembly, said, "I bless God for America, for her temperance and her revivals ; we need them here ; but there is one thing she needs from us, the principle of UNIVERSAL EMANCIPATION." And, said Dr. C. I have come to the conviction by calm inquiry, and some prayer, that this cause will go, and that it is the only cause which will go.

Mr CHARLES STUART, of England, said it was cause of gratitude in his mind, that God had permitted him to land on these be-loved shores, just in season to second this resolution. He saw in this meeting a proof that the American Eagle and the Dove of Peace are even now rising clear and casting off the weight that our brother has so beautifully alluded to. He had been pained to hear, just before he left England, that his dear brother, who had just sat down, was denounced in America as a slanderer of his country. William Lloyd Garrison never slandered his country. No man had ever done so much to wipe off from his country the stain which in Britain attaches to your country on account of domestic slavery.

He was also grieved to hear that a report had been circulated here, that Wilberforce, the sainted Wilberforce, signed the celebrated document against colonization under the influence of sickness, and the debility of approaching death. It was false. He knew it was done while he was in the full possession of his holy mind, and in the enjoyment of his usual health, *before* he was attacked with the brief sickness which removed him from the world. He knew, too, that so far from having retracted the protest, it formed one of the excellent recollections which cheered his spirit when going into the presence of God, that he had left that testimony in favor of righteousness and humanity, against false political principles and oppressive prejudices. Mr. S. then alluded to the circumstances which made him not a stranger and a foreigner. The ashes of his parents are here, and his sisters live here, and he came here to be a friend and a brother.

The meeting was one of the deepest solemnity, and was pronounced by an experienced pastor who bore no part in the exercises, to be the most religious meeting that he ever attended in the anniversary week. The meeting was then adjourned to Thursday evening, at Dr. Lansing's church.

THURSDAY EVENING.

ADJOURNED PUBLIC MEETING IN REV. DR. LANSING'S CHURCH.

The American Anti-Slavery Society, by adjournment from the anniversary meeting of Tuesday, in Chatham-street Chapel, assembled again, on Thursday evening at half past 7, in the new church of the Rev. Dr. Lansing, in Houston-street. ARTHUR TAPPAN, Esq. the President, in the chair.

Prayer was offered by Rev. O. Wetmore, of Utica.

Rev. S. S. Jocelyn of New Haven, offered a resolution,

That the American church is stained with the blood of "the souls of the poor innocents," and holds the keys of the great prison of oppression; that while she enslaves, she is herself enslaved; and that she can never go forth to millenial triumph until she shall wash her hands from blood—open the prison door—and let the oppressed go free.

Mr. Jocelyn proceeded to sustain these positions. The poor innocent infants were sacrificed to Moloch by the idolatrous and rebellious Jews. Among the more than two million of slaves in this land, there were computed to be more than 500,000 infants, helpless and dependent. These "poor innocents" at their birth, were offered to the Moloch of American oppression. Their entire existence was sacrificed on this bloody and obscene altar. Not less than 200 of these innocents were born daily. Yes! this day 200 had been added to the number. And not less than 300,000 of the slaves of this land were held by Evangelical Christians! They were held essentially in the same debasing and degrading bondage—subject to the same system of cruelty and oppression with the rest of their race: —denied the means of education—forbidden to read the bible—unprotected by the laws —uncultured in their minds—unreformed in their morals.

Slavery is a system of pollution. It recognizes not the law of purity. It knows no marriage for the slave. It annuls the seventh command of the decalogue. It is a common thing for a female slave, a member of a church, to change husbands, and yet remain in fellowship with the church! This is done because females, as well as males are sold from one plantation to another, as the interests of the masters require, and husbands and wives are separated, to see each other's faces no more. And there are not wanting Christians and ministers to justify this breach of the commands of God, on the part of the slaves, on account of the peculiar circumstances in which they are placed. Yet the laws and practices which create these circumstances, are permitted to go unreproved.

Again, there are churches whose funds for the support of the ministry consist, not in glebe lands, or money at interest, but in slaves! the flesh and bones, and bodies and souls of men! It is computed that at least 300 Christian ministers hold slaves, not merely a few household domestics, but gangs of field slaves, to cultivate large plantations Many ministers, even from the north, become large slave-holders. This is frequently in consequence of their becoming connected in marriage with a wealthy heiress of a slave fortune. As the Canaanitish women were snares to God's ancient people, and led them into the most abominable practices, and the most grievous departures from God; even so in our own nation at this time, a most fruitful source of corruption to the church was the unhallowed alliances of Christians with families whose houses were founded in blood. And is not the church thus stained with blood? Is not the blood of the "poor innocents" found in her skirts?

2. The resolution charges the church with holding the keys of the great prison of oppression. Slavery, the world over, is that great prison. Its doors are not broken by violence. No. They are unlocked only by moral power. But the moral power of the whole world is held by the church. The keys of the prison are in her hands. But she refuses to unlock the doors. How was it in England? The church there held the keys, and so long as she refused to unlock the doors, the slave remained in bondage. But when, by the instrumentality of her Clarkson and her Wilberforce, she unlocked the doors, (if indeed it be done,) then the mandate went forth, that the captives be made free. The American church now holds the same key, and refuses to unlock the doors of the prison. She does it at the south—by her general example. There might be individual exceptions, but in general terms it might be said her members were oppressors. She does it, by decrying discussion—and by the influence of her religious press. Has the southern church ever petitioned for a repeal of the slave laws? Has she even asked that the horrid system of abominations should be done away? Has she been ashamed, or could she blush? The Methodist church in its Conferences, and the Presbyterian church in its General-Assembly, had sanctioned slavery. The Methodist church by altering her salutary discipline:—the Presbyterian church by blotting out, in 1818, the noble testimony against the oppression, which, until then, had stood recorded in its standards. Among the Baptist, the Episcopalian, and other churches, no favorable movement on the subject had been made.

The Friends, indeed, a long time since, had taken a correct stand, but they stood alone. And at the north, the church refuses to unlock the prison—by apologizing for the sins of the south—by making exceptions and provisos where the law of God had made none—by fostering unholy hatred and prejudice—by denying the power of the gospel to eradicate the hatred she cherishes—by her pulpits—by her presses—by her reviews—by upholding the prejudice that upholds slavery—by adducing scripture in its support—by caressing slave-holders—by denouncing emancipation—by branding even her members as cut throats, fire brands, and madmen, whenever they uttered a note of remonstrance or of warning. Here is a moral power, but wielded as Satan would have it wielded. Her's were the keys: but the doors were closed, and the church refused to open them. Yes! In the church is lodged the moral power of the nation. But it is a moral power prostituted in prolonging the system of outrage, pollution and death.

3. But, sir, while enslaving, the church is herself enslaved. At the south she is enslaved by her fears—by conscious guilt—by her vexations—by her slave-stained luxuries—by sensuality—by her poverty in pecuniary means. With a defiled conscience —inconstant in love and fickle in action— the practical enemy of man, soul and body. Oh, how is the southern church enslaved! and notwithstanding her splendid papal delusion of an oral instruction that can supersede the necessity of the written word of God, how groveling is her standard of Christian duty and enterprise. And the northern church, too, is enslaved—by her sycophancy—by her silence—by her prejudice. Poisoned, shut up, with the fetters on her feet, and a death chill in her veins, the WHOLE CHURCH is enslaved. The whole head is sick and the whole heart is faint.

And now, sir, how is this enslaved and languid church, defiled as she is with guilt, and steeped in the "blood of the poor innocents"—with all this moral apathy and mental imbecility—aye—and with all this practical infidelity, how is she to go forth to millenial triumph? How shall *she* give knowledge, that withholds education? How imitate papists, and destroy the beast? How withhold the Bible, and convert the heathen? How throw down the bloody altars of human sacrifice, and yet sacrifice souls to slavery?

Never, no, never can the church begin her millenial warfare, till cleansed of this pollution. Even her prayer shall become sin. "When ye make many prayers I will not hear." "Wash you—make you clean. Put away the evil of your doings. Cease to do evil. Learn to do well."

Yes. The church must repent. At the north and at the south must she repent, and do works meet for repentance. Deliver the captive. Plead for the oppressed. Raise high the moral standard. Unfold the depths of this iniquity, and let them be seen and read of all men.

Oh, sir, we may boast of our benevolent institutions and of our revivals in vain, in vain, till we are washed of this blood! We are holding back the latter day glory. O let us arise, and banish prejudice and oppression. Brothers, sisters, fathers, listen. Time is short. The judgment will soon set. Alas! if the "blood of the innocents" shall then be laid on our own souls! Rather let us break off our iniquities by righteousness, and our transgressions by showing mercy to the poor. Then shall the light of our Zion go forth like brightness: Every knee shall bow and every tongue confess that Jesus is Lord, to the glory of God the Father.

———

From the Emancipator.

CHRONICLES OF KIDNAPPING IN NEW-YORK.

This disgraceful business within a week or two has been pushed forward with new vigor. At this moment there are *eleven* persons confined in the city prison as *slaves*. Five of them have been arrested within a few days. They are thrust into cells about 7 feet by 3 1-2, with no light but that which straggles through a grating in the door. Their names are Wm. Miller, James Carter, William Carter, Wm. Scott, and Peter Martin. The arrest of the latter was peculiarly cruel. He has resided in New-York about four years, has a wife and one child. For the last year he has been in the employ of Forstall & Berthoud, No. 57 Water street. The salesman, Mr. Bailey, commends Martin as a most faithful, trustworthy man, and as having no fault but that of being "too modest and unassuming." Martin was opening the store when the kidnappers came upon him. One of them told him he must go with them. He replied that he was engaged, and could not. Upon this he was violently seized and received a blow on the face. The horrible fact now came upon him, that he was taken as a slave. He happened to have in his hand a knife, which he was accustomed to use about the store, in mending cotton bags, &c. and with this he defended himself to the considerable injury of Westervelt, the deputy sheriff. But a sufficient *posse* was in attendance, and a number of butchers were brought to their assistance by the cry of " Thief! thief! he has stolen a thousand dollars." [That is, gentle reader, *he had stolen himself!*] The whole rabble rushed in, bruised him, and trampled him under foot, till he was reduced to a physical necessity of being passive. In this wounded and forlorn condition, he was thrown into such a cell as I have described. There he lies, while the " priest" and the " Levite" pass by, far on the other side. But he had one friend who did not forsake him. His faithful wife, in an agony of feeling, has been laboring night and day for his comfort and release. This man was a member of the Sabbath school attached to the Chatham street Chapel. Americans! *Do circumstances like these attend the recovery of any other kind of property?*

These men have all filed their writs of homine replegiando, as allowed by the common law of England, fortified by the statute of this state, by means of which they will have the benefit of a trial by jury, unless prevented by the machinations of their ruthless persecutors. This law, the birthright of every Englishman, which allows to every man when called into jeopardy of his liberty, a trial before twelve disinterested men, who must *agree* in his condemnation, stands mightily in the way of the *owners of human flesh!* They have attacked it as *unconstitutional!* A prodigious effort is now making to bring the Supreme Court to set it aside. An opinion of the Superior Court has already been obtained in favor of the slave-holders. The Hon. Court, however, did not venture practically to set aside the law, but recommended that the matter should be carried higher. They reason thus: The Constitution requires that fugitives from service shall be given up. The United States' law

provides that any magistrate shall be competent to adjudge the claim set up to any fugitive. Therefore, the law which compels the claimant to abide by the decision of a *jury*, contravenes the Constitution and the United States' law. Most profound thinking! But does the Constitution provide that a man shall be given up who is NOT A FUGITIVE? Does the law of Congress enjoin that the liberty of a man who has never been a slave shall turn upon the decision of an individual magistrate? If so, then are the free citizens of New-York deprived of a RIGHT which is the pride of the English Common Law—we are all carried back, for the convenience of slave owners, to the usages of feudal despotism. Citizens of New-York! shall this humane law be overthrown?

A few weeks since a fugitive by the name of Robinson or Sweeny, was taken from on board a revenue cutter in our harbor and cajoled away without a trial. When he arrived in Richmond, he was prevailed upon, (according to a letter just received from that place,) to inform against an aged free black by the name of Lewis, as accessary to his escape. Upon this Lewis was brought before the mayor and sentenced to 300 *lashes on the bare back!* Robinson also disclosed the names and residence of a large number of fugitives in this city, in consequence of which several persons immediately left Richmond to recover their property. They are without doubt here, and aided by the talents of BOUDINOT and his HONOR the RECORDER, there is too much reason to fear they will succeed.

The most afflicting case is yet to be told. It occurred last Friday. Stephen Downing, otherwise called Levi Ames, had been in prison about 18 months;—a fine young man, whom every body commends that knows him. He had been adjudged a slave by a jury, but owing to a heavy bill of expenses he was kept in prison—in the hope that humane people might *buy him.* By this delay the claimant lost his legal right to remove the slave. This opinion had been given by Judge Edwards, who only declined to release him on the ground that the case came more properly under the jurisdiction of the Supreme Court. The case was to have been brought before that court at its session in this city this week. The Hon. Richard Riker, Recorder of the city, promised that he would do nothing in the mean time without giving notice to Robert Sedgwick, Esq. Attorney for the prisoner. But, as was apprehended, George Wilson, Esq. in behalf of the claimant, applied to the Supreme Court at Albany, who incautiously granted a mandate to the Recorder to give a certificate for removal. And the Recorder *did* grant such certificate, without giving notice to the other party, as he had solemnly promised! And in consequence of this base neglect, the liberty of an honest man was lost! He was stolen away from the city-prison on Friday morning, and put on board a Richmond packet which sailed before the fact was discovered.

On the 14th inst. I was requested to visit a schooner just arrived from Newbern, N. C. to see if any thing could be done for some children, who, it was said, were about to be carried to the New Orleans slave market. I found there an old Frenchman by the name and title of Dr. Mairs, who had in his possession four mulatto children, the oldest a girl of about fifteen, and the others little boys. He said that the children were his own offspring—that they were free—that he was carrying them to New Orleans to reside—and that their mother had gone there *three years ago.* Was their mother his wife? No, not exactly—they had never been married. Was she his slave? No, he had lived with her as a wife, and intended to, still. But why had he sent the mother of his children to New Orleans *three years* before he went himself? No answer, except that he did as he pleased with his own family.

There is a credible person in this city, who witnessed the sale of the mother of these children at Newbern, and saw her bound and carried on board a vessel for New Orleans. There can be no doubt that the *father* intends to *sell his children* as slaves; and that he took the route by this city to avoid the odium which even in Newbern must fall upon such a fiendish transaction.

There is no law of the land that I know of, to prevent a father from carrying his children to a slave market. Fearing that the law which is written on the hearts of men might interfere, this honorable slave-breeder made haste to be off—he sailed in the ship Huntsville on the morning of the 15th.

The children were too young and too ignorant to know what was before them. The oldest, however, evidently went reluctantly. I asked her whether she wished to go. With a cowering glance towards the unnatural father, she murmured, "I suppose I shall have to go."

Here, gentle readers, is a loop-hole into that *"delicate subject,"* with which, "as we value the *Union,"* we are adjured not to meddle!   E. WRIGHT, Jr.
May 16, 1834.

PRESENT CONDITION OF LIBERIA.

Two important documents are now before the public, which shed a strong light upon the condition of Liberia, and will probably settle the question with many, that the colony can no longer be supported by Christians, either as a desirable home for our colored fellow citizens, or for its *missionary influence.* The first is a letter from the Rev. J. B. Pinney, the acting governor of the colony. The second is the Examination of Thomas C. Brown, from Liberia, in the Chatham-st. Chapel. These documents disclose nothing novel, to those who have closely watched the progress of the colony, with their eyes open to both sides.

As they have been published very extensively, we shall only call the attention of the readers of the Reporter to them, by a slight notice of some of their contents.

Gov. Pinney "anticipated many difficulties, but has found them vastly exceed his imaginings."—The "military" companies had no sooner escorted him to the Agency House, than he discovered that it was in a falling condition, hardly tenantable, the foundation having given way, "from the united attack of the *ant* and the weather,"—and this, notwithstanding he found an unpaid bill of $600 for *repairs,* for which he was obliged to draw on the bankrupt society at home.

"You are doubtless aware," says the Governor, "that affairs were very much deranged, and that very many things needed immediate attention; but the reality, in either respect, you cannot know, for you have not seen. Almost every public building needed repairs and expense. Unsettled bills for ☞ COFFINS, ⚰ nurses, rented stores and houses, mechanics, &c. in addition to floating acceptances and orders of my predecessor, to the amount of two or three thousand dollars, and the current expenses of the colonial officers and school teachers, after his departure, came in upon me like a flood."

"The provisions on hand," [in the public store,] "from which more than fifty infirm persons and *widows* were drawing, consisted only of 4 barrels of beef, 300 kroos of rice, and some damaged meal."

The government schooner from lying still was damaged and worm eaten, and had to be repaired at an expense of about $300.

The emigrants who accompanied the governor, were at first accommodated in the *Hospital.* He speaks of them as having passed through the seasoning *remarkably* well.

The flag staff had tumbled down, and the colonial flag was exhibited from the limb of a tree.

"The Eboes and Congoes," re-captured Africans, we suppose, "were in a state approaching to war." They had been placed on land claimed by individual colonists. The Governor could not reconcile it with his sense of duty "to leave them at the mercy of the colonists," and to settle the difficulty, gave them other land in exchange for that which they had occupied. "When informed of this plan, *their joy seemed to know no bounds*; and in their efforts to evidence it by firing a great gun, three were very severely burned."

The governor has left no means unemployed to excite a spirit for *agricultural improvement*, and with good reason, for he says that "with the exception of gardens for families, and twelve acres planted with coffee trees by Rev. C. M. Waring, he might venture the assertion that not *fifty acres* are cultivated in the colony." He recommends as a matter of the first importance, as connected with the agriculture of the colony, the erection of a Poor House, in which to "employ *the numerous old women*, WIDOWS, &c., who are now eating from the agency store the bread of idleness."— "They might be employed," says he, "in *picking oakum*, carding and spinning cotton, weaving and making up their own apparel." How wonderful that our *free* colored people should not be attracted by the prospect of leaving their widows to *pick oakum* in the *Poor House at Liberia!*

Mr. Pinney assigns two causes for the neglect of agriculture. First, "The fascinations of trade." This he hopes will cure itself. The captains who, by their long credits, have pandered to this depraved appetite, are now reaping its bitter fruits.— Consequently they will "stop credits," and thinks Mr. P. "of course hundreds of strong men must return to the long deserted farms." We think they will return farther than that.

Second. A cause which shows up the "comforts" of Liberia to perfection. We must describe it in the governor's own graphic language.

"But this [the propensity to trade] has not been the principal cause of agricultural neglect. I am convinced the evil has its source farther back, and is deeper seated in the system. A colonist arrives in Monrovia at any time during the year. He is entitled to support six months. If anxious to do well, he looks forward to the day when this aid is to cease, and is prompted to make efforts to provide against it. If he gives way to these promptings, the result is generally severe illness, and greater and longer continued weakness. If, as all experience proves is most prudent, he sits down to await and escape the fever, the six months are soon gone and he is cast upon his own resources. If in health, which is not often the case, he starts under the most favorable circumstances; but what are they? A pennyless stranger, without house or food!! What is he to do under such circumstances? If his land is ready at the moment, he cannot wait to plant a crop and have it grow; his own wants and his family's, if he have any, demand immediate relief. Sawing timber has heretofore been the dernier resort. The new emigrant hires or borrows a saw, and with a companion proceeds to the woods to earn his bread. A tree is selected in the swamp, and having no oxen to draw it out, they are under the necessity of pitting it on the spot. Here, *alternately standing in the water from knee to waist deep, and sawing four days*, they are enabled, after carrying their wood to market, (which occupies the other two,) to purchase enough to support themselves; and possibly he may be enabled to secure a lot in two years by building a plain frame house. In the mean time his system has become, in most cases deeply injured or diseased, an aversion to farming contracted, and the man's usefulness to himself and the colony almost ruined."

It seems that a large tract of country has been purchased of the natives VERY CHEAP! And also,

that a title to six acres back of Cape Mount, "is becoming quite a subject of dispute." "I have firmly asserted our right," says the missionary governor, "and the determination of the colony to ENFORCE it if necessary; and thus the matter rests for the present!! [What would be said if abolitionists should propose to "*enforce*" the "right" of the slave to his liberty?]

We have not attempted a synopsis of governor Pinney's letter, but the few extracts we have made will enable the reader to judge what must be the value of those pretensions, which are set up for the colony, as a comfortable home for our colored brethren. Its claim to be a missionary establishment, or a "foot-hold for missionaries," may be still further illustrated.

Gov. Pinney has sent out the colonial schooner without *ardent spirits*, "which is considered," he says, "indispensable to successful trade at any season." In his honesty, he will no doubt report her success in due time. By the way, we like Mr. Pinney, and are bold to say that if all his predecessors had been as frank, we should have had little need to attack the colonization scheme at the present time.

In relation to the moral and religious state of the colony, Mr. P. remarks:

"There, is, as in all other communities, so here, a larger portion of vice than the good would wish to see: yet I am persuaded that a large portion of the community is virtuous and inclined to favor a severe construction of the laws. There have been no revivals of religion among us for a long time, and at present there are no very encouraging appearances."

It seems that the colony itself is missionary ground, and ground which is scarcely broken; for, writes Mr. P.,

"Let the Christian community know, that to extend knowledge and promote sound piety, a quire of paper is, at the present moment, of more worth than a Bible. Bibles and tracts have been sent here, and either used as waste paper, or made food for worms. Why? Not because the people despise either, but because we have not a reading population. Until this is secured, their Bibles would be of more value in China."

And after all this, does not the Christian community of America understand, that to cure Africa of her complicated and dreadful moral maladies, they have sent out, not a skillful physician, but a tyro, ignorant of the first rudiments of the healing art, and needing to be healed himself? Of what use to the real missionary of the cross, in evangelizing Africa, can be such a population? Such a sample of American Christianity? We do not condemn the Colonization Society simply because there are vicious people or ignorant people in Liberia. There are such at home. But then we do not send *them* to convert the heathen, or to help to convert the heathen. If the colony is claimed as a *missionary* establishment, it must be compared with other missionary establishments. It must hope to succeed on similar grounds. What would be said of the American Board, if it should send out such sort of people to convert the world? Missionaries that have no one qualification for their work but the supposed one of a *similarity of color* to the natives on whom they are to operate. But the colony, it is said, *may* be made a good *foot-hold* for missionaries hereafter. And so the sacred funds of benevolence are to be employed, not in preaching the gospel to every creature, but in making "footholds" for preachers hereafter.— The same policy would teach us to send out a colony of irreligious people to Canton, to trade with the Chinese, in the hope that hereafter they might be converted to God, and furnish a good foothold for operating upon the immense mass of "Celestial" superstition!

We think it would be cheaper and better in every point of view, to bring back the colonists for whom Mr. P. pleads so eloquently, and educate them in our schools here at home.

The readers of "Brown's Examination" will see that similar statements are made by him. The two accounts are mutually corroborative. Gov. Pinney's statements show a strong bias in favor of the Colonization Society, with an honesty which will not permit him to withhold unwelcome facts ; Mr. Brown's show the straight-forwardness of a man who means simply to tell what he knows.

From the Liberator.

VINDICATION OF WILLIAM WILBERFORCE.

To Messrs. Garrison & Knapp :

Gentlemen—Finding that reports have been widely circulated, on the subject of the "Protest," which are as hostile to truth, as they are derogatory to the character of William Wilberforce, I beg through your paper to expose the falsehood of these reports, and to clear the character of that beloved and lamented friend of man.

The reports to which I allude, are, that Wm. Wilberforce signed the "Protest" respecting the American Colonization Society, under the feebleness of existing illness, of approaching death, and of undue influence. I know that all these allegations are utterly false.

William Wilberforce gave his noble mind to the solemn inquiry, with all his characteristic intelligence and candor. In a state of health rather better than usual, and yielding to the force of truth, he deliberately signed the Protest in question, in conjunction with some of the oldest and best friends of liberty. Of the sickness which soon after suddenly seized him, at that time he had no indications. It came upon him like a thunderbolt, and hurried him into eternity—into the immediate presence of the God whom he had long loved, and whose work of love had long been his delight; and I am assured by some of his best friends, that the recollection of having signed that Protest, and of thereby doing what he could to efface the influence of the error on that subject, into which he had been unwarily led, was one of the sweetest solaces of his departing hours.

C. STUART.

The following advertisements are forwarded by a correspondent of the New York Evangelist.

☞ They are from the capital of a nation that declares the African slave trade piracy, and supports armed vessels to crush it !!

CASH FOR ONE HUNDRED AND FIFTY NEGROES.

We will pay the highest prices in cash, for one hundred and fifty likely young negroes, of both sexes, families included. Persons wishing to sell, will do well to give us a call, as we are permanently settled in this market. All communications will meet attention. We can at all times be found at Mr. W. Robey's, on 7th street, south of the Centre Market House, Washington City, D. C.

June 4—eodtf   Joseph W. Neal & Co.

CASH FOR NEGROES.

We will pay the highest cash price for any number of likely young negroes, from 12 to 25 years of age. As we are at this time permanently settled in the market, we can at all times be found at Mr. Isaac Beers' Tavern, a few doors below Lloyd's Tavern, opposite to the Centre Market, in Washington, District of Columbia, or at Mr. McCandless's Tavern, corner of Bridge and High Street, Georgetown. Persons having servants to dispose of, will find it to their advantage to give us a call.   Birch & Jones.

June 10—dw&swtf

NOTICE.

Was committed to the prison of Washington County, Dist. of Columbia, on the 19th day of May, 1834, as a runaway, a negro man who calls himself David Peck. He is 5 feet 8 inches high.— Had on, when committed, a check shirt, linen pantaloons, and straw hat. He says he is free, and belongs to Baltimore. He is a bright mulatto, stout, and well made, and about 22 or 23 years of age. The owner or owners of the above described negro man, are hereby requested to come forward, prove him, and take him away, or he will be sold for his prison and other expenses, as the law directs.

James Williams,
Keeper of the Prison of Washington County, District of Columbia.

June 7—8t   For Alex. Hunter, M. D. C.

DONATIONS TO THE AMERICAN ANTI-SLAVERY SOCIETY.

Received since the annual meeting, cash of the following individuals :—C. P. Grosvenor, $1 ; Dr. Weeks, .50 ; E. M. P. Wells, 1 ; H. Kingsbury, 1 ; R. B. Hall, .50 ; Dr. Atlee, 5 ; Alex: Paber, .25 ; O. Wetmore, 1 ; S. J. May, 2; A. Kingsley, 1 ; Dr. Parrish, 2 ; R. Jenkins, 1 ; George Bourne, 1 ; E. P. Wetmore, 1 ; E. Lyman, 1 ; N. Blount 1 ; Amos Freeman, 1 ; Martin Cross, 1 ; S. H. Cox, Jr. .25 ; Wm. A. Tappan, .25 ; L. H. Tappan, .25 ; P. A. Bell, 1 ; Wm. Adams, 1 ; T. S. Wright, 1 ; R. P. G. Wright, 1 ; John Dudley, 1 ; R. H. Seely, .50 ; Robt. Jackson, 1 ; U. M. Gregory, 2 ; Rowland Bourne, 1 ; Thos. Williams, 2 ; Lewis C. Gunn, .50 ; Wm. Smith, .25 ; E. A. Marsh, .25 ; John Jones, .50 ; E. Ellsworth, 1 ; S. Howard, 1 ; P. Howard, 1 ; a friend in Westchester, 10 ; Isaac Barton, 5 ; Thos. Shipley, 5 ; John Frost, 10 ; J. A. Lane, 1 ; L. Tappan, 38 ; Abraham L. Pennock, 50; Dr. J. A. Paine, .25 ; A. Ashton, (Philadelphia,) 4 ; D. Fanshaw, 5 : Hudson Fem. Auxiliary, 5 ; Philadelphia Fem. Aux. 10 ; collections at the anniversaries, in cash, 149 61 ; monthly concert, 2 08.

AMERICAN

ANTI-SLAVERY REPORTER.

VOL. I.]   JULY, 1834.   [NO. 7.

THE DOMESTIC SLAVE-TRADE.

We have on hand a large number of facts in relation to the traffic in American citizens, proving beyond question that if it falls behind the African slave-trade in any department of atrocity, it is not the fault of those who conduct the business. But an able report of a committee of the New England Anti-Slavery Convention, from the pen of D. L. Child, Esq., will save us the trouble of arranging the matter which we had intended, while it developes some facts which had not previously come to our knowledge. We ask those who are always making exceptions in favor of *kind masters*, to reflect whether any man can be *kind*, who knows, as every intelligent man at the south must know, these appalling facts, and yet holds slaves;—holds up the abominable tree which bears all this bitter fruit. Most earnestly do we intreat all our fellow-citizens to read and ponder these FACTS.

From the Liberator.

REPORT ON THE SLAVE TRADE.

The Committee on the Domestic Slave Trade of the United States, ask leave respectfully to submit the following Report:

The Federal Constitution, in the same clause which empowers Congress to regulate commerce with foreign countries and the Indian tribes, also authorizes it to regulate commerce among the several States. The three subjects, foreign commerce, commerce with the Indian nations, and between the different States, stand on precisely the same footing. It was so well understood at the time of framing the Constitution, that the power to abolish the *foreign* slave trade was conferred by the above-mentioned clause, that it was thought necessary by dealers in the flesh of foreigners, and by their patrons and instigators, the slave-holders here, to except from the operation of that clause, the trade to Africa and other places abroad. "*Twenty years'*" continuance of unutterable woes and unpunishable crimes, was stipulated and guaranteed by us to the *republican* masters and traders of slaves. And this plenary indulgence to the south to sin during that term, was one of the items in that price of principle, which the north paid for the Union! How completely does this fact put the seal of hypocrisy upon that boast, which has been so often made by masters in the slave states, and still oftener by their apologists in the free, that Virginia *did* petition his majesty George the III. to prohibit the foreign traffic, which his majesty in council refused to do. Even if this were done with earnestness, good faith, and right motives, which we deem very problematical, it was more than cancelled by the pertinacious and unprincipled demand of that shocking stipulation for the continued existence of the traffic, when it was about to expire without their aid, and would have expired but for their opposition. When we view that stipulation in connection with the slave representation in Congress, and the power and influence which it exerts upon every ramification and measure of the government, and upon every important interest of society, our sorrow and indignation cannot fail to be at the highest, and to defy the power of language adequately to give them utterance. By these provisions *combined*, the slave states acquired an ascendancy in the government, in proportion as they committed crime; the

---

☞ *When gratuitous, please to read and hand it to your neighbor.* ☜

right to give law to a free country, in proportion as they violated the rights of freedom; and thus political power, the dearest object of earthly ambition, (including as it does the control of the purses and employments of the people, and the honors and emoluments of the government,) was given as a bounty for murder, and every other crime destructive and brutalizing to the bodies and souls of men.*

But the domestic trade, which is now carried on in these states, without an attempt to restrain it, does not differ essentially from the foreign. In its great and leading characteristics, it is the same. It is commenced and attended in its progress by the same heart-breaking separations from kindred, friends and home—the same terror, anguish, and despair; it is conducted with the same violence, kidnapping, and in case of resistance or pursuit, murder and massacre, as in Africa; and it is unquestionably accompanied with more fraud than was ever perpetrated on the African coast. Your committee feel it their duty, at the risk of being thought tedious, to illustrate by facts the tremendous guilt and misery of this business.

Hezekiah Niles, Esq. editor and publisher of the Baltimore Weekly Register, is situated in the focus of the domestic slave trade. He has ever shown himself, though a *feeling*, yet a faithful apologist of slaveholders. His testimony, therefore, so far as it is against those persons, and their agents and *protegees*, (for slave traders are nothing more,) is peculiarly valuable. It is the confession of the adversary. To that testimony your committee invite your attention.

In the Register for 1829, vol. 35, p. 4, we find the following statement, under the head of " *Kidnapping.*"

----

*In a very late work, entitled "Transatlantic Sketches, comprising visits to the most interesting scenes in North and South America and the West Indies, with notes on negro slavery and Canadian Emigration, by Capt. J. E. Alexander, of the British Army, London, 1833," we find the following passage:
"The most remarkable circumstance connected with slavery in America is the following. A planter in Louisiana, of forty years standing, assured me that there are a set of miscreants in the city of New Orleans, who are connected with the slave traders of Cuba, and who at certain periods proceed up the Mississippi as far as the Fourche mouth, which they descend in large row boats, and meet off the coast slave ships. These they relieve of their cargoes, and returning to the main stream of the Mississippi, they drop down it in covered flat bottomed boats or arks, and dispose of the negroes to those who want them." Vol. 2. p. 26.

" The Winchester (Va.) Republican has an interesting narrative of a case of kidnapping, in which a woman was rescued, though the wretch who sold her to a trader in human flesh escaped. Dealing in slaves has become a LARGE BUSINESS. Establishments are made at several places in *Maryland and Virginia*, at which they are sold like cattle. These places of deposit are strongly built, and well supplied with iron thumbscrews and gags, and ornamented with cowskins and other whips,—oftentimes bloody. But the laws of these states permit the traffic, and it is suffered. *All good men obey the laws !*"

Dr. Jesse Torrey, of Philadelphia, one of the earliest, and therefore most meritorious laborers in the anti-slavery field, has collected a number of cases, from which your committee select a few, recommending to all who hear this report, to read Dr. Torrey's book.†

" A youth, having learned the subject on which I was occupied, and being prompt to communicate whatever he might meet with relative to it, informed me, on returning from school on the evening of the 18th of December, 1815, that a black woman destined for transportation to Georgia, with a coffle about to start, attempted to escape, by jumping out of the window of a garret of a three story brick tavern in F. street, about day break in the morning, and that in the fall, she had her back and both arms broken. I remarked that I did not wonder; and inquired whether it had not killed her? To which he replied, that he understood she was dead, and that the *Georgia-men* had gone off with the others. The relation of this shocking disaster excited considerable agitation in my mind, and fully confirmed the sentiments which I had already adopted and recorded, of the multiplied horrors *added* to slavery, when its victims are bought and sold, frequently for distant destinations, with as much indifference as four-footed beasts. Supposing this to be a recent occurrence, and being desirous of seeing the mangled slave before she was buried, I proceeded with haste early on the following morning in search of the house. Calling at one near where the catastrophe occurred, I was informed that it had been three weeks since it took place, and that the woman was still living. I found the house, and having obtained permission of the landlord to see her, I was conducted by a lad to her room. On entering the room, I observed her lying upon a bed on the floor, and covered with a white woollen blanket, on which were several spots of blood, which I perceived was *red*, notwithstanding the *opacity* of her skin. Her countenance, though very pale from the shock she had received, appeared complacent and sympathetic.—Both arms were broken between the elbows and wrists, and had undoubtedly been well set and

----

† "Portraiture of Domestic Slavery in the United States—Philadelphia, published by the Author, 1817,

dressed, but from her restlesness, she had displaced the bones so that they were perceptibly crooked. I have since been informed by the mayor of the city, who is a physician, and resides not far distant from the place, that he was called to visit her immediately after her fall; and found, besides her arms being broken, that the lower part of her spine was badly shattered, so that it was very doubtful whether she would ever be capable of walking again, if she should survive. The lady of the mayor said she was awakened from sleep by the fall of the woman, and heard her heavy struggling groans. I inquired of her, whether she was asleep when she sprang from the window? She replied, " *No: no more than I am now.*" I asked her what was the cause of her doing such a frantic act. She answered, ' *They brought me away with two of my children, and would not let me see my husband —They didn't sell my husband, and I didn't want to go; I was so confused and 'istracted, that I didn't know hardly what I was about—but I didn't want to go, and I jumped out of the window;—but I am sorry now I did it—They have carried my children off with them to Carolina.*'

I was informed that the slave trader who had purchased her near Bladensburgh, gave her to the landlord as a compensation for taking care of her. Thus her family was dispersed from north to south, and herself nearly torn in pieces, without a shadow of hope of ever seeing or hearing from her children again. ' He that can behold this poor woman, (as a respectable citizen of Washington afterwards remarked,) and listen to her *unvarnished* story without a humid eye, possesses a stouter heart than I do.' "*

" I have been informed by several persons in the District of Columbia, that a woman who had been sold in Georgetown, *cut her own throat* ineffectually, while on her way in a hack to the same depository ; and that on the road to Alexandria, she completed her purpose by cutting it again mortally."

" A statement was published in the Baltimore Telegraph a few months ago, that a female slave who had been sold in Maryland, with her child, on her way from Bladensburgh to Washington, heroically cut the throats of both her child and herself, with mortal effect. This narrative has been since confirmed by a relative of the person who sold them."

Mr. Henry B. Stanton, in a recent letter to the editor of the New York Emancipator, dated April 23, 1834, states the following case, as among the disclosures made in the late remarkable discussion at Lane Seminary in Ohio.

" I will now relate briefly a few facts of a different character, showing the unspeakable cruelty of this traffic in its operations upon slaves left behind. The following was related during our debate by Andrew Benton, a member of the theological department, who was an agent of the S. S. Union for two or three years in Missouri. A master in St. Louis sold a slave at auction, to a driver who was collecting men for the southern market. The negro was very intelligent, and, on account of his ingenuity in working iron, was sold for an uncommonly high price— about 7 or 800 dollars. He had a wife whom he tenderly loved—and from whom he was determined not to part. During the progress of the sale, he saw that a certain man was determined to purchase him. He went up to him and said, ' If you buy me, you must buy my wife too, for I can't go without her. If you will only buy my wife, I will go with you willingly, but if you don't, I shall never be of any use to you.' He continued to repeat the same expression for some time. The man turned upon him, and with a sneer and a blow, said, ' Begone, villain ! don't you know you are a slave ?' The negro felt it keenly. He retired. The sale went on. He was finally struck off to this man. The slave again accosted his new master, and besought him with great earnestness and feeling to buy his wife, saying, that if he would only do that, he would work for him hard and faithfully—would be a good slave— and added with much emphasis, ' If you don't, I never shall be worth any thing to you.' He was now repelled more harshly than before. The negro retired a little distance from his master, took out his knife, *cut his throat from ear to ear*, and fell, weltering in his blood ! Can slaves feel ?"

A member of this convention,* to whom we were indebted on yesterday for so much interesting information, touching the disreputable exclusion of colored persons from republican seminaries of learning, has related to your committee the following case. It occurred in Maryland, his native state, while he was yet a resident there.

A woman, a cook belonging to a gentleman on the eastern shore, was sold by him to Georgia. The first time he entered his kitchen after the tidings were received by her, she stabbed him with a carving knife, quite through the breast, and he fell dead instantaneously. Then, with the same instrument, she slashed her arm in the part opposite to the elbow, severing the flesh, cords and arteries, and fell and expired on her master's corpse.

---

* After this part of this report was read to the Convention, the Rev. Amos A. Phelps, agent of the American Anti-Slavery Society, rose and said that he had just had the privilege of seeing this woman who still survives; that one of her arms and hands was perceptibly crooked, as Dr. Torrey described it at the time; that she had become the mother of three children by her husband, who was not sold; that her master, who gave her away as above, allured by the *children* had recently laid claim to them and their mother !

---

* Rev. William Monro, of Portland.

One of your committee* was informed by a Methodist clergyman in Georgetown, in the District of Columbia, of the case of a husband, who, upon his wife being sold and carried to the south, pined away, and in a few weeks died of a broken heart.

The case of another husband in Washington, in the same District of Columbia, was narrated to the same gentleman, by a member of a church in that city. Upon the sale and departure of his wife, he became, from being an industrious and sober man, a drunkard, and in a short time crazy, and remains so.

Your committee recur with a painful satisfaction to the testimony of Mr. Stanton's letter. He says:—

"The slaves at the north have a kind of instinctive dread of being sold into southern slavery. They know the toil is extreme, the climate sickly, and the hope of redemption desperate. But what is more dreadful, they fear that if they are sold, they will have to leave a wife, a sister, or children whom they love. I hope no one will smile unbelievingly when I say, *that slaves can love.* There is no class of the community whose social affections are stronger.—The above facts illustrate this truth. Mr. Benton, of whom I spoke above, tells me, that while prosecuting his agency in Missouri, he was applied to in more than a hundred instances by slaves, who were about to be sold to southern drivers, beseeching him in the most earnest manner to buy them, so that they might not be driven away from their wives, their children, their brothers and their sisters. Knowing that his feelings were abhorrent to slavery, they addressed him without reserve, and with an entreaty bordering on frenzy. Mr. B. related the following. He was an eye-witness. A large number of slaves were sitting near a steam-boat in St. Louis, which was to carry them down to New Orleans. Several of their relatives and acquaintances came down to the river to take leave of them. Their demonstrations of sorrow were simple but natural. They wept and embraced each other again and again. Two or three times they left their companions—would proceed a little distance from the boat, and then return to them, when the same scene would be repeated. This was kept up for more than an hour. Finally, when the boat left, they returned home, weeping and wringing their hands, and making every exhibition of the most poignant grief. Take the following facts as illustrative of the deep feeling of slave mothers for their children. It is furnished me by a fellow student who has resided much in slave states. I give it in his own words. 'Some years since when traveling from Halifax in North Carolina, to Warrenton in the same state, we passed a

large drove of slaves on their way to Georgia. Before leaving Halifax, I heard that the drivers had purchased a number of slaves in that vicinity, and started with them that morning, and that we should probably overtake them in an hour or two. Before coming up with the gang, we saw at a distance a colored female, whose appearance and actions attracted my notice. I said to the stage-driver, (who was a colored man,) 'What is the matter of that woman, is she crazy?' 'No massa,' said he, 'I know her, it is ——. Her master sold her two children this morning to the soul-drivers, and she has been following along after them, and I suppose they have driven her back. Don't you think it would make you act like you was crazy, if they should take your children away, and you never see 'em any more?' By this time we had come up with the woman. She seemed quite young. As soon as she recognized the driver, she cried out, 'They've gone! they've gone! The soul-drivers have got them. Master would sell them. I told him I could'nt live without my children. I tried to make him sell me too; but he beat me and drove me off, and I got away and followed after them, and the drivers whipped me back: and I never shall see my children again. Oh! what shall I do!' The poor creature shrieked and tossed her arms about with maniac wildness—and beat her bosom, and literally *cast dust into the air,* as she moved towards the village. At the last glimpse I had of her, she was nearly a quarter of a mile from us, still throwing handfulls of sand around her, with the same phrenzied air.' Here we have an exhibition of a mother's feelings on parting with her children."

On the subject of the dreadful apprehensions under which slaves, and even free negroes in free states labor, in consequence of this odious trade, Dr. Torrey relates a remarkable instance. An African youth, in the city of Philadelphia, lately cut his throat, almost mortally, merely from the apprehension, as he said, of being sold.—This information was obtained from several respectable citizens of Philadelphia, who had personal knowledge of the fact.

Mr. Garrison relates, on the authority of a clergyman of Kentucky, the case of two little boys, which is not surpassed by the most affecting incident recorded in the annals of the African trade. The boys were tenderly attached to each other, and constant companions from their infancy. Their owner sold one of them, and not without some anticipation of the consequences upon the other, and therefore he used deception to prevent and quiet his sorrow. When the traded lad was removed, the other was told that it was but for a little while, and that he would soon see him again. The boy became uneasy at the unwonted absence of his playmate. He was again assured that he would come back. This pacified him only to increase his alarm, when he found himself again balked. Again he was soothed by falsehood in some new form, and with more solemn protestations, and this cruel mockery of the most beautiful and sacred affection, was repeated with less and less effect, until the lad lost all confidence in his perfidious comforters, and gave himself up to despair. He drooped a few weeks, pined away and expired. His heart was crushed.

Your committee have entered into these authentic details, notwithstanding their painful nature, with the hope of convincing some of those persons, who are in the habit of replying to all instances when presented singly, that they are of doubtful authority, or that they are too rare to be reasoned upon. The feelings of that person are not to be envied, nor his principles admired, who cannot be affected even by a solitary instance of excessive and deliberate barbarity, especially when he *knows* that the same tyrant who has committed one, may commit an hundred with equal profit and impunity; and that half a million of owners are at liberty, and very likely to do the same.

One of the objections to the domestic slave trade, most grievous in its nature, though not the most extensive in its effects, is the great temptation and facility which it affords for kidnapping freemen, both in the slave and free states. Some examples will prove and illustrate this proposition.

A member of this convention,* who formerly resided in the District of Columbia, has communicated to your committee a case, which was within his own knowledge, he having interfered to prevent the unrighteous result. A drunkard and spendthrift, named Laskey, having dissipated his money, took this method to replenish his pockets. He procured a newspaper, (no difficult task,) containing an advertisement of a runaway slave, and presented himself before a judge of the United States Court in the District, and made oath that a certain *free* colored man, residing there, was the slave intended by the advertisement. The accused was brought before the judge, and upon the testimony of this miscreant, and

an accomplice, he was adjudged a slave, and was carried south, in spite of the zealous exertions of our friend. It is the opinion of the same gentleman that by a conspiracy of one or two needy and profligate men with a domestic slave trader, any free colored man in *any* state, may be, and a very considerable number annually are kidnapped *according to law!* The liberty of colored free men has not been sufficiently guarded by the laws of the United States, nor of any of the separate states; for in none, even of the free states, on the question of *liberty or slavery,* is the supposed slave allowed a trial by jury, any more than he is on the question of life and death in the slave states. New York has lately provided for such trial where a man is claimed as a slave, but it seems to be considered very doubtful if the judicial tribunals of that state will sustain the enactment. If they should not, it will be high time that Congress should revise the act for restoring men to slavery, who have escaped from it, so that it may not be used as an instrument for enslaving those who are by birth or manumission free. Suppose such a statute as the one above mentioned had been applied to the pilgrims, who fled from ecclesiastical tyranny, or to their descendants; for no length of time, no number of generations, can by the slave code render the posterity of slaves free! Or, suppose the British Parliament should pass an act to reduce these states to colonial dependence once more. We should fight, immediately, and justly. And what does this show? It shows that the reclaiming of fugitive and self-emancipated slaves, is an affair of *mere power,* and *not of right;* and is submitted to on the same principle that we surrender our purse to a highwayman, who points a pistol at our breast.

The following is from the testimony of the Rev. George Bourne, in a recent publication,* abounding with useful and afflicting details.

"Nothing is more common than for two of these white partners in iniquity, Satan-like, to start upon the prowl, and if they find a freeman on the road, to demand his certificate, tear it in pieces or secrete it, tie him to one of their horses, hurry to some jail, while one whips the citizen along as fast as their horses can travel.—There, by an understanding with the jailer, who SHARES in the spoil, all possibility of intercourse with his friends is cut off. At the earliest pos-

---

* Mr. Abner Forbes, teacher of the Boston Grammar and Writing School for colored youth.

* "Bourne's Picture of Slavery in the United States, p. 121, Middletown, Con. E. Hunt, 1834."

sible period, the captive is sold to pay the felonious claims of the law, bought through jugglery by this trio of man-stealers ; and then transferred to some of their accomplices in iniquity, who fill every part of the southern states with fraud, rapine and blood."

Mr. Bourne mentions several other cases, where the most subtle frauds, and the most revolting cruelties, are by turns displayed. The committee recommend the whole book to the attention of anti-slavery friends. The author probes with a firm hand, this fever-sore of the body politic.

Mr. Munro and Mr. Forbes, whose testimony has before been referred to, concur in declaring that the practice of whites to *search* any colored persons, bond or free, male or female, whom they meet in the slave states, is universal; and indeed any one who reflects upon the laws of those states, must be aware that this right of search would necessarily result from them. This is very important in its bearing on the kidnapping branch of the domestic trade. For generally speaking, a free colored man deprived of his free papers, can entertain very little hope of vindicating his freedom.— Your committee are fully satisfied that where the liberty of a slave is in question, it is extremely difficult to obtain the testimony of whites to facts in favor of the slave, however clear or notorious they may be.— Mr. Forbes says, that he has known white witnesses, whose love of truth, justice and humanity, impelled them to come forward, and enabled them to defy persecution, to give their evidence amidst the hisses of the whole court-house. When it is considered that the sheriffs and constables or other persons serving subpœnas for witnesses, must all be white—that they must be *paid*—that the negro has very little to pay with, and can never, on the score of expense, compete with his master—that even if he should be able to bring his witnesses into court, he can seldom, from these causes, have legal counsel—and that at last he is to be judged by a slave holder—it must be seen and acknowledged, that any free colored man, without his certificate in his pocket, *is a slave*—not of one man, but of every man he meets ! Such are some of the consequences of substituting a bit of parchment for that great law of God, that all men are free, that universal law, which the Roman code in its worst state fully acknowledged, and applied to the condition of slavery in that empire ; so that there in the worst of

times, every man was *presumed to be free*, *until the contrary were proved*. Here he is presumed to be a slave, unless he proves himself to be free !

Your committee would now recur to the work of Dr. Torrey. The evidence which that gentleman has recorded is the more valuable, as it has been before the whole country for *sixteen* years, and no contradiction, or even qualification of his statements has been attempted. This is the best proof that they will admit of none. He says:

" The others whom I found in the same garret, (meaning where the poor woman with broken limbs was lying,) and at the same time, were a young black widow woman, with an infant at the breast, both of whom were born free. Her husband had died a few days previous to her seizure, and she was in a state of pregnancy at the time. She stated that the man in whose house she resided, together with his brother, and three other persons, (two of whom she said then stood indicted for having seized and carried her off at a former time,) came into the room (a kitchen) where she was in bed, seized and dragged her out, fastened a noose round her neck to prevent her from screaming, and attempted to blindfold her, which she resisted with such violence that she prevented them from succeeding. She said, while one of them was endeavoring to fix the bandage over her eyes, that she seized his cheek with her teeth, and tore a peice of it entirely off. She said one of them struck her head several times with a stick of wood, from the wounds of which she was almost entirely covered with blood. She showed me a large scar upon her forehead, occasioned by one of the blows, which a gentleman, who saw her the day previous to the seizure, has since informed me was not there before. She said, while she was struggling against them, and screaming, the man in whose house she lived bawled out, ' Choak the —— —— ; don't let her halloo ; she'll scare my wife !' Having conquered her by superior force, she said they placed her with the child in the chaise, and refusing to dress herself, three of them, leaving the two who belonged to the house, carried her off in the condition that she was dragged from the bed, to a certain tavern in Maryland, and sold them both to the man-dealer, who brought them to the city of Washington. She stated that one of her captors drove the carriage and held the rope which was fixed to her neck, and that one rode each side, on horseback ; that while one of them was negociating a bargain with her purchaser, he asked her who her master was, and replying that she had none, her seller beckoned to him to go into another room, where the business was adjusted without troubling her with any further inquiries. She stated that her purchaser confessed, while on the way to Annapolis, that he believed she might have had some claim to freedom, and intimated that he would have taken her back, if the man of whom he bought her had not run away ; but requested her, notwithstanding, to say nothing to any body about her being free, which she refused to comply with. She affirmed that he offered her for sale to several persons, *who refused to purchase her, on account of her asserting that she was free.* She stated that her purchaser had left her in Washington for a few weeks, and gone to the eastern shore, in search of more black people, in order to make up a drove for Georgia."

" These facts clearly exemplify the safety with which the free born inhabitants of the United States may be offered for sale and sold, even in the metropolis of liberty, as oxen ; even to those who are notified of the fact, and are perhaps convinced that they are free !"

" A mulatto youth had been purchased in the city of Washington, and kept in it in irons several weeks by a person who confessed his regret, that he had not removed him before the suit for the recovery of his freedom had commenced ; and that, if he had known it sooner, he would have taken him on to ——, (the place of his residence,) even if he had been satisfied of his being free. One slave trader to whom he had been offered, was however so conscientious, that he refused to purchase him or the lad who was with him, (before mentioned,) being confident that they were illegally enslaved."

" I have been assured by a gentleman of the highest respectability, that a former representative to Congress, from one of the southern states, acknowledged to him that he held a mulatto man as a slave, having purchased him in company with slaves, who affirmed that he was free born, and had been kidnapped from one of the New England states, who was well educated, and who, he had no doubt, was born as free a man as himself or my informant. Upon being asked how he could bear then to retain him, he replied that the customs of his part of the country were such, that these things are not minded much."

" Mr. Cooper, one of the representatives to Congress from Delaware, assured me that he had often been afraid to send one of his servants out of his house in the evening, from the danger of their being seized by kidnappers."

It appears by the following passage, that Dr. Torrey was powerfully struck by that resemblance, or rather identity of the American slave trade and the African slave trade, which your committee have asserted. He says :

" Thomas Clarkson states, in his History of the Abolition of the Slave Trade, that the arrival of slave ships on the coast of Africa, was the uniform signal for the immediate commencement of wars for the attainment of prisoners, for sale and exportation to America and the West Indies. In Maryland and Delaware, the same drama is now performed in miniature.— The arrival of the man-traffickers, laden with cash, at their respective stations, near the coasts of the great American water, called justly, by Mr. Randolph, ' *a Mediterranean sea,*' or at their several *inland posts,* near the dividing line of Maryland and Delaware, (at some of which they have grated prisons for the purpose,) is the well known signal for the professed *kidnappers,* like beasts of prey, to commence their nightly invasions upon the *fleecy flocks,* extending their ravages, (generally attended with bloodshed, and sometimes murder,) and spreading terror and consternation amongst both freemen and slaves, throughout the *sandy regions,* from the western to the eastern shores. These ' *two-legged featherless animals,* or *human blood-hounds,* when overtaken, which is rare, by the messengers of the law, are generally found armed with instruments of death, sometimes with pistols with *latent* spring daggers attached to them."

On the subject of the difficulty of a kidnapped free man or woman holding any communication, by which assistance could be procured, Mr. Munro states the following facts, as having come under his own observation.

In the droves, which are marched inland from Maryland south, and from the prisons, depots and public houses to the vessels, none is allowed to address a bystander of any color or condition. Now and then, a negro raises his head and calls out, " Good bye," to his friends and acquaintance. This is all. It is exceedingly rare that one hears more. I was once present, when a woman cried that she was *free,* and had been kidnapped. A gentleman of respectable character attempted to inquire into the particulars of her case, but *Woolfolk,* the ferocious merchant of souls, rode up to him on the side walk, and drew his pistols upon him. Of this action, no notice was taken by the police or public authorities of any kind.— Woolfolk's servants follow him, armed with pistols and daggers.

It may be observed in general, that the kidnapping of freemen is common all over this country, and prevails to an extent of which few are aware.

Mr. Jude Hall, a colored man of New Hampshire, a valiant soldier during the whole of our revolutionary war, and at the time of his death a pensioner of the United States, lost three sons by kidnapping from New England vessels. One of them, after ten years bondage, escaped to England, and wrote from there a few years ago, an account of his being sold by *his captain,* of his continuance in slavery during the above period, of his escape thence, and of his success and prosperity after arriving in England, where he had become the captain of a coasting vessel, and was happily married. This news was received after the death of the father. The other two, if living, are still in slavery—and it is not known where.*

A colored seaman of Boston, was lately kidnapped at New Orleans, and committed to the *calaboose*, preparatory to being sold and sent into the interior. He supposes that his captain, a Scotchman named Bulkley, was privy to the outrage. There he remained in the most filthy and infected of prisons, and believes he should have been in slavery at this time, if he had not been able to speak French. Availing himself of this advantage, he conveyed a message through a creole French soldier who was on guard, to two friends in the city, who obtained his release.

This sailor saw in the prison *nine* colored men, whom he knew to be free, having known several of them as stewards on board of northern vessels. Two of them belonged to Boston, one to Portland, and three to New York. After twenty days, they were to be sold. The witness adds the following remarkable declaration, which it is to be hoped may operate, if not as a help to reform this horrid abuse, at least as a caution to all colored seamen, both against their own officers, and the caitiffs who infest the shores of the Mississippi.

"*There is a continual stream of free colored persons from Boston, New York, Philadelphia, and other seaports of the United States, passing through the* CALABOOSE *into slavery in the country.*"

A member of this convention† states, among five cases of kidnapping within his own knowledge, that of his brother. We quote his own words.

About eighteen years ago, Robert H. Barbadoes was kidnapped in New Orleans, imprisoned, handcuffed and chained, for about five months or longer, and deprived every way of communicating his situation to his parents. His protection was taken from him, and torn up. He was often severely flogged to be made submissive, and deny that he was free born. He was unluckily caught with a letter wrote with a stick, and with blood drawn from his own veins, for the purpose of communicating to his father his situation; but this project failed, for the letter was torn away from him and destroyed, and he very severely flogged. He then lost most every hope; but at length the above Peter Smith* was kidnapped again in this garden of paradise of freedom, and being lodged in the same cell with him, he communicated to Smith the particulars of his sufferings. At the examination of Smith he was found to have free papers, signed by the governor; in consequence of which, he was set at liberty. He then wrote to Barbadoes' parents, and likewise arrived in Boston as soon as the letter. Free papers were immediately obtained, and signed by his father and Mrs. Mary Turel, Mr. —— Giles, and Mr. Thomas Clark, town clerk; and by the governor of this state, demanding him without delay, he was returned to his native town, Boston, where all these other persons belonged."

The following is from Mr. Stanton's letter.

"A member of this institution, recently visiting among the colored people of Cincinnati, entered a house where was a mother and her little son. The wretched appearance of the house and the extreme poverty of its inmates, induced the visitor to suppose that the husband of the woman must be a drunkard. He inquired of the boy, who was two or three years old, where his father was? He replied, 'Papa stole.' The visitor seemed not to understand, and turning to the mother, said, 'What does he mean?' She then related the following circumstances. About two years ago, one evening, her husband was sitting in the house, when two men came in, and professing great friendship, persuaded him, under some pretence, to go on board a steamboat, then lying at the dock, and bound down the river. After some hesitation he consented to go. She heard nothing from him for more than a year, but supposed he had been kidnapped. Last spring, Dr. ——, a physician of Cincinnati, being at Natchez, Miss. saw this negro in a drove of slaves, and recognized him. He ascertained, from conversation with him, that he had been driven about from place to place since he was decoyed from home by the slave drivers, had changed masters two or three times, and had once been lodged in jail for safe keeping, where he remained some time. When Dr. —— returned to Cincinnati, he saw the wife of the negro, and engaged to take the necessary steps for his liberation. But soon afterwards this gentleman fell a victim to the cholera, which was then prevailing in Cincinnati. No efforts have since been made to recover this negro. No tidings have been heard from him since the return of Dr. ——. He is probably now laboring on some sugar or cotton plantation in Louisiana, without the hope of escaping from slavery, although he is a free born citizen of Philadelphia."

---

* Affidavit of Robert Roberts of Boston.
† James G. Barbadoes of Boston.

* One of the four persons previously mentioned by Mr. Barbadoes.

Mr. Stroud, author of the Sketch of Southern Slave Laws, states that more than thirty free persons of color were carried off from Philadelphia in *two years*. Five with great difficulty and expense had been released. The rest were still in bondage.

Torrey says, that in many cases, whole families have been attacked by night, knocked down, gagged, and dragged away, leaving no traces behind, except trails of their blood. He further says, on the authority of an "ingenuous slave trader," which reminds us of the title of a comedy, ("Honest Thieves,") that "several thousand free citizens of these United States, are held in hopeless captivity in this land of freedom."

The star-spangled banner in triumph shall wave
O'er the land of the free, and the home of the—slave.

The laws of the slave states concur with private depravity, to keep up this abominable trade. Their prisons, as well as that which we all pay and support in the District of Columbia, stand ever ready to fly open for the accommodation of soul-sellers and stealers, and to close upon their captives. The statutes of the old slave-breeding and slave-trading southern states provide every means for rendering man-merchandizing easy and lucrative. Thus they authorize the county courts to issue under seal, certificates of the good character of any slave about to be sold to Georgia, Louisiana, &c. which greatly enhances his merchantable value, and is analogous to an invoice or bill of health in a lawful commerce. The inhuman, and worse than heathen principles, universal in the slave states, that any colored man shall be taken and deemed to be a slave, and shall be incompetent as a witness, whether slave or not, augment, prodigiously, the facility of enslaving free men. Thus any colored man may be imprisoned by any white, and if no white witness appears, he must be sold to pay the advertising, jail fees, and for apprehending him. The laws in some states are so conscientious as to direct that in such cases he shall be sold only for a term of years to pay the above expenses; but all accounts of the *practise* agree that this restriction is generally nugatory. Once sold, they are taken to Georgia and other states more south, and disposed of as entire slaves, to those who know not the contrary, or disregard it if they do; and after this they must inevitably remain slaves for the residue of their lives. The awful motto was not more applicable to Dante's hell—

"*O ye who enter here, abandon hope!*"

than to the entrance of Georgia or the Mississippi to these men.

It is true that "free papers," as they are called, are some protection so long as they are retained, but what are they worth when every white ruffian has the RIGHT OF SEARCH, and in nine cases out of ten, (we use the language of Mr. Monro,) finds those papers, however carefully concealed, and tears them in pieces?

Another law, which if not universal, is very general in slave states, is that a slave, or any person for him, who shall sue for the freedom of the slave, in case such slave shall fail in the action, shall pay to the master DOUBLE COSTS, and no slave can prosecute such action without first giving security for costs.

With such multiplied impediments in their way, let the convention judge how many free men held in bondage, will be likely to vindicate their freedom. The negroes must have a white man in some states to prosecute for them; in all, they must have white sureties and witnesses, either of which it renders a white man unpopular with his *caste* to be. Then he has counsel to fee, and clerk's and jury fees to advance. All these things require money of men, whose very condition it is to have no right to acquire property, and to be incapable of possessing a farthing? Supposing him by some miracle to have surmounted these, still his judges and jury are slaveholders.

Your committee forbear at this time to multiply examples, not because they are few, but because they are so many.

It may be reckoned as among the great evils of the domestic slave trade, that to an owner, who abuses his power in such a manner as not to destroy life, but yet to render the victims disagreeable to his sight, disquieting to his conscience, or dangerous to his reputation, or their resentment, or the sympathy of their companions formidable to him—it affords the means of getting rid of them as effectually as if they were buried. "Dead men tell no tales," is likewise true of traded men.

From a manuscript for which your committee are indebted to a member of this convention,* we extract the following case.

A gentleman of Baltimore was the father of a mulatto girl, by his slave. He determined to fulfil his natural duty towards her,

---

* Rev. George Bourne.

and gave her an excellent education, and she grew up a very accomplished young lady. When she was arrived almost at womanhood, her father died. By a codicil to his will he emancipated her, and bequeathed her a handsome property. Her white brother, who was the executor, destroyed the codicil of the will and the modesty of the maiden, and when she was about to become a mother, sold her for an enhanced price to Louisiana.

Many cases have been stated of slaves, whose masters had voluntarily contracted with them to give them emancipation, when they should have earned a certain sum, (the full value of their persons,) over and above their usual tasks ; and after they had earned and paid it over, have sold them, and removed them to a safe distance. This cruel deceit seems to be resorted to for gain or revenge.

The affecting case of a barber, who attempted to cut his throat on being informed that he was sold, when he had just paid over to his master the last of the purchase-money for his own body, has been generally published within a few months in the newspapers. It may be considered as some proof of the power of that story, that it should have found its way into those vehicles of information, which systematically suppress the truth, touching the condition and fate of our enslaved countrymen.

The following is from a recent publication.*

" A master had repeatedly promised to manumit a slave who was an excellent blacksmith, but he had as often violated his promise. The slave had worked earlier, later and harder, upon the expectation of becoming so much the sooner a man. At length, however, his heart grew sick. Disappointment, sharper than a serpent's tooth, relaxed the sinews of his arm, and poisoned his coarse and scanty fare. The master, to revive his spirits and restore his vigor, finally promised with unwonted solemnity, that if he would earn by extra labor a certain sum of money, amounting to several hundred dollars, he should be free. The slave fell to work once more with redoubled energy. He toiled long and hard, and at last the blessed day dawned, on which, according to the stipulation, he was to be enfranchised. But his treacherous and brutal master had sold him to a slave trader, to be carried to New Orleans ! and on that day he was destined to receive—not his promised freedom

but a new suit of chains. The heart-stricken man told his tale to the trader ; how he had been promised, how he had toiled, what cherished and often deferred hopes would be blasted forever.— He entreated him in the most touching language, to renounce the sacrilegious bargain. But " there is no flesh in the heart" of a slave trader. Seeing that his prayers and tears were vain, the slave became desperate. He told the dealer that if he did take him, one or the other of them must die ; and that he then gave him fair warning. The trader was highly diverted, and said " he liked such a spirited fellow." They went on board a vessel, and, during a serene evening in that delicious climate, the trader reposed himself upon the deck. In the dead of the night, the slave contrived to rid himself of his handcuffs, and groped until he grasped an axe, and, thus armed, stood over the sleeping man. He waked him and told his purpose. ' Then God have mercy on me,' said the slave trader. ' God will not have mercy on you, neither will I,' said the slave, and beat out his brains."

There cannot be a reasonable doubt that the American " Middle Passage" abounds in horrors very similar to those of the African. The victims collected for the southern market, are consigned to prisons attached to private establishments, or to county jails, or to the jail in the District of Columbia. There they suffer from hunger, heat and cold, in chains and in cells, which all witnesses describe as filthy and loathsome in the extreme, and even in this situation the traders still find or make occasion for using the " bloody lash."

If from these receptacles they are transported by sea, they are crowded between decks and into the hold in just such numbers as the captain pleases, and their fare is such as pleases him or the owner of them. Of course, it is not likely to be *expensive*.— The ship-room to be reserved for each slave coming from Africa was prescribed by the British Parliament long before they abolished the trade. Our Congress has found it necessary to prescribe the ship-room which captains shall reserve *for passengers* on foreign voyages to and from the United States. If these enactments were necessary, is it not probable that the unlimited liberty of crowding unreasonably and uncomfortably our coasting *slavers*, is abused in nearly every voyage ? Will not the captains make money by abusing it ? Will not traders save by it ? The ordinary cargo appears to be from one hundred and fifty to two hundred slaves. It seems to your committee that there *must* be suffering, excessive suffering from straightness of room ;

* " Speech of David L. Child, Esq. at the first anniversary of the N. E. A. S. S. published by the Boston Young Men's Anti-Slavery Society for the Diffusion of truth, 1834."

and we have a painful suspicion that it is much greater from this cause, and also from badness and scantiness of provision and harsh treatment on board, than is either known to us, or generally suspected. No one has yet told the secrets of an *American coasting slaver.*

The following from the letter of Mr. Stanton, may serve to give an inkling of what may be.

"A trader was recently taking down nine slaves in a flat boat. When near Natchez, his boat sprung aleak. He was compelled to abandon her. He put his slaves into a small canoe. Being manacled and fettered, they were unable to manage the canoe. It upset—they were plunged into the river—and sunk, being carried down by the weight of their chains. The water was deep and the current rapid. They were seen no more. My informant conversed with a man who accompanied a cargo of slaves from some port in Virginia, round, by sea, to N. Orleans. He said the owners and sailors treated them most unmercifully—beating them, and in some instances literally knocking them down upon the deck. They were locked up in the hold every night. Once on the passage, in consequence of alarm, they kept them in the hold the whole period of four days and nights, and none were brought on deck during that time but a few females—and they, for purposes which I will not name. Mr. Editor, do the horrors of the middle passage belong exclusively to a by-gone age?

"There is one feature of this nefarious taffic which no motives of delicacy can induce me to omit mentioning. Shall we conceal the truth, because its revelation' will shock the finer sensibilities of the soul, when by such concealment, we shut out all hope of remedying an evil, which dooms to a dishonored life, and to a hopeless death, thousands of the females of our country? Is this wise? Is it prudent? Is it *right?* I allude to the fact, that large numbers of female mulattoes are annually bought up, and carried down to our southern cities, and sold at enormous prices, for the purposes of private prostitution. This is a fact of universal notoriety in the south-western states. It is known to every soul-driver in the nation. And is it so bad that Christians may not know it, and knowing it, apply the remedy? In the consummation of this nameless abomination, threats and the lash come in, where kind promises and money fail. And will not the mothers of America feel in view of these facts?"

"Those who are transported down the Mississippi river, receive treatment necessarily different, but in the aggregate no less cruel. They are stowed away on the decks of steamboats, (our boats are constructed differently from yours,) males and females, old and young, usually chained, subject to the jeers and taunts of the passengers and navigators, and often, by bribes, or threats, or the lash, made subject to abominations not to be named. On the same deck, you may see horses and human beings, tenants of the same apartments, and going to supply the same market. The *dumb* beasts, being less manageable, are allowed the first place, while the *human* are forced into spare corners and vacant places. My informant saw one trader, who was taking down to New Orleans one hundred horses, several sheep, and between fifty and sixty slaves. The sheep and the slaves occupied the same deck. Many interesting and intelligent females were of the number. And if I were satisfied that the columns of a newspaper were the proper place to publish it, I could tell facts concerning the brutal treatment exercised towards these defenceless females while on the downward passage, which ought to kindle up the hot indignation of every mother, and daughter, and sister in the land."

Let it be remembered that this testimony comes from the very scene of these atrocities, and from the mouths of the sons of slaveholders.

There is much testimony which might be heaped up on the subject of the cruelties to the droves, which move to market by land. In the works of Torrey, Rankin,[*] Bourné, Mrs. Child, the Liberator, and the New York Anti-Slavery Reporter, facts may be found sufficient to oppress the soul of any one, whom custom has not rendered insensible to human misery and the blackest crimes. On this subject Mr. Stanton says:

"The slaves are taken down in companies, varying in number from 20 to 500. Men of capital are engaged in the traffic. Go into the principal towns on the Mississippi river, and you will find these negro traders in the bar-rooms, boasting of their adroitness in driving human flesh, and describing the process by which they can ' *tame down*' the spirit of a ' *refractory*' negro. Remember, by ' refractory,' they mean to designate that spirit which some high-souled negro manifests, when he fully recognizes the fact, that God's image is stamped upon him. There are many such negroes in slavery. Their bodies may faint under the infliction of accumulated wrong, but their souls cannot be crushed. After visiting the bar-room, go into the outskirts of the town, and there you will find the slaves belonging to the drove, crowded into dilapidated huts—some reveling—others apparently stupid—but others weeping over ties broken, and hopes destroyed, with an agony intense, and to a free man, inconceivable. Many respectable planters in Louisiana have themselves gone into Maryland and Vir-

[*] " Letters on Slavery, by Rev. John Rankin." p. 80—4.

ginia, and purchased their slaves. They think it more profitable to do so. Brother Robinson conversed with one or two of them when on their return. This shows that highly respectable men engage in this trade. But those who make it their regular employment, and thus receive the awfully significant title of '*soul drivers*,' are usually brutal, ignorant, debauched men. And it is such men, who exercise despotic control over thousands of down-trodden, and defenceless men and women."

"The slaves which pass down to the southern market on the Mississippi river and through the interior, are mostly purchased in Kentucky and Virginia. Some are bought in Tennessee. In the emigration they suffer great hardships.— Those who are driven down by land, travel from two hundred to a thousand miles on foot, through Kentucky, Tennessee, and Mississippi. They sometimes carry heavy chains the whole distance. These chains are very massive. They extend from the hands to the feet, being fastened to the wrists and ancles by an iron ring round each. When chained, every slave carries two chains—i. e. one from each hand to each foot. A wagon, in which rides 'the driver,' carrying coarse provisions, and a few tent coverings, generally accompanies the drove.— Men, women, and children, some of the latter very young, walk near the wagon; and if, through fatigue or sickness they falter, the application of the whip reminds them that they are slaves. Our informant, speaking of some droves which he met, says, 'the weariness was extreme, and their dejected, despairing and woebegone countenances I shall never forget.' They encamp out nights. Their bed consists of a small blanket. Even this is frequently denied them. 'A rude tent covers them, scarcely sufficient to keep off the dew or frost, much less the rain. They frequently remain in this situation several weeks, in the neighborhood of some slave trading village. The slaves are subject, while on their journeys, to severe sickness. On such occasions the drivers manifest much anxiety lest they should lose—*their property!* But even sickness does not prevent them from hurrying their victims on to market. Sick, faint, or weary, the slave knows no rest. In the Choctaw nation, my informant met a large company of these miserable beings, following a wagon at some distance. From their appearance, being mostly females and children, and hence not so marketable, he supposed they must belong to some planter who was emigrating southward.— He inquired if this were so, and if their master was taking them home. A woman, in tones of mellowed despair answered him :—'Oh, no, sir, we are not going *home!* We don't know where we are going. *The speculators have got us!*' "

The cruelties exercised in these passages are not always unavenged by the miserable slaves. It is in the recollection of most men, that a company of sixty slaves, while march-

ing through the west some years ago, killed two of their drivers, and severely wounded their purchaser. Two slave traders were slain by the slaves they were driving to market, near Prince Edward Court House, Va., about a month since.

The anguish, wailing and despair which are daily witnessed at the slave market, are themes familiar, alas! too familiar to us all; and your committee will not now dwell upon them. The brutal examination of women which takes place, is less spoken of than other particulars relating to that mighty instrument of torture, a slave auction.

On this topic your committee refer to the testimony of Mr. Robinson, a member of the Lane Seminary, a citizen of Nashville, Tennessee, where he was graduated, and has resided.

"After slaves arrive in market they are subjected to the most degrading examinations. The purchasers will roll up their sleeves and pantaloons, and examine their muscles and joints critically, to ascertain their probable strength, and will even open their mouths, and examine their teeth, with the same remarks, and the same unconcern, that they would a horse."

"The females are exposed to the same rude examinations as the men. When a large drove of slaves arrives in a town for sale, placards are put up at the corners of the streets, giving notice of the place and time of sale. Often they are driven through the streets for hours together (for the purpose of exhibiting them) exposed to the jeers and insults of the spectators. About a year since, Mr. Robinson saw about a hundred men, women and children, exposed for sale at one time in the market place at Nashville ; and while three auctioneers were striking them off, purchasers examined their limbs and bodies with inhuman roughness and unconcern. This was accompanied with profanity, indelicate allusions, and boisterous laughter."

"There are planters in the northern slavestates, who will not sell slave families, unless they can dispose of them all together. This they consider more humane—as it in fact is.— But such kindnesses are of no avail after the victims come into the southern markets. If it is not just as profitable for the traders to sell them in families, they hesitate not a moment to separate husband and wife—parents and children, and dispose of them to purchasers, residing in sections of the country remote from each other. When they happen to dispose of whole families to the same man, they loudly boast of it, as an evidence of their humanity."

What a condemnation of the general practice of the slave traders, and indeed of their whole traffic do these boasts imply ! Your committee had long entertained a painful *suspicion*, that corrupt and degenerate persons from the United States were fraudulently introducing and holding slaves in the Texas, notwithstanding that slavery was abolished forever, throughout all Mexico, in the year 1829. This suspicion was founded upon the confident calculations of southern planters and politicians upon Texas, as a future market of slaves, and upon their known eagerness to purchase or conquer it. Nevertheless, we did indulge the hope, that even fugitives and intruders from the United States, who should set down in that fair country, would have too much respect for their native land and her apparent institutions, to attempt to convert a friendly and free, into a slave state. Or, if this were not so, that the government and people of Mexico would have too much respect for themselves to permit those base men to contemn their laws, or even to pollute the soil with their presence. But we now regret to say, that we have met with evidence on this subject, which reduces suspicion to reality. Capt. Alexander, whose work we have before cited, makes the following statement.*

"The Mexicans complain with justice that instead of industrious and respectable settlers being introduced into Texas, in general the most worthless outcasts enter their territory. I heard of people there quarrelling and shooting one another with pistols in the open day with impunity;—of a dialogue between two friends, who unexpectedly met there. One asked what brought the other there. 'The murder of his brother-in-law.' The other 'had fled after being detected in kidnapping free negroes.'— Again, the Mexicans complain that they are insulted by the Americans, who, contrary to express stipulations, introduce slaves into the colony, under pretence of their being indented servants; and indeed it seems quite evident that the Americans are endeavoring to obtain possession of the country, (a very tempting prize) as they did Florida, by encouraging squatters to enter it, who, when they are sufficiently numerous, will rise under pretence of being oppressed, and an American force will be marched in to succor them, which, retaining possession of the country, a compulsory sale will ensue." Vol. 2, pp. 43—4.

It is supposed by many persons residing at the south, that if the planters could not *sell* and send off a few slaves *annually*, to make up the deficiency of income from their agriculture, they would be obliged to abandon immediately so bad a system of la-

bor. The domestic trade, in this view, is chargeable with the whole guilt of the continuance of slavery in several of the states.

It is impossible to form any satisfactory idea of the number of slaves annually sold in the United States, by the regular traders. There is no other branch of commerce, concerning which our government has given us no statistical information. It would be unseemly for a republican government to publish these things, but not at all for a republican people to do them.

One of your committee* has information, on which we can rely, that one house in the District of Columbia exported *one thousand*, in the year 1833, and will export more the present year. They employ two vessels constantly. There is another house in the same District. A third, located in Georgetown, has been given up; not, however, on account of the decline of the trade, for that is allowed to be increasing. The price is depressed at this moment, owing to the derangement of the currency, but the trade is unquestionably brisk and profitable.

The high price of cotton and the ravages of the cholera last year, and the return of the same *blessing*, (for such it has been said the poor slaves esteem it,)—and the new tracts of cheap and fertile land, wrested from the Indians, conspire, and will conspire to increase the demand for slaves, in the south and south-west, for some time to come.

Mr. Niles in his Register, states that in the week, ending Sept. 16th, 1831, three hundred and seventy one slaves were reported in the New Orleans papers as landed from Baltimore, Alexandria, Norfolk and Charleston. Supposing this to be an average number, it would follow that the domestic maritime slave trade supplies that city with no less than twenty thousand slaves every year, three times the annual importation from abroad into the United States, when the foreign trade was most brisk. We may add ten thousand for those landed in other states and territories, without touching at New Orleans, and twenty thousand for the inland trade, making a total of *fifty thousand men*, trafficked yearly, like swine and turkeys from Kentucky. It is supposed by one gentleman in this convention,† that the number will this year exceed one hundred thousand.

---

* See Debates of the Virginia Convention.

* Rev. Mr. Frost.

† Rev. Mr. Blain, of Pawtucket.

It is a fact worthy of observation, that just at the precise time that the foreign slave trade was *permitted* by our Constitution to cease, the domestic was ready to begin. The turn of the tide could not have been calculated with more accuracy! Perhaps we owe it to this circumstance, that the law of 1808 was passed at all! Extensive arrangements would seem, by all accounts, to have been made in the northern slave states, to prepare a supply for the market, and to profit by the monopoly.— And now this dreadful result takes place, that ☞ *slaves are the only domestic article, the production of which, is encouraged by a prohibitory tariff.* ☜

In conclusion, your committee recommend an earnest and early appeal to Congress on this subject, that a petition, setting forth the constitutional law, and the practical horrors and atrocities relating to this trade, be drafted under the direction of the New England Anti-Slavery Society, and printed with the minutes of this convention, and sent to all parts of the country and to all Anti-Slavery Societies, for circulation and signatures, and they recommend the passage of the following resolve :

Resolved, As the opinion of this convention, that the domestic slave trade of the United States is equally atrocious in the sight of God with the foreign, that it equally involves the crimes of murder, kidnapping and robbery, and is equally worthy with the foreign to be denounced and treated by human laws and tribunals as piracy, and those who carry it on as enemies of the human race.

Signed,   D. LEE CHILD,
                   JOHN FROST,
                   RAY POTTER,
                   JESSE PUTNAM,
                   JOSEPH SOUTHWICK.

[The length of the preceding article has crowded out of this number an excellent communication from J. G. WHITTIER, addressed to the society of Friends. We especially regret this, because that article should have appeared in the last Reporter. If Providence permit, it shall appear, the first article in our next.]

LAWS AGAINST LIBERTY.

We ask, has human liberty ever been more effectually trampled down by any *laws*, than by those which pertain to slavery in this country? Even in Sparta, the pride and cruelty of whose institutions entitle it to be called a republic of incarnate fiends, among all the atrocities practiced upon the poor Helots, they were not liable to be bought and sold asunder, or driven ·hundreds of miles in chained coffles, to gratify the sordid avarice of their oppressors.— Though obliged to support their haughty conquerors by their unrequited labor, and to wear a distinct garment as a badge of contempt, and though occasionally butchered off, merely to gratify their masters' cherished propensity to murder; their general condition relative to their masters must have been better than that of our slaves. The free Spartans in the madness of their military phrenzy, gave up to the Helots by law, both the theory and the practice of agriculture and the mechanic arts, and indeed every thing which had a tendency to humanize and elevate the mind. If the Helots were publicly whipped once a year, to remind them that they were slaves, it must be remembered that the masters also whipped themselves, that they might not lose that hardihood and ferocity, by virtue of which they kept in subjection a population five times as great as their own. It is remarkable too, that in the Peloponesian war, 2000 Helots were freed for their bravery in battle, a plain proof that they were not always held in contempt. But, the slavery of the Helots was the most cruel upon ancient record. It excited the abhorrence of all Greece. The earthquake which overthrew Sparta was generally considered as the Divine vengeance upon her for her cruelty to these slaves.

We are not aware that in any of the ancient republics, it was made a crime for a master to teach his slave letters, or to make him free. At Rome, it was common for slaves to be learned men, and to acquire both freedom and wealth by their excellence in liberal studies. The Roman or civil law protected the property of the slave, and thus enabled him to buy his own liberty. This provision was vitally important. It had the effect of cutting a window in the prisoner's cell, for the light of hope to come in. This very code of law, in relation to slaves, has been adopted by all the *continental* powers of Europe to govern their slaves in the Colonies. It is for this reason that the slavery which our government is so anxious to have preserved in Cuba, is so much milder than ours. There, instead of a law against emancipation, is a law which has freed its tens of thousands, by *compelling* the master to take the fixed price of the slave when presented by him, instead of his services. The British laws in regard to slavery are more severe. They of course formed the basis of our own. The only difference as to the manner in which this consummate robbery is legalized in the United States and in the British West Indies is this ; for half a century their laws have been growing milder, while ours have been growing more severe. While they have passed laws against separating husband and wife, and in favor of teaching slaves, with a view to their ultimate emancipation, we have passed laws making it criminal to teach, and throwing obstacles in the way of emancipation.

There are laws in all our slave-holding states which do in fact put the slave, except for any purpose of benefitting him, entirely under the irresponsible control of the master. It avails nothing to say that this government, as it is actually administered, is mild and humane. In the general, it cannot be true. Human nature is the same in all ages. It is the uniform testimony of past history that despots have, in general, abused power. Even the responsible agents of a free government are sufficiently prone to do so. That there are mild and humane slave-holders, as there have been liberal minded autocrats, and tender hearted highwaymen, we do not deny. But that the aggregate of those who make and sustain the laws, are more humane than the laws themselves, is altogether incredible. A single provision of slave laws makes the protection of the slave a mere mockery. *Neither the evidence of a slave, nor of any one colored like a slave, can be taken by a court against* ANY WHITE MAN ! The enactment in Virginia is as follows: " Any negro or mulatto, bond or free, shall be a good witness in pleas of the Commonwealth for or against negroes or mulattoes, bond or free, or in civil pleas where free negroes or mulattoes shall alone be parties, *and in no other cases whatever.*" Similar enactments exist in Missouri, Mississippi, Kentucky, Alabama, Maryland, North Carolina, Tennessee, and, with shame be it spoken, in the free state of Ohio. In the other slave states, custom supplies the place of this law.

In regard to a slave's holding property, the law of Louisiana may be taken as a fair specimen of the prevailing legislation. " A slave is one who is in the power of a master to whom he belongs. The master

may sell him, dispose of his person, his industry, and his labor; he can do nothing, possess nothing, nor acquire anything but what must belong to his master." In South Carolina the law is as follows: " Slaves shall be deemed, sold, taken, reputed, and adjudged in law to be CHATTELS PERSONAL in the hands of their owners and possessors, and their executors, administrators and assigns, *to all intents, constructions, and purposes whatsoever.*"

But the climax of this despotism of law is, that while the master may do what he pleases with his slave as a slave, he is not at liberty to make him a freeman. It is not enough for these immense bands of robbers to permit every member to plunder at his pleasure—*they make it a crime to restore any thing!!* In South Carolina, Georgia, Alabama, and Mississippi, a valid emancipation can be effected only *by authority of the legislature specially granted.* In Georgia, an attempt to free a slave, or even to permit him in any way to enjoy the avails of his own labor, may subject the *humane transgressor* to a fine of *a thousand dollars!!*

In North Carolina, emancipation to be valid, must be made on account of " *meritorious services, to be adjudged and allowed by the county court.*" Under this law, if a slave purchase his freedom and receive a quit-claim from his master, he is liable still to be sold for his master's debts.

ATTEMPT TO PUT DOWN ANTI-SLAVERY BY FORCE.

On the Fourth of July there broke out a most bitter and violent persecution of the abolitionists of New York. We have not time now to detail a tenth part of the atrocities which have been enacted here, within the last week. The daily presses of the city, almost without exception, reckless of truth on the subject of slavery, have, by giving utterance to unmeasured fiction and obloquy in regard to the doctrines and measures of abolitionists, prepared the populace for the most ruthless violence. It commenced by disturbing the meeting in the Chatham St. Chapel on the Fourth of July and preventing the oration. On the subsequent Monday evening, a meeting of colored people, of the most respectable character, was violently interrupted, and an attempt made to expel them from the house. Even some of the daily papers admitted that the aggression was altogether on the part of the whites. A conflict ensued after the main part of the audience retired, in which the seats and lamps supplied the place of arms, till the house was cleared by the interference of the police.

Since that, the nightly mobs have proceeded in their work of destruction with almost as much effect as if the city had been given up to their *law.* They have broken open the house of Mr. Lewis Tappan, and made a bonfire of the furniture in the street. They have attacked the house of Rev. Dr. Cox, and broken the windows and door. They have attacked his church in Laight St., and those of Rev. H. G. Ludlow, and Rev. Peter Williams, with considerable injury. They have nearly demolished a school house and numerous dwellings of the colored people in Mulberry St. And not yet satisfied, they threaten to demolish the house of every leading abolitionist, and to EXTERMINATE *the people of color !*

We do not mean to be understood that the civil authorities are not faithfully exerting themselves to put an end to this state of things, but they certainly did not begin in time. They suffered the outrage on the Fourth of July to proceed, without an attempt to arrest it,—and the next morning the daily papers pronounced the rioters a "civil set of fellows," &c. The reins were thus laid upon the neck of the disorderly, and how soon they will be again in the grasp of authority, it is difficult to foresee.

The public have now before them, a palpable proof of the depth and virulence of that *prejudice* upon which *slavery is founded.* "A *white* man who will descend to a social equality with a *black,*" say the persecutors, "ought to be expelled from society."— "Hurrah for liberty," "Down with AntiSlavery" are the cries with which an overwhelming mob, cheered on by the daily press, blazon forth the political hypocrisy of our nation, while they essay to answer *arguments* by *pulling down houses!* Surely the rioters and their sage abettors little know what they do. They are constructing for us an argument, which will sweep into the ranks of anti-slavery every *thinking* and *honest* man from Maine to Georgia. The day of anarchy is necessarily short ;—when men have returned to their sober senses, they will begin to inquire, *why* was all this commotion ? they will begin to see where it

was that they trampled on Truth as the mire of the street—and repent of their folly.

ORIGINAL HYMN.

BY JOHN G. WHITTIER.—Sung on the 4th of July, at the Chatham Street Chapel.

" Oh, Thou, whose presence went before
Our fathers in their weary way,
As with Thy chosen moved of yore
The fire by night—the cloud by day !

When from each temple of the free
A nation's song ascends to Heaven,
Most Holy Father !—unto Thee
May not our humble prayer be given ?

Thy children all—though hue and form
Are varied in Thine own good will—
With Thy own holy breathings warm,
And fashioned in Thine image still.

We thank Thee, Father !—hill and plain
Around us wave their fruits once more,
And clustered vine, and blossomed grain
Are bending round each cottage door,

And peace is here—and hope and love
Are round us as a mantle thrown,
And unto Thee, supreme above,
The knee of prayer is bowed alone.

But, Oh, for those, this day can bring
As unto us—no joyful thrill.
For those, who, under FREEDOM'S wing,
Are bound in SLAVERY'S fetters still :—

For those to whom thy living word
Of light and love is never given,
For those whose ears have never heard
The promise and the hope of heaven !

For broken heart—and clouded mind,
Whereon no human mercies fall,
Oh, be thy gracious love inclined,
Who, as a father, pitiest all !—

And grant, Oh, Father! that the time
Of Earth's deliverance may be near,
When every land and tongue and clime
The message of Thy love shall hear—

When, smitten as with fire from Heaven,
The captive's chain shall sink in dust
And to his *fettered soul be given*
THE GLORIOUS FREEDOM OF THE JUST !"

DONATIONS TO THE AMERICAN ANTISLAVERY SOCIETY.

Cash received since 20th June.—Piladelphia Female A. S. Soc. $10 ; Abm. L. Pennock, Philadelphia 50 ; Mr. Ibbotson, 20 ; Joel Parker, 1 ; Rev. Mr. Dunbar, 5 ; Rev. S. J. May, collection at monthly con. Brooklyn, 10 ; Libertus Van Bokkelin, Flushing, L. I. 5 ; sundry persons at Athens, N. Y., Chas. Marriott, 23 ; Norwich 4th July collection, 40 ; Springfield, N. J. Aux. 18 ; Mr. Charles Bishop, 2 ; $184.   W. G., jr. Treas.
New-York, 11th July, 1834.

AMERICAN

ANTI - SLAVERY REPORTER.

VOL. I.]   **AUGUST, 1834.**   [NO. 8.

TO THE MEMBERS OF THE SOCIETY OF FRIENDS.

The following epistle on the subject of slavery was issued by our friends in Great Britain, at their meeting in London, on the 4th of 1st mo. 1833.

All that is said of colonial slavery applies with equal force to the slavery which now exists in the United States.

Nay, more—the obligation imposed upon us, as a religious body to exert ourselves for the speedy and total extinction of slavery in this country, is stronger than that which rested upon our friends in Great Britain.

The slaves of the British colonies were only 800,000. Ours are more than *two millions.*

The laws regulating colonial slavery were less severe and inhuman than those of many of our states,—and

As subjects of a kingly government, our friends in Great Britain had less direct influence and responsibility than we have, in the enactment and continuance of laws.

Yet, animated by that holy principle of love which knows no distinction of caste or color, they made the case of the miserable slave their own, and " put their souls in his soul's stead."

They constituted the most efficient and active members of those anti-slavery societies of the United Kingdom which have been made instruments in the hand of Him who maintaineth the cause of the afflicted, and the right of the poor, for the entire deliverance of their land from the sin and danger of slavery.

They rejoiced to find the members of other religious denominations awakened to the sin against which they had so long borne their testimony; and they welcomed them with open arms, as brethren in a cause of righteousness.

They entered into no *compromise* with the iniquity,—no scheme for re-acting the horrors of the " middle passage" of the slave trade, by offering the slave the miserable alternative of *transportation,* or *perpetual slavery :* but

The only remedy they proposed for the SIN *of slavery, was total and immediate cessation from the* PRACTICE *of it.*

Constantly, earnestly, with tongue, and pen, and substance, they sought, through good report and evil to awaken the slumbering sympathies of their countrymen to the wrongs and sufferings of their brethren in bondage.

And greatly have their efforts been blessed by Him who as a father careth for all his children. The iron of colonial slavery has been broken off from human necks.— Eight hundred thousand beings have been lifted from the condition of brutes, into the pale of humanity.

Thus have our friends in Great Britain borne their testimony. *How are we bearing ours ?*

Are we using all the moral means which God has placed in our power wholly and speedily to remove this national evil ?

Are we affording our countenance and sympathy to those of other denominations who are faithfully bearing the same Christian testimony against slavery, which our own discipline advises ?

Do we, as a people, in view of the sins of our slave-holding, as well as the condition of our enslaved brethren, regard the solemn language of holy writ ?

☞ *When gratuitous, please to read and hand it to your neighbor.* ☜

"When I say unto the wicked, O, wicked man thou shalt surely die; if thou dost not speak to warn the wicked from his way, that wicked man shall die in his iniquity, but his blood will I require at thy hand.—*Ezek.* 33: 8

"If thou forbear to deliver them that are drawn unto death, and those that are ready to be slain; if thou sayest, behold we knew it not: doth not He that pondereth the heart consider it? And He that keepeth thy soul, doth not he know it? And shall he not render to every man according to his works?— *Prov.* xxiv. 11, 12.

Dear friends!—The cries of our oppressed and suffering brethren in bondage have not risen in vain. He hath heard them in His holy habitation, whose tender mercies are over all his works.

In the recent manifestations of his providence He has smiled upon the cause of Emancipation. Shall we not, ere long, by our backwardness and coldness, expose ourselves to the bitter curse of Meroz, who came not up to the help of the Lord against the mighty?

If in thought and word and deed we keep not ourselves far from oppression,—if, seeing the thief, through fear of men, we consent with him,—if, from a regard to our worldly interests, we do not " in any wise rebuke" our brother in his sin—" what shall we do when God riseth up?—and when He visiteth, what shall we answer him? Did not He that made us make them —even our suffering brethren?"

The words of that eminent laborer in the cause of truth and humanity JOHN WOOLMAN, uttered at the Philadelphia yearly meeting in 1758, have been revived in my mind as strongly applicable to the present time. May the awful weight of their truth rest upon all hearts!

" My mind is often led to consider the purity of the Divine Being, and the justice of his judgments; and herein my soul is covered with awfulness. Many slaves on this continent are oppressed, and their cries have reached the ears of the Most High. Such are the purity and certainty of his judgments that he cannot be partial in our favor. In infinite love and goodness, he hath opened our understanding from one time to another, concerning our duty to this people; and *it is not a time for delay.* Should we now be sensible of what he requires of us, and through a respect for the private interest of some persons, or through a regard to some friend-

ships which do not stand upon an immutable foundation, neglect to do our duty in firmness and constancy, still waiting for some extraordinary means to bring about their deliverance, it may be *by terrible things in righteousness God may answer us in this matter.*"   A FRIEND.

Haverhill, Ms. 16th of 4th mo. 1834.

SOME REFLECTIONS ON THE SUBJECT OF SLAVERY, RESPECTFULLY SUBMITTED ON BEHALF OF THE RELIGIOUS SOCIETY OF FRIENDS TO THE CHRISTIAN PUBLIC IN THE BRITISH DOMINIONS.

The Society of Friends, having long believed it to be their duty to advocate the inalienable right of the injured sons of Africa and their descendants to the enjoyment of civil and religious liberty, feel themselves constrained, in Christian love, at this important period, not only to maintain the cause of the oppressed, but to plead with those who are upholding the system of British colonial slavery.

One quarter of a century has now elapsed since the British government abolished the slave-trade on the coast of Africa; but to this very hour, within our colonial territories, the subjects of this empire are legally sanctioned in buying and selling their fellow-men as the beasts that perish. Year after year has passed on; the cry of justice and mercy has been raised; the cause of these oppressed and degraded children of our Heavenly Father has been advocated; the practice of slavery has been clearly proved to be utterly unchristian, so that though sophistry has been employed in attempts at refutation, it has been employed in vain; and reason and religion have gained greater triumphs by the contest; it is nevertheless still suffered to disgrace our country.

The character of slavery has within the last ten years been faithfully depicted by means of official documents laid before parliament, as well as by the testimony of unquestioned veracity, eye-witnesses of the enormities of the system. It has been proved that the invariable tendency of this condition of society is to weaken moral principle, and to benumb and to destroy the best sympathies of the human heart. Its atrocities and its horrors, as now exposed to public view, are not beheld as its occasional fruits, but as its natural and uniform results. What, indeed, but the unrestrained and licentious indulgence of the basest passions can be expected from the prevalence of the most abject servility on the part of one portion of the human family, and uncontrolled power on the part of another? Whoever allows himself to examine more in detail the barbarity often exercised upon the victims of slavery, and the degradation into which they are plunged, a degradation marked by the prostration of every feeling that ennobles man, must regard as truly awful the situation of those who, from mistaken policy, are concerned in directly upholding this system.

It requires but a very slight acquaintance with the laws of Christ to convince us that nothing is more repugnant than slavery to the spirit and precepts of his holy religion.

"All things whatsoever ye would that men should do to you, do ye even so to them," was the command of our blessed Savior; and again, "Thou shalt love thy neighbor as thyself," under which term we believe are comprehended our fellow creatures of every nation, tongue and color. These divine laws are of perpetual obligation. Our Lord further declares, "If thou wilt enter into life, keep the commandments;" "If ye love me, keep my commandments." If, then, we wilfully violate his commandments are we not in danger of losing an inheritance in eternal life? Are we not giving practical proof that we do not love Jesus Christ? Can there be a greater violation of his righteous law than to buy and sell our fellow men, to claim a right of property in them and their offspring, to hold in perpetual bondage those for whom, as well as for us, Christ died? Is not this practically denying the Lord who bought us?— And ought not these considerations to bring with them solemn reflections on looking forward to that day when we must all appear before the judgment seat of Christ?

We earnestly beseech our fellow-countrymen, our Christian brethren of every denomination, to lay these things to heart.— As subjects of the same government, as fellow-believers in the truths of the pure and holy religion of our blessed Redeemer, we are called upon to cherish feelings of kindness and love to one another. We therefore affectionately desire that we may all be wholly clear of any longer supporting this unrighteous system, and contributing to frustrate the gracious and beneficent designs of our Almighty Parent respecting his rational creation. We believe that amongst the proprietors of slaves there are those who are amiable in the various relations of private life, and who are seeking to live as becometh the gospel.—To these we would especially appeal. Permit us, in sincere good will, to ask you—Can you, as believers in Christ, and desirous to be numbered with his disciples both here and hereafter, continue to be connected with a system so entirely opposed as slavery is to the scope and design of his gospel? When you contemplate the moral state of the countries where it prevails, when you consider their blighted prospects, notwithstanding all the unallowed gains which it has yielded, can you doubt but that this system is signally marked by the righteous displeasure of the Supreme Governor of the world?

The present circumstances of the slaves and of the free people of color in the British colonies, the troubles in the Mauritius, the insurrection in Jamaica, and the religious persecutions which have followed, are momentous signs of the times as regards the continuance of slavery. Contemplating these events, and the increased interest for the oppressed, which so manifestly pervades every class of society in this land, the time is surely arrived when all should co-operate in Christian endeavors wholly and speedily to remove this national sin. When a people have become enlightened on the enormity of a crime, the guilt of continuing that crime is aggravated. Ignorance of the real character and tendency of slavery can no longer be pleaded. Warning, has, of latter times succeeded warning with portentous rapidity. Divine revelation teaches us, and the history of mankind exemplifies the truth that the retributive justice of the Most High does fall on individuals and on nations when they wilfully continue in their guilt, and take not heed to the solemn warnings conveyed in the exercise of his over-ruling providence.

Now is our time: protraction accumulates the guilt. It is fearful to look at the present state of society in the colonies; it is still more fearful to look forward. As we believe that the continuance of slavery is an offence in the sight of God, so we also believe, that if, from a conviction of its sinfulness, we in repentance towards God put away this evil from before him, he will graciously turn unto us and bless us; and if laws for its IMMEDIATE AND ENTIRE EXTINCTION, accompanied by judicious and equitable provisions, are forthwith made, that our Heavenly Father will prosper this work of mercy. And we further believe, that by the substitution of the paternal care of the government in the place of the arbitrary power and authority of the master, the peace of society will be secured, and the comfort, the happiness, and the prosperity of all be greatly promoted.

We offer these reflections with no feelings of hostility to any class; we sincerely pity those who are involved in a system from which the conduct of our predecessors in religious profession has warned and guarded us.

We cannot doubt but that many of the colonial proprietors would gladly disencumber themselves from the burden of any longer upholding slavery, and that they would unite in such measures for its abolition as they might deem safe and equitable. We feel for them as possessors of estates which may have descended to them by inheritance with the clog of slavery attached to them. At the same time, being fully persuaded that men are most likely to prosper in the world when, in the conducting of their temporal affairs, they act according to the eternal principles of justice, we are strongly impressed with the belief that the immediate provision for the termination of slavery at the earliest possible period will, in this respect, greatly benefit the colonial proprietor.

May our legislators, and all in authority, both at home and abroad,—may every one in his individual allotment, who can sympathize with the sufferings of the oppressed, and to whom it is given to feel for the present and future well-being of his fellow men, —be so influenced by the power of Christian love and of Christian truth, as that we may all cordially co-operate in endeavoring to effect this righteous object, and not relax in our efforts until its final accomplishment.

In conclusion, it is our earnest prayer, that it may please Almighty God to continue to regard this kingdom for good; and to direct its councils in this and other acts of justice and mercy so as to promote his glory in the harmony of his rational creation.

Signed in and on behalf of a meeting representing the religious society of Friends, in the interview of its yearly meeting, by

GEO. STACEY, Clerk.

London, 4th of 1st mo.

ST. DOMINGO.

RESULTS OF EMANCIPATION.

Nothing is more common than to hear the condition of St. Domingo or Hayti appealed to, as proof of the inexpediency of emancipation. If we propose at once to substitute the mild sway of law for the tyrannous domination of individual avarice, we are warned of the HORRORS OF ST. DOMINGO, *as if liberty, and not slavery,* had shed all the blood that once drenched that now *happy* island! It shall be our task to bring to light FACTS—most strangely hid from the American public—in regard to the results of emancipation so far as it has been tried. If after all the disadvantages of a sanguinary struggle to reinstate themselves in their rights, the Haytiens are rising in the qualities of freemen, surely they would not have made less progress, had they never been disturbed in the enjoyment of that freedom, which in 1793[*] was conferred upon 500,000 of them at a single dash of the pen.

It is true that the blacks were immensely the majority of the population, and indeed, in the event of the struggle of 1802–4 they were the sole population. They were left little better than naked and houseless on a soil devastated by a most ferocious and protracted warfare. But what then? If it shall appear that from this condition they have become industrious, comfortable, wealthy and well-ordered, is not their example the stronger in favor of liberty? *If such a people* can make a benefit of freedom, cannot the boon be *safely* conferred by a nation like ours upon a mere fraction of its population?

The following is extracted from the "Report from the select committee on the extinction of slavery throughout the British dominions, with the minutes of evidence. Ordered by the House of Commons, to be printed, 11th August, 1832."

Mr. ROBERT SUTHERLAND, called in, and examined.

"Where do you reside?—At No. 132 Regent street.

"Are you conversant with the state of the population in the island of Hayti?—I

---

[*] See Clarkson's Thoughts—Anti-Slavery Reporter, No. 3.—Where it is stated, on unquestioned authority, that the act of emancipation restored tranquility to the island, which was only interrupted by the endeavors of the former masters to re-enslave the people.

resided there for some time, and I think I do understand something of the state of that country.

"When did you first go to the island?—My first visit to the island was in 1814 or 1815.

"When did you leave the island?—I left it also in 1815.

"When were you last there?—In 1827.

"For how long?—I think about a fortnight or three weeks, but I had been there previous to 1827; I was there about the end of 1819, 1820, and part of 1821, without leaving the island.

"When did you return the next time?—I returned, I think, in 1823, or the beginning of 1824, for a few days; I called in at Jacmel, and rode to Port-au-Prince, and then I was there again in 1827.

"In all, therefore, since the year 1815, you have visited the island four times?—Yes.

"Had you any official duty there?—No, on private business; my father resided in the island, and had resided a considerable time; he was a merchant and British agent there; we had no established British agent, but he was recognized as British agent; my father died in 1819, and I was serving in my regiment at Canada; I had just been reduced on half pay; I received a letter from the executor calling me over to arrange my father's affairs, and it was in consequence of that I was there so long a time.

"In 1815, when you were first there, did civil war prevail?—When I first went there the island was divided into three governments; there was a monarchial government established in the north under Christophe; there was a republican government under the mulatto Pechon; and there was the Spanish part, which still adhered to Spain. Those parties were not precisely at war, but there had not been any thing like a definitive peace; the fact is, there was no treaty of peace between them; they could attack one another at any period they liked, without any breach of faith.

"Under the black monarchy and the mulatto republic had not freedom been obtained by the negroes?—Yes; the Spanish part was still under the Spanish government, and the negroes were in a state of servitude, but it was a mild state of slavery; they were obliged to maintain a mild system, in consequence of the neighborhood of the other parties.

"Did you visit the Spanish part at that time?—I did not visit the Spanish part till 1821.

"In the year 1821 had complete emancipation been obtained by the Spanish slaves?—No, the Spanish slaves were still in a state of slavery.

"In 1821 had you the means of comparing the state of the free blacks in the other two parts, with the slaves in the Spanish part?—No, I cannot say that I had; I had an opportunity of knowing every thing that was going on in Christophe's part, and in the republic under Pechon, but I did not visit Christophe's part till 1819 and 1820. I went from Port-au-Prince with Sir Home Popham, and I resided at the Cape for a few days; I went to court with the Admiral, and dined at Christophe's. I had then very little opportunity indeed of ascertaining what was going on with reference to the negroes in Christophe's dominions, because Christophe looked upon me with some jealousy, in consequence of my father living under a republican government, and my father had always sustained Pechon's cause in preference to Christophe's, because he considered Christophe rather arbitrary.

"When you were there in 1823, had you the means of comparing the situation of any part of the free black population with the situation in which you had left them in 1815?—Yes, I had.

"What part of the population was it?—It was in Pechon's part.

"Will you state what was the result of that comparison; had there been progressive civilization and improvement in their condition or otherwise?—I have already stated that the country was divided into three governments; it is necessary to enter into the views of the different parties. Pechon's policy was this: by giving the people as much liberty as possible, in fact, a liberty almost amounting to licentiousness, to undermine the absolute monarchy of Christophe, and ultimately to lay the foundation of a policy which would succeed in placing the whole of the island under his wing. That policy succeeded, and his successor, the present man, is now at the head of the island of St. Domingo. Christophe, in consequence of his arbitrary way of dealing with the people, was completely undermined by his own soldiers, who shook off his authority. He committed suicide in the year 1821. I recollect going to the Cape in the year 1821, with the army of Boyer, merely to see how those people carried on their warlike operations. With respect to the state of the people in 1820, there was a decided improvement as compared with the former period.

"In what particulars was that improvement most perceptible ?—They were generally in better obedience to the laws. I will just mention one circumstance to give an idea of the state of the country: I have known foreign merchants who resided there who were in the habit of going to the capital from different parts of the island with sometimes one hundred, sometimes two hundred, and sometimes three hundred dollars, without any person except merely those who led the mule and himself accompanying it, and I have seen them go unmolested from one part of the island to another; and I do not know any thing that can answer better for a state of civilization than that circumstance.

"Was that in consequence of the excellence of the police ?—No ; but the fact was, that such was the mild disposition of the natives themselves, that they required no police. I will say that there were not many instances of petty thefts and many things of that kind.

"Were there no murders or crimes of that kind ?—I never recollect hearing of any murder during the time I was in the island.

"Did not such a state of society surprise you ?—Yes, I must confess that I was very much surprised, because I did not expect a set of emancipated negroes could be so mild.

"As to their industry, had you any means of observing whether they cultivated the land ?—I frequently heard the proprietors of large estates say that they felt a difficulty in obtaining laborers ; I believe that that difficulty proceeded chiefly from the real comfort of the native Haytians; that they felt no wants. There was an Agrarian law passed by Pechon, by which almost all the negroes who could take the charge of any little plantations of their own were located upon them.

"Then an Agrarian law took place, leading to a minute subdivision of property, and giving to each man a portion of land ?—Yes.

"Would it not be impossible to argue from such a state of society to any other state, in which no such division of property took place as a consequence of emancipation ?—Yes; I think if all the negroes in the West

Indies are like the negroes of Hayti, I will venture to assert that they might be fixed upon their plantations, and, under proper fiscal regulations, might be obliged to work, and might become useful free laborers. I have no hesitation in saying that, judging from the negroes of Hayti ; but I am not prepared to say that any slave, not possessing the same intelligence with the negroes of Hayti, would be fit to be placed upon the same footing with them: but it must be recollected that the people of Hayti have imbibed a great deal of intelligence from being constantly in a state of warfare.

"Does Hayti afford an example of a free black population working for wages ?—I think it does.

"You were understood to say that they all possessed land of their own, and that they worked upon that land; and that you had understood from the large proprietors that there was great difficulty in their obtaining laborers for hire; if that be so, does it not fail to afford an example of free labor for hire ?—No, it does not ; there are some who have no lands, and who are located upon the plantations, of which there are a great many. The Agrarian law only extends to the more intelligent part of the population ; land was allotted to almost all the old soldiers, who were of sufficient intelligence to become proprietors and to cultivate the soil ; and I believe there was an article of that very Agrarian law, which stated, that if the land, or so much of it, was not cultivated at a certain period, it was forfeited.

"Are there many persons who work for hire in Hayti ?—Yes, the whole cultivation is carried on by free labor.

"Do those persons work with industry and vigor ?—I have no reason to think that they do not. The proof that free labor in Hayti answers is this, that after the French were expelled there was absolutely no sugar work, there was no mill; there was nothing of that kind which could be put in use, it was so destroyed ; and since that period various plantations have grown up in Hayti ; men have gone to the expense of laying out twenty, thirty, and forty thousand dollars to build up those sugar works, and there are a vast number of plantations in the island ; and it stands to reason that unless those men were repaid for their capital, they would not continue that sort of work. And there is another thing to be observed, that sugar is not the staple commodity of Hayti; they only make sufficient for consumption: coffee is the staple commodity of the island.

"Have you heard complaints generally as to the industry of those who were employed in free labor?—I have heard the great proprietors frequently complain of the great difficulty of obtaining laborers, but those were men accustomed to the old colonial custom; their complaint was, not that those that did work were inefficient, but they complained of the difficulty of getting a sufficient number to cultivate.

"Have you seen any of the negroes at work on sugar estates?—Yes, on several plantations.

"Have you traveled much in Hayti?—Yes, I rode through a great part of the island.

"From what you have seen of it, should you consider yourself to have obtained a competent knowledge of the state of society generally in it?—Yes, I think I have.

"You say that large sums of money have been laid out in the erection and restoration of sugar works?—Yes.

"Are those sugar works carried on with success?—They were not carried on with very good success when I was there in 1821, and 1822, and 1823, although there were several plantations that were doing remarkably well in those years. I do not know what may be the difference since, because since, they have been at war.

"When you were there in 1827, had you an opportunity of knowing?—No; in 1827 I was unwell, and I could not ride about so much.

"Have you reason to think any of those sugar works have been abandoned since?—No, I have not heard that they have been abandoned.

"Was there any scarcity of sugar when you were there?—No.

"Was it cheap or dear?—I cannot state the price.

"Did they import sugar for their own consumption?—I never heard of it; on the contrary, they use very little sugar; they use syrup, which is a sort of distillation from the cane. Foreigners get a little refined sugar; for instance, I used to get my refined sugar from Jamaica, but the natives of the country never use any thing but a little syrup, so that they have sufficient sugar for their consumption.

"You stated that you thought a state of warfare made the people more intelligent; should you think it would have a tendency to promote that great mildness of character which you expressed to exist there generally?—It might be supposed that a state of warfare would have led to a contrary disposition, but it is difficult to conceive the mild way in which every thing was carried on among those people; in fact, at that time the government was obliged to act mildly, because its very existence depended upon the mildness with which it treated the population; but I believe that no chief could exist ten days that attempted to tyrannize over the people; in fact, if there was any fault in them, it was that they were too relaxed; but the reason of it was, that they wished to pursue a policy that should unite the whole island; they succeeded, and since that they have assumed more energy.

"Was not the war there attended with bloodshed, as it usually is?—Very little indeed; sometimes where people are required to be taken out of the way, it is done in a sly way; but I never saw those fellows come to cross bayonets.

"By taking people out of the way, do you mean assassination?—I was referring to a very tragical circumstance that occurred during my residence in that island; it was the death of the children of General Christophe: there were two young princes who were shamefully butchered by Christophe's own party, but I do not mean to say that there is a disposition on the part of the natives of the country to do any thing like assassination.

"Do you recollect in 1820 and 1821, when you went up with Sir Home Popham, the circumstance occurring of the judges having given a decision contrary to the opinion of Christophe, and their having been ordered out upon the batteries in chains by way of punishment?—I do not recollect the circumstance, but I think it is very likely to have occurred, because I have always considered that Christophe's government has been, in fact, a severe government; the fact is, Christophe governed like an uneducated slave, as every slave would do when he gets the upper hand; a gentleman will always rule with the feelings of a gentleman, but every upstart that gets into power will naturally be overbearing.

"You say that you think oppression would not be borne there; do you think that the

Code Rurale is not oppressive ?—The Code Rurale did not come into operation till after I had an opportunity of judging of it, for it did not come into operation till the year 1824, 1825, and 1826.

"Was not that the Code established by Toussaint ?—It was founded upon that, according to the Lex Scripta of the Code Rurale; I do not consider it in any way too severe; I think it shows, rather, that the government are becoming energetic, and it is nothing more or less than the sort of vagrant law we have in this country ; the fact is, that I have a very high opinion of the government of Hayti, from the very energy it displays in enforcing cultivation.

"Then do you think that the contracts are, on the whole, free contracts, rather than compulsory labor?—Decidedly, there is no such thing as compulsory labor; I do not suppose that government would exist one week, if it attempted any thing like the re-enslaving of those people; the government is essentially an absolute government; it is what you may call a constitutional government *de jure*, and an absolute government *de facto*, which is decidedly the best calculated for that state; but, at the same time, it must be observed, that an absolute government is not maintained for the internal rule of the people; it is more maintained to prevent any foreign intrigues that may be attempted to be introduced into that island for the purpose of possessing it.

"Do you think a pure despotism is necessary to govern emancipated slaves ?—I do not, if the slaves are like the negroes of Hayti; but I say that a sufficiently energetic system is necessary; and one of the reasons why I admire the prudence and the conduct of the present man who rules that country, is that, when he got the whole island under his power, he immediately set to at passing laws for the cultivation of the soil, and applied all idlers to it, but not by force.

"How did the President induce those idlers to work upon it?—According to the Code Rurale, every vagrant may be applied to work as a free man any where, and he is paid for his work ; I believe we have the same regulations in this country ; if we had not a surplus of population in this country, we should be obliged to resort to the same measure.

"If a man can show that he has the means of subsistence of his own, is he com-pelled to labor under the Code Rurale?—Decidedly not; I should think a negro would shoot a man that was to make any attack upon his personal liberty; there are no people in the world so jealous of any thing like an attempt to degrade them, or to make them feel that they are not really free men, as the people of Hayti.

"Do you think there is any sort of resemblance between the person called the conducteur under the Rurale Code and the driver in the colonies where slavery exists ?—Certainly not, by the very meaning of the word conducteur ; the one is a leader, while the other is a driver ; the word conducteur means a person to lead the rest, as a captain leads his party.

"Do you believe that corporal punishment is inflicted upon any of the laborers in Hayti ?—I believe it is impossible.

"Is it not contrary to law?—I believe it is.

"What is the inducement to work there ?—Wages when I was there; one-fourth or one half of the proceeds of the plantation were distributed among the negroes.

"Was that after the Agrarian law, which divided all the property of the island among the blacks ?—Yes.

"Did all the blacks receive land?—No ; the great object was, after the sudden emancipation, to bring them gently to work, that they might not consider it any sort of degradation; by becoming proprietors of the soil, they worked for themselves, and several of them bring down their coffees from an immense distance.

"Was then that division of the soil the basis on which the emancipation rested ?—No, the emancipation took place by force of arms;* this was upon the settlement of Pechon's government.

"After the violence of the revolution had subsided, the first settlement that took place was the settlement of the land by the Agrarian law ?—No, I cannot speak of what first took place after the revolution; when I was there in 1821 and 1822, I found a great number of the negroes that had fought in the revolution, and their families, squatted upon different tracts of the country, and cultivating yams for their own subsistence, as

---

* The witness must refer to the second disenthralment of the blacks, after the destruction of the French army under Le Clerc. The general emancipation in 1793 was in no sense procured by force on the part of the enslaved.

well as coffee for exportation, and living in the happiest state in the world; in fact I have seen the peasantry in the Highlands of Scotland, where I was brought up, and I declare that the negroes in St. Domingo are comparatively as much superior to them in comfort, as it is possible for one man to be over another.

"The peasantry in the Highlands in Scotland live upon the property of others; were not those squatters living upon land which had belonged to others, and of which they had become possessed?—Precisely, land given to them by government.

"Do you know what first took place immediately after freedom was proclaimed?—No; any thing I know of is only from hearsay.

"Do you know any thing of what was the state of the colony in 1804, when it became free?—I have got a very curious document here; it is an old letter, dated in 1804 or 1805, from the late Mr. Sutherland; it is a draft of a letter addressed either to Earl Spencer or to Lord Auckland, and I will just read an extract from it.

"What is the date of it?—It is without date; my father had a license, which is dated the the 10th day of October, 1806, which is a license giving him the exclusive privilege of trading to that island: this letter must have been dated about that period; it is my father's hand-writing; he says,

"Sir,—By desire of the Right Honorable Lord Auckland, I take the liberty of addressing this letter to you, on the subject of the trade of St. Domingo, to state the result of my observations during my residence in that country, from personal knowledge and intercourse:" the material part is this; he says, "The exports of the colony in 1801, a little time previous to its being given up by the unfortunate Toussaint to the government of France, was 69,000,000 lbs. of coffee, and other produce in proportion; but, from the frequent revolutions that have since taken place, the total exclusion of the whites, the great diminution of the blacks and people of color, the numbers taken from the cultivation of the soil to keep up the army, the annual crops do not exceed 15,000,000 lbs of coffee, 10,000,000 lbs of cotton, 4,000,000 lbs of cocoa, with a variety of other articles of less value, and which cannot be particularly enumerated; the cultivation of the sugar-cane, which used to be the first

staple, from the destruction of the works, the want of laborers as well as of artificers to replace ———— are totally abandoned;" therefore, I infer, from the commencement of the sentence, that all the works were totally abandoned. He says, "But this branch may again revive, and other produce experience gradual and considerable increase, as this government becomes more settled, civil commotions put an end to, and tranquillity and confidence completely restored amongst the remaining inhabitants, and which must now be nearly, if not entirely, accomplished, every objection of ———— to the ruling party being now removed; and I am fully authorised in stating that, from what I know of the attachment Desaline bears to this country, as well from principle as from policy, prudence and self-interest, a commercial treaty may be entered into with him, so as to secure the principal part of the lucrative trade of this Island to Great Britain, and which cannot fail to prove an immense source of national wealth, as nearly the whole of its rich productions will be received in exchange for British manufactures."

"In the description you have given of the great abundance of food, and the great variety of comforts that the people enjoy in Hayti, and in the comparison you have made of those people with the peasantry of Scotland, do you mean to include the people that work upon other persons' estates, as well as those that cultivate their own land? —I mean to state that the general state of the population is fully equal to that of the Highlands of Scotland, or the Squatters in North America, both of which I have seen. I conceive that a man that goes a laborer to cultivate an estate, and makes his two gourdens a day, is a happier man, decidedly, than a man who is obliged to hire land to work for his maintenance, and then to give three days' labor to the farmer, as the subletters in Scotland and Ireland are obliged to do.

"Do you believe that it is the practice in Hayti for those that work on the estates of their masters to work for their masters either on Saturday or Sunday?—No, they always have Saturday as a market day; and there are no people so strict with regard to the Sunday, as the Roman Catholic Sunday is a day of amusement after church.

"Are there any Wesleyan Missionaries in Hayti?—Not one; I recollect the French sent them a bishop out, and they walked him off again.

"You have read an extract of a letter from your father to Lord Spencer, for the purpose of showing that in the year 1801, after the negroes had been free for eight years, still a very considerable quantity of colonial produce was exported?—Yes, and that the sugar works were all destroyed; and to show that all the sugar works that have since been erected have been erected by the free labor of those very negroes.

"Was not that before the Agrarian law?—Yes, I believe it was.

"Is it or not the fact, that peace did not prevail in the Island till the Agrarian law was passed?—There was no peace till Christophe was cut off.

"Had the Agrarian law the effect of pacifying the natives?—It had the effect; there were contending parties in the island, and the great object of Pechon was, by giving every man a hold in the soil to give him an interest in it, so that, in the event of France attempting to invade them, every man had his own little hamlet, and his wife, and his family, and his property to defend.

"Did that produce peace?—No; the peace was produced in consequence of the parties ceasing from hostilities, and that gave the government of Pechon an opportunity of passing the Agrarian law to reward the old soldiers.

"Then before the passing of the Agrarian law was the country in a state of civil war?—The Agrarian law had nothing to do with the state of peace or war.

"Was not the Agrarian law confined to a division amongst the soldiery?—In fact, amongst all classes, soldiery and others; in fact any man could have land by an application for it.

"Do you know of your own knowledge that there was this Agrarian law passed?—I have never seen the Lex Scripta, but I have seen the Lex practice by seeing the people in possession of the land; I have rode into the mountains in the very heat of the day, for the express purpose of examining the state of civilization amongst them.

"Then are the Committee to understand that, just in the same way as you said before, whatever the constitution may have been *de jure*, it was *de facto* absolute; do you say now that, whatever the Lex Scripta may have been upon this subject, there was *de facto* a subdivision of property?—Yes.

"Was not it essential that there should be something of that kind, as all the white persons had been driven out at the time of the invasion of the French?—No doubt of it; because they were at the time almost all upon an equality.

"Then you do not consider it to have been a violent seizure of the property of the proprietors, but in point of fact a subdivision of the soil which the proprietors had abandoned?—There was no such thing known as a proprietor in Hayti, the old colonists were all driven out.

"Do you mean to say of your own knowledge, that all the white proprietors were expelled in 1793?—Not of my own knowledge.

"What reason have you for thinking that was the case?—It must be recollected that all the French, with the exception of a very few, were driven out of the island; long before the period I speak of, no white man held any property in the island.

"How do you know that?—I know that, because there is a law existing that no white man can hold property in Hayti.

Of what date is that law?—I cannot state, but I believe it is the constitution of Hayti.

"When was that law made, was it made in 1793, when the slaves were emancipated, or in 1804, when Dessaline became Emperor, and the French abandoned the colony?—I cannot positively state, but I know that the law does exist.

"Do you know whether the French, the white proprietors, abandoned the colony in 1793 or 1803?—I rather think there were some that were protected under Toussaint, but I merely take my information from history; and, in fact, *many of them would have been allowed to retain their possessions if they had not attempted to reinstate the old state of things.*

"Is it your impression that the larger part of the white proprietors were expelled in 1793 or in 1803?—I should think it was much more likely that they were expelled in 1800.

Do you mean to say that any French inhabitants continued in the island of St. Domingo after it was evacuated by the English troops?—I cannot say; in the first place, it was before I was born; and I do not pretend to state any thing I do not know."

BRITISH EMANCIPATION.

The results of the act of the British Parliament, which went into effect on the 1st of August, will be watched in this country with the deepest interest. A strong disposition is manifested by the pro-slavery presses to hail with delight any mischance or failure in the experiment. Should the products of the colonies diminish, or should the planters, by their obstinate infatuation provoke their former slaves to any acts of hostility, we shall doubtless be told that Slavery is better than Freedom, and that Emancipation is dangerous. It will be recollected, however, that while Slavery was declared to be totally abolished on the 1st of August, the planters were permitted to put instead of it a system of apprenticeship —*for full grown men!*—as absurd as it is unjust. Should evil grow out of this ungenerous arrangement, " Immediate Emancipation" will not be responsible for it.

We have not yet received any important news from the colonies since the act went into effect. By the politeness of Stephen Dilett, Esq. a *colored* member of the Legislature of New Providence, we have been put in possession of a file of Jamaica papers of previous dates, by which it appears that the only ground of apprehension in the West Indies was that feature of the *plan* to which we have alluded. The reasoning of the Editor of the Jamaica Watchman is worthy of insertion. When will the press of our own slave-holding states dare to promulgate truth so salutary ?. ED. REP.

" There can be little doubt, we should think, about the impolicy and impracticability of the apprenticeship plan, as it now stands. Very many are of opinion it would be for the interest of the laboring population, as well as the proprietors, to dispense with it altogether, and taking proper precautionary measures, enter, on the 1st of August, on emancipation. Others are of opinion that there ought to be some intermediate or probationary state, in which those who are to be benefitted may be prepared for the change which is to take place in their condition, and these admit that whatever may be the duration of that state, every inducement should be held out to industry and good conduct. And how is this to be done? As yet we have heard of no plan more likely to succeed than that of paying hire according to the quantity of work performed. One stimulus has been removed. It is therefore necessary to substitute another. This has not been done in the ministerial plan, which the persons we allude to think might be amended in this respect, and so made to answer all the purposes for which it was intended. It appears to us, however, that the advocates for the probationary state with wages will find that it is freedom under another name, with this inconvenience attending it on the part of the present masters—that they will be burthened with those whom they would rather be without. If the system of wages is to be resorted to, then there does not appear the slightest necessity for indenting the laborers, whilst the proposed probation will be purely ideal.

" Should it be thought desirable, however, to confine the laborers to the various properties to which they are now attached, by the strong arm of the law, rather than the affection which it is admitted they cherish for the place of their nativity—the home of their fathers, we do not see that any harm can result from it. There can be but one objection, and that is the uselessness of enforcing, by pains and penalties, what might be done without invoking the aid of the law, when no such aid is necessary—and furnishing a legal stimulus, when a much stronger one already exists in the mind of almost every laborer in the island. Self-interest, that powerful principle of the human heart, will certainly prevent the man or woman from quitting the place to which he or she has been accustomed from infancy, and on which their huts and grounds and every thing else they possess, are to be found, so long as its proprietor will allow them the same rate of wages that is paid by others."

THE EXAMPLE OF BRITAIN.

The cause which produced the British abolition act, is admirably demonstrated by a paper which will by no means be accused of any fanatical tendencies. We quote the article entire, forbearing any comment except that the writer, in glorifying Wilberforce and Clarkson, seems to have forgotten that, whatever may have been their prudence, they did not fail to receive the same treatment as the modern abolitionists on this side the Atlantic. They were regarded in their day as madmen and fanatics

—and Clarkson especially, was more than once threatened with the vengeance of those whose criminal gains were endangered by his labors. Perhaps a similar space of time may clarify the murky vapors which have arisen from a profligate pro-slavery press, around the names of the men who have *here* labored to produce the conviction that "Slavery is inconsistent with Christianity." It is consoling, at any rate, to reflect that with all our demerits, we are embarked on precisely the principles which achieved the glorious victory over British slavery, and we have the cordial sympathy and co-operation of the very men who, by the blessing of God, carried the "conviction" of the SIN OF SLAVERY home to the heart of the British nation. ED. REP.

From the Baltimore Gazette & Daily Advertiser of Aug. 1, 1834.

" This day, the 1st of August, 1834, will be a memorable one in the annals of history, for on this day SLAVERY CEASES THROUGHOUT THE BRITISH EMPIRE.— What a host of reflections rise in the mind on considering this important fact! How wonderful the change effected in the condition and relative situation of millions of beings within our own time! Masters deprived of the power of retaining in bondage those whom they had bought or inherited; nominally free blacks raised to be free citizens, possessing all the rights of the hitherto privileged class; slaves proclaimed by law to be no longer the property of others, but to be ranked as apprentices for a term of years, and then declared completely free :— these are the changes we have lived to witness, changes which, it was formerly supposed, it would require centuries to effect. In what way and by what means have they been produced? By rebellion on the part of the blacks ? No. By the fear, on the part of the whites, that rebellion was about to break out? No. Other causes have been at work, to understand which properly, it is necessary to revert to a period about fifty years ago! At that time Clarkson, Wilberforce, and other philanthropists, formed themselves into an association, whose object was to put an end to the African slave trade, then carried on extensively with the British West Indies. They labored in this cause with but little intermission for twenty years; but very differently from the course pursued by the wild and fanatic abolitionists in our country, whose imprudent

zeal has defeated the very object they intended—still they persevered till success finally crowned their labors, and they were proclaimed by the public voice of both hemispheres as benefactors of mankind. The act of the British Parliament abolishing the African slave trade, was passed in the year 1807, being just one year before the period fixed by Congress for the same purpose, as far as the United States were concerned; and which period was the earliest that could be adopted constitutionally. The example set by the two countries was not lost, others successively falling into the measure, till at length the African slave trade was declared by both to be piracy. After the adoption of this measure little was done by the friends of the blacks for several years, except calling the attention of the government to the necessity of active measures for effecting the total suppression of the abominable traffic. At length, however, slowly and by degrees, the public attention in England was directed to the total abolition of slavery itself; and here we arrive at the cause of the changes which this day take place. It was not policy; it was not humanity; it was not fear; no, it was none of these singly considered, though each might have been brought forward as subsidiary : *it was a general conviction in the nation that Slavery was incompatible with Christianity.* This was evidenced by the debate which took place in the House of Commons about ten years back, on Mr. Berxton's [Buxton's ?] resolution declaring this as an incontrovertible truth. Canning, then Premier, did not offer a formal negative to the resolution, but proposed a set of resolutions in lieu of it, the purport of which was, that it was expedient to abolish slavery as soon as possible, consistently with the safety of those whose interests might be affected by the measure. The abolitionists, glad to see such a declaration emanate from the ministry, readily adopted it, so that the original resolution was not passed. But though not passed by the House of Commons, it continued to gain advocates both in and out of Parliament, till, as above stated, it became an almost universally established [adopted ?] axiom.

But how, it may be inquired, should that be deemed inconsistent with the Christian religion at the present day, which was not so regarded in past ages, by men as pious, and as devoted to their convictions of truth, as their successors of the present? To this we have only to allege, that as, in the New Testament, no express prohibition of slavery is to be found, it is not to be wondered at that different men, in different ages should have arrived at opposite conclusions. The African slave trade was, as we have seen, carried on for upwards of two centuries by Christian nations, and yet it was finally adjudged to be no better than piracy. The same gradually spreading conviction has brought slavery, so far as England is concerned, *to be placed on the same level.* We simply state the fact without commenting on it; but, as the subject of slavery is highly important we shall shortly revert to it, with the view of enabling such of our readers as are not aware of the real state of the question, to form a correct judgment of the folly or wisdom of the British Parliament in desiring its entire abolition."

These editorial remarks called forth from Gen. Duff Green, of the United States Telegraph, the charge against the Baltimore Gazette of advocating the cause of the abolitionists, and falsifying in regard to British abolition. A part of the reply of the Baltimore Gazette is striking. Let the reader remember that it comes from a *southern press.*

" The Editor of the Telegraph says that policy, and policy only, was the cause. Now it is true, as we have since shown, that it became a matter of policy with the British ministry—if they had not adopted it, they would have lost the support of their best friends, and must have resigned their seats. But why would this have been the inevitable result? Because the conviction we have mentioned [that slavery was inconsistent with Christianity] had taken so strong a hold of the public mind, that nothing could remove or even shake it."

PRO-SLAVERY AT THE NORTH.

We are constantly told by a certain class of presses, that the north is opposed to slavery, and consequently our arguments are wasted here for want of an aim. But let the reader ponder the following extract from the Richmond Inquirer. Will it any longer be pretended that there is not work to be done at the north, and that the sentiment of the North has nothing to do with slavery at the South?

From the Richmond Inquirer, Aug. 5.

ABOLITIONISTS.

" We learn from private sources that many of the most respectable citizens in New York were originally concerned in putting down the abolitionists. We understand that plans were in agitation to *mark* Dr. Cox and others, and to keep down their fanaticism in the most signal manner. As the scene deepened, however, other persons stept in, who were actuated by different passions, and who endeavored to turn the riots to purposes of their own. It was, however, the impression of the most intelligent observers on the spot, that the outbreaking of the public sentiment was so decided against the abolitionists, that it is likely to keep down the zeal of the fanatics for many years to come—at all events, that there is not the slightest disposition in the great mass of the community to encourage their schemes, and to tamper with this most delicate of all subjects. This is unquestionably the conclusion which every man but a violent political partizan would draw from the late development of public sentiment in New York. A correspondent of the Charleston Courier strongly confirms this idea, in an intelligent letter he addresses on the 17th from New York.

" The recent anti-abolition riots in this place, which now seem to have ceased, although strong precautionary measures against their recurrence are still continued, however evil in themselves, as instruments of mischief, cannot but be highly gratifying to the people of the south, as a strong, and indeed, conclusive manifestation that the public sentiment of the north, will of itself suffice to put down that fanatical spirit of false philanthropy and real incendiarism, which but yesterday, as it were, boded over us in dark and threatening clouds. What more can the south desire, than that northern mobs should assemble to put down and punish those who could plot ruin to southern interests, and desolation to southern plains, *and that the great mass of the respectable population of the great city should stand by and behold the operations of these mobs, with that unequivocal evidence of approbation, which* NON-INTERFERENCE *on such an occasion clearly implies?* The language of the northern press too, is cheering in the extreme—it condemns *mobbing* it is true; but it, at the same time, visits its censures chiefly and justly, in unmitigated severity, on the heads of the abolitionists themselves, as furnishing, by their vile machinations, and indecent outrages upon public feeling, the occasion, and, in some measure, the justification of those mobs, which the obligations of social order have constrained the civil authorities to suppress, with prompt action, but almost reluctant sentiment. Mob violence in such a city as New York, is justly held to put in peril the life and property of every citizen—it is a moral (?) tempest, in which many may ride, but which none can control — and the municipal authorities here, cannot be too highly commended for their energetic measures (carried it is said to the extent of putting 8000 militia under arms at one time,) in preventing the farther demonstration of popular indignation even against fanatical abolitionists, in a mode too fraught with danger to the dearest interests of society to be tolerated even for the promotion of the best ends. From all that I can see, hear, and learn, public sentiment at the north, in reference to southern interests was never in a sounder state than it is now—the feeling in favor of the south, and against the abolitionists, is deep and almost universal—the disposition is general to recognize the SANCTITY of southern RIGHTS OF PROPERTY, [Do northern colonizationists recognize THE *right of property* in question ? ED. REPORTER.] and the conviction of the duty and the policy of non-interference with the domestic institutions of the South, seems to be as sincerely felt as it is openly acknowledged."

"THE MARYLAND SCHEME."

The last Liberator (Aug. 23) contains a full exposition of the scheme of the Maryland Colonization Society, as it stands connected with the laws for thrusting out the " poor and the needy" from that tyrannous republic. It is sufficient to say that the Colonization Society proposes to *co-operate* with the *state* on the basis of the following law. For such a *benevolent* purpose they have sent agents throughout the north to solicit *charity ! !* We shall not trust ourselves to speak of the merits of this *co-partnership*, for two reasons ; first, we are busily engaged in disseminating documents which will open the eyes of our fellow citizens sooner than any thing we might say. Secondly, our compass of English furnishes no epithets which would not be

tame and inadequate. We would simply ask our readers to put themselves for a moment, in imagination, into a colored skin, within the boundaries of Maryland, and then turn over all their recollections of the union of " CHURCH AND STATE" for a parallel to this.

" A LAW OF THE STATE OF MARYLAND."

" An Act relating to the People of Color of this State."

" Sect. 1, Provides for the appointment of a ' Board of Managers, consisting of three persons,' to superintend the whole business of the removal of ' the people of color now free, and such as shall hereafter become so.'

" Sect. 2, Makes it the duty of the Treasurer of the Western Shore to pay to the Board of Managers such sums as they shall from time to time require, not exceeding in all $20,000 for that present year, to be applied by them, at discretion, in the work of removal, and in taking measures ' to obtain and place before the people of color of the state, full and correct information of the condition and circumstances of the colony of Liberia, or such other place or places to which they may recommend their removal' !

" Sect. 3. And be it enacted, That it shall hereafter be the duty of every clerk of a county in this State, whenever a deed of manumission shall be left in his office for record, and of every Register of Wills, in every county of this State, whenever a will, manumitting a slave or slaves, shall be admitted to probate, to send within five days thereafter, (under a *penalty of ten dollars* for each and every omission so to do, to be recovered before any justice of the peace, one half whereof shall go to the informer and the other half to the State ;) an extract from such deed or will, stating the names, number and ages of the slave or slaves so manumitted, (a list whereof, in the case of a will so proved, shall be filed therewith, by the executor or administrator) to the board of managers for Maryland, for removing the people of color of said State; and it shall be the duty of the said board on receiving the same to notify the American Colonization Society, or the Maryland State Colonization Society thereof, and to propose to such society that they shall engage, at the expense of such society, to remove the said slave or slaves so manumitted to Liberia ; and if the said society shall so engage, then it shall be the duty of the said board of managers to have said slave or slaves delivered to the agent of such society, at such place as the said society shall appoint, for receiving such slave or slaves, for the purpose of such removal, at such time as the said society shall appoint; and in case the said society shall refuse so to receive and remove the person or persons so manumitted and offered, or in case the said person or persons shall refuse so to be removed, then it shall be the duty of the said board of managers to remove the said person or persons to such other place or places beyond the limits of this state, as the said board shall approve of, and the said person or persons shall be willing to go to, and to provide for their reception and support at such place or places as the said board may think necessary, until they shall be able to provide for themselves, *out of any money that may be earned by their hire,* or may be otherwise provided for that purpose ; and in case the said person or persons shall refuse to be removed to *any* place beyond the limits of this state, and shall persist in remaining therein, then it shall be the duty of said board to inform the sheriff of the county wherein such person or persons may be, of such refusal, and it shall *thereupon be the duty of the said sheriff* FORTHWITH TO ARREST, *or cause to be arrested, the said person or persons so refusing to emigrate from this State,* and TRANSPORT THE SAID PERSON OR PERSONS BEYOND THE LIMITS OF THIS STATE ; and all slaves shall be capable of receiving manumission, for the purpose of removal as aforesaid, with their consent, of whatever age, any law to the contrary notwithstanding.

"Sec. 4. And be it enacted, That in case any slave or slaves so manumitted, *cannot be removed without separating families,* and the said slave or slaves, unwilling on that account to be removed, shall desire to renounce the freedom so intended by the said deed or will to be given, then it shall and may be competent to such slave or slaves so *to renounce in open court the benefit of said deed or will, and* TO CONTINUE A SLAVE.

"Sec. 5. And be it enacted, That it shall and may be competent for the Orphan's Court of this state, and for the Baltimore city court, to grant *annually,* a permit to any slave or slaves so manumitted as aforesaid, to remain as free in the said county, in cases where the said courts may be *satisfied* by

respectable testimony that such slave or slaves so manumitted *deserve such permission on account of their extraordinary good conduct and character;* Provided, such permit shall not exempt any manumittor or his representatives, or his estate, from any liability to maintain any hereafter emancipated slave, who, at the time his or her right to freedom accrues, may be unable to gain a livelihood, or be over forty-five years of age at said time, and afterwards become unable to maintain himself or herself.

" Sec. 6. And be it enacted, That the said board of managers shall in ALL cases where the removal of a slave or slaves manumitted as aforesaid, shall devolve upon them, have *full power and authority,* whenever the same shall be necessary, and can be done with advantage, to *hire out such slave or slaves so manumitted and so to be removed, until their wages shall produce a sufficient sum to defray all expenses attending their removal, and necessary support at the place or places of such removal.*

" Sec. 7, Authorises the treasurer to borrow the requisite funds, never exceeding $200,000 in all. Section 8th, authorises the levying of a tax to raise the said specified funds. The 9th, directs the sheriffs of the several counties to cause the number of the free people of color, their names, sex, and age, to be carefully taken, noted, and sent to the said board of managers. The 10th, fixes the compensation of the sheriffs. The 11th, defines the duties of the managers, when informed by the sheriffs of persons wishing to remove. And the 11th, provides that the act have no *ex post facto* operation.

" *By the House of Delegates, March* 14, 1832.—This engrossed bill, the original of which passed this House the 9th day of March, 1832, was this day read and assented to.

"By order:

" GEO. B. BREWER, Clerk.

"*By the Senate, March* 14, 1832.—This engrossed bill, the original of which passed the Senate the 12th day of March, 1832, was this day read and assented to.

" By order.

" JOS. H. NICHOLSON, Clerk.

" GEO. HOWARD."

" The wicked have drawn out the sword and have bent their bow to cast down the poor and needy."— *Psalm* xxxvii. 14.

APPEAL TO THE FRIENDS OF THE AMERICAN ANTI-SLAVERY SOCIETY.

The violence of our enemies has in a few days accomplished for us the work of years. It has thoroughly aroused public attention. Thousands of ears are now open, that had remained deaf to our arguments. Thousands of minds are now excited to study our doctrines, who before were unconscious of our existence as well as asleep to the sin and peril of their country. But it must not be concealed that the American Anti-Slavery Society is not possessed of the funds necessary to take advantage of this favorable crisis, nor even to continue its past rate of operation, feeble and inadequate as that has been. No *end*, however desirable, can justify the dishonesty of incurring debts without the ability to pay. *The executive committee are resolved, therefore, not to proceed a step farther in their operations than the means are put into their hands to pay those whom they employ.* Accordingly they have voted *to suspend the publication of the A. S. Reporter after this month till the treasury is replenished.* Other very important publications must be kept back for the same reason.

The burden hitherto has fallen chiefly upon a few friends in New-York. They have been willing to spend and be spent in this holy cause. But is that a reason why they should be permitted to bear all? It should be remembered that those who compose the Executive Committee have given not only their money but their *time*, in no measured portion. Will not the members of more than *one hundred* anti-slavery societies, the advocates of *immediatism* in all that is good, reflect on this? Compared with the whole nation we are few and feeble; but if we stand shoulder to shoulder, by one united and easy effort the moral power of the nation will be won. It need only be said that if the donations of our friends are not sent in to the treasurer without delay, the publications of the society, instead of being increased as they ought to be an hundred fold, will be very much diminished. It is very desirable that all the anti-slavery societies which have not done so already, should send us a complete list of their officers, with the post-office addresses of each. Donations may be safely remitted *by mail*, and should be addressed to "WILLIAM GREEN, Jr. No. 7, *City Hall Place, New-York.*"

E. WRIGHT, JR., *Sec. Dom. Cor.*
Anti-Slavery Office, 130 Nassau-st. }
New-York, August 8, 1834. }

DONATIONS AND SALES.

The following sums have been received since the last number was published.

From a Friend, . . .	by Wm. Goodell . .		4 00
Mr. G. A. Avery, . .	of Rochester, N. Y. .		25 00
Mrs. G. A. Avery, .	" "		5 00
Mrs. Susan Stanton, .	" "		5 00
Mr. A Tappan, . .	New-York City . .		600 00
Mr. John Rankin, . .	" "		100 00
4th July Collection, .	Hallowell, Maine .		80 00
Ebenezer Dole, . .	" "		20 00
4th July Collection, .	Pawtucket, R. I. .		30 00
" "	Reading, Mass. . .		6 00
Mr. John Usmar, . .			50
Mr. Seth Conklin, .	Syracuse, N. Y. .		5 00
Rev. P. Williams, . .	New-York City . .		1 00
Mr. Joseph Carpenter,	New-Rochelle, N. Y·		1 00
Rev. Sam. E. Cornish,	New-York City . .		1 00
Mr. A. Townsend, .	New-Haven, Con. .		5 00
Anti-Slavery Society .	Norwich, Con. . .		6 00
Ladies A. S. Society, .	" "		7 00
John Taylor, . . .	Bath, Maine . . .		3 00
Theo. Sem. Aux. . .	Auburn, N. Y. . .		8 00
Thomas J. Gillelan	. . . .		62
Wm. Garribrance,	. . . .		50
Louis Sheridan,	. . . .		1 00

[The following sums were collected by C. Pepper, Jr. Esq.]

From Colored People in	Albany, N. Y. . .		14 62
" "	Lansingburgh, N. Y.		4 95
" "	Troy, N. Y. . .		11 19
" "	Schenectady, N. Y.		12 52
" "	Utica, N. Y. . .		6 55
" "	Whitesboro', N. Y.		2 99
" "	Little Falls, N. Y. .		3 61
" "	Auburn, N. Y. . .		10 49
" "	Rochester, N. Y. .		16 22
" "	Geneva, N. Y. . :		4 65
" "	Canandaigua, N. Y.		5 12
" "	Buffalo, N. Y. . .		16 28
Mr. Perry Hardy, . .	Canandaigua . . .		1 00
Sales at the office from 21st April to 2d July	.		77 83
Sales at the office from 2d July to Aug. 30th	.		140 09
Benjamin Perry, .	Schaghticoke, N. Y,		2 50
Sarah Dizoose, .	" "		1 00
Dr. E. Barker, .	" "		50

Total . . $1246 73

WM. GREEN, JR. Treasurer.
No. 7 City Hall Place, New-York,
Aug. 30, 1834.

NOTICE.

We trust the friends of the enslaved will not suffer us to intermit our labors in time to come, so long as we seem to have done in issuing this number at the close instead of the beginning of the month. A pressure of important duties connected with the cause have rendered it impracticable to publish this at an earlier date. Should the work be relinquished, those subscribers who have paid will be furnished with other publications to the amount due to them.

TERMS.

☞ This periodical will be furnished to subscribers at $1 00 per annum, done up in a neat cover; or 50 cents, without the cover. To those who take several copies a discount will be made as follows: 15 per cent. for 10 copies, 25 per cent. for 25 copies, and 33 per cent. for 100 copies.